ROAD TO THE BIG TIME

A CENTURY-LONG DREAM LEADS CREIGHTON TO THE BIG EAST

STEVEN PIVOVAR

Omaha World-Herald

ROAD TO THE BIG TIME

BY STEVEN PIVOVAR

EDITOR
Dan Sullivan

DESIGNER
Christine Zueck-Watkins

PHOTO IMAGING
Jolene McHugh

EXECUTIVE EDITOR
Mike Reilly

PRESIDENT AND PUBLISHER
Terry Kroeger

ON PRECEDING PAGE: Grant Gibbs, Gregory Echenique and Doug McDermott celebrate a victory over Wichita State in the 2013 Missouri Valley Conference tournament title game.

THIS PAGE: Jim Karabatsos scores on a layup against Omaha University at the Creighton gym in 1949.

ON FACING PAGE: Anthony Tolliver dunks in the 2006 Valley tournament.

Omaha World-Herald Co.
1314 Douglas St. Omaha, NE 68102-1811
First Edition
ISBN: 978-0-615-89513-0
Printed by Walsworth Publishing Co.
Marceline, MO

Table of Contents

A century-long dream fulfilled

GREG MCDERMOTT AND HIS CREIGHTON BASKETBALL TEAM boarded a plane the morning of March 20, 2013, bound for the NCAA tournament. But McDermott knew that by the time the wheels touched down in Philadelphia, his program would be in a much different place in more ways than one.

The university's president, the Rev. Timothy Lannon, and Athletic Director Bruce Rasmussen were in New York for the official announcement that Creighton would be leaving the Missouri Valley Conference to join the new Big East Conference.

Greg McDermott directs the Bluejays' practice before their NCAA tournament game in Philadelphia.

In December 2012, seven schools — DePaul, Georgetown, St. John's, Villanova, Providence, Seton Hall and Marquette — announced their intention to break away from the old Big East and form a new basketball-centric conference. Months of speculation followed, and every rumor seemed to start a social-media firestorm among Creighton's fans, even in the midst of a memorable season in which their team was nationally ranked. Would the Bluejays get into the Big East, or would they be passed over, as the seven sought additional members to begin play in the 2013-14 season? The March 20 announcement that Creighton, Xavier and Butler had been selected to join the league brought massive joy, and relief, to Bluejay fans.

The new Big East, with a lucrative television contract in hand, provides Creighton an opportunity to join college basketball's "big time."

Big time. Creighton has been chasing that dream almost since students started bouncing basketballs on the Hilltop campus in 1911. An Omaha World-Herald story in 1916 told of the school's plan for a "big time" schedule, and 12 years later the Bluejays changed conferences in an attempt to boost their stature.

Creighton's century-long journey to the Big East has been filled with grand accomplishments and agonizing frustrations. The program has been perched on the mountaintop of college basketball, but it also has been all but disbanded. And in the past 15 years, the Bluejays have enjoyed their greatest level of fan support.

"I think the fact that our fans are very passionate about our team and our program is one of the reasons we're going to the Big East," said McDermott, who will coach Creighton's first game in the new conference. "Would we be going to the Big East if we were averaging 9,000 per game instead of 16,000? My guess is no.

"On one hand, I'm sad to leave the Valley," he said. "But I'm excited to move to the Big East."

McDermott's emotions were shared by other Creighton officials, including Kevin Sarver. With the exception of a brief stint after graduation, Sarver has been at Creighton — either as a student or an employee of its athletic department — since 1985.

With Lannon and Rasmussen in New York in March, Sarver was at D.J. Sokol Arena, the school's on-campus athletic facility, preparing for a public announcement of the Big East move. He was approached not once but twice by longtime Creighton boosters. Each had tears in his eyes.

"They were choked up," Sarver said. "They were saying that this is the greatest day ever and can you believe that this is where we are? They were just going on and on.

"I knew getting into the Big East was important, but it really hit me what a momentous day this was for our fans, for our donors. I hadn't thought about it in that context, and it was very moving to me to see that kind of reaction."

The small Jesuit school on the fringe of Omaha's downtown embraces its basketball tradition, even though it doesn't match that of Duke, UCLA, North Carolina and others on the short list of the sport's elite programs.

November 19, 1916:

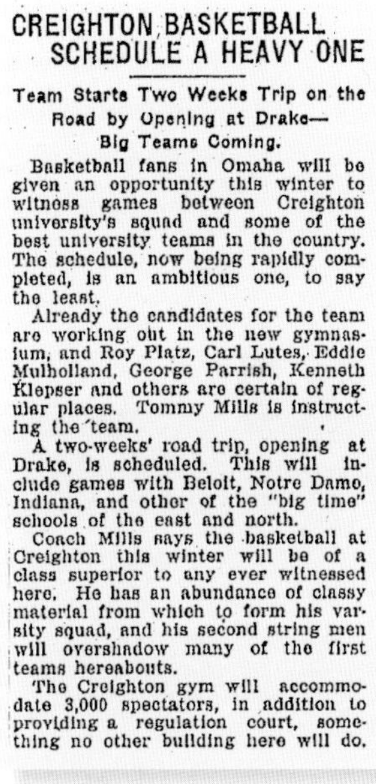

CREIGHTON BASKETBALL SCHEDULE A HEAVY ONE

Team Starts Two Weeks Trip on the Road by Opening at Drake—Big Teams Coming.

Basketball fans in Omaha will be given an opportunity this winter to witness games between Creighton university's squad and some of the best university teams in the country. The schedule, now being rapidly completed, is an ambitious one, to say the least.

Already the candidates for the team are working out in the new gymnasium, and Roy Platz, Carl Lutes, Eddie Mulholland, George Parrish, Kenneth Klepser and others are certain of regular places. Tommy Mills is instructing the team.

A two-weeks' road trip, opening at Drake, is scheduled. This will include games with Beloit, Notre Dame, Indiana, and other of the "big time" schools of the east and north.

Coach Mills says the basketball at Creighton this winter will be of a class superior to any ever witnessed here. He has an abundance of classy material from which to form his varsity squad, and his second string men will overshadow many of the first teams hereabouts.

The Creighton gym will accommodate 3,000 spectators, in addition to providing a regulation court, something no other building here will do.

By 1911, north and south wings had been added to the original main building at Creighton, founded in 1878. It was time to add a basketball team.

Bluejay teams have produced 21 conference championships, beginning with the Western Catholic College and Nebraska Intercollegiate titles in the school's first official season of 1916-17. The most recent was the Missouri Valley crown the 2012-13 team claimed in dramatic fashion on the final day of the regular season. Creighton teams have played in 18 NCAA tournaments and made 10 appearances in the National Invitation Tournament. Twenty-nine Bluejays have earned some form of All-America recognition, and three hall of fame coaches spent part of their careers on the Hilltop. Those achievements have fostered a fierce sense of pride in Creighton's coaches, players and fans, bolstered by the knowledge that the Bluejays over the years have done more with less in terms of facilities, athletic budgets and player talent level. Yet the Bluejays were able to compete with — and beat — some of the sport's biggest names.

"Creighton basketball has always had this little dichotomy," said Tom Apke, who played for the Bluejays in the 1960s and later coached the Jays. "It's a school not sure if it was big time, and on the other hand making great strides in showing that it was pretty darn big time."

In recent years, the artificial delineation of college basketball into high, mid- and low majors created frustration for schools such as Creighton that found themselves on the second tier. It also motivated the players and coaches.

"We had a chip on our shoulders," said Kyle Korver, an All-America sharpshooter from 1999 to 2003. "We were out to prove that we belonged, that we could play with anybody and beat anybody."

In addition, players and fans often have felt that Creighon's basketball accomplishments go relatively unnoticed in a football-crazed state. The campus sits about 50 miles northeast of the University of Nebraska in Lincoln, home of a powerhouse football program that has won five national championships. "With Nebraska being so close and all the hype that the football team gets, you always felt like you were on a lower tier," Korver said. "That always bothered me. It was like, 'We're winning a whole lot of games here. Is anyone noticing?' "

The move to the new Big East may change that. Almost all of the Bluejays' games will be shown on national television, providing Creighton with additional prestige, not to mention a lot more money that can be used to support an already strong basketball program. The fact that Creighton will be banging elbows with Georgetown and Marquette in the conference tournament at New York's Madison Square Garden each March also stands to polish the perception of the program. The Garden, where Creighton teams occasionally played in the formative years of the program, calls itself the world's greatest arena, and Creighton now is assured of playing there at least once a year.

"The new league gives us a chance to compete on a national stage that we've never had before," Sarver said. "We have to make sure we do everything we can and fight like crazy to make sure it works."

As Creighton prepares to make the bold step into the new Big East, it's time to glance back and acknowledge those who helped reach that century-long dream of the big time. Creighton wouldn't be headed in its new direction without the contributions of coaches such as Arthur Schabinger, Eddie Hickey, Red McManus, Eddie Sutton, Tom Apke, Tony Barone and Dana Altman, or players such as Ed Beisser, Bob Gibson, Paul Silas, Bob Portman, Gene Harmon, Bob Harstad and Kyle Korver.

"We're in this position now," Rasmussen said, "because we've been fortunate enough to stand on the shoulders of giants."

DAKTRONICS
20:00
35
ECHENIQUE
00
CREIGHTON
1

A
B
D
E
F

1911-1959

Building a foundation

Creighton closed its 1923-24 season against Marquette at the Hilltop gym. The two schools played four games that year, with each school hosting two. They split in Milwaukee, while Creighton won both games in Omaha over the Golden Avalanche, as Marquette was known at the time. After the final game, a 32-12 Creighton rout, The World-Herald called the team "probably the greatest in Blue history."

Creighton and Marquette prepare to square off in the Hilltop gym in 1924. Creighton players, from left, are Johnny Trautman, Ike Mahoney, Jimmy Lovely, Joe Speicher and Sid Corenman.

Willing to pay to play

JULIUS FESTNER AND HIS BUDDIES just wanted to play some basketball. The year was 1911. Creighton had been competing in football since 1900 but had yet to field a team in the indoor sport that James Naismith had invented two decades earlier. One problem for Creighton was that it had no place on campus to hold games or practices. But Festner and his buddies wanted to play basketball, and they approached the school's administration about starting a team. On their own dime.

"We put it up to the president and the athletic board and requested to use the university name and schedule what games we could," Festner recalled a half-century later. "This was granted, but since there were no funds, we financed ourselves, buying our own uniforms and providing the coaching without cost."

Claus Delfs, a Creighton medical student who had played basketball at Drake, served as the team's player-coach. The team practiced and played some of its games at Omaha University, which at the time was near 24th and Pratt Streets.

Creighton faced the YMCA Pirates on Dec. 14, 1911, in its first basketball game. The World-Herald carried a report the next day: "In a hot and fast game of basketball, the YMCA Pirates swamped the Creighton varsity five by the score of 58 to 18. Although at times the collegians exhibited flashes of individual brightness, a lack of teamwork was evident. The Pirates played hand in hand with a swift sureness that invariably landed the ball in the basket. They covered the field well and excelled their opponents in general teamwork and goal throwing. The game was rough and fiercely contested."

A young man from Wilber, Neb., emerged as Creighton's first star. Frank Prucha had played basketball in high school and, according to a 1912 article, had "few equals of his age in the state. ... He brought many a victory to Wilber."

November 19, 1911:

CREIGHTON TO HAVE BASKETBALL TEAM

First Varsity Five Will Play in Omaha University Gymnasium

Manager Delfs Is Working on Schedule and Has Many Fast Players.

At last the desire of the students will be fulfilled and Creighton university will have a varsity basketball team. The authorities of the college have long wanted a basketball five, but as no suitable gymnasium or hall for practice was available no action was taken. Through the generosity of Omaha university, with whom Creighton recently formed an athletic association, Creighton is now able to organize a team, being offered the use of Omaha university's gymnasium twice a week.

A practice game between Creighton and Omaha universities has been scheduled for Tuesday evening, in which Creighton will try out a number of men who are candidates for the varsity five.

Among the prospective players Delfs, Hoffman, Hawes, Prucha, Balderson, Madden and McGrane seem likelihoods, as each has had considerable experience in the game with high school teams throughout the state and on college fives.

January 7, 1912:

CREIGHTON BASKETBALL FIVE HAS FAST COACH AND CAPTAIN

Claus Delfs

Frank Prucha

Creighton finished the 1911-12 season with a 15-3 record against a schedule that included games against Omaha University, Doane College and Tabor College. The Blue and White — Creighton didn't adopt Bluejays as its official nickname until 1924 — also played local high school and YMCA teams. The school continued to field a basketball team, on an unofficial basis, for the next four seasons.

But in 1915, the school hired Tommy Mills as its football coach, and he later took over basketball duties, too. A former star halfback for the Beloit College football team, Mills put Creighton's first official basketball team on display for the 1916-17 season and set the tone for change.

In assessing his team's prospects before the season, Mills promised that basketball at Creighton that winter would be "of a class superior to any ever witnessed here." A story noted that Mills had "an abundance of classy material from which to form his varsity squad, and his second string men would overshadow many of the first teams hereabouts."

The school also had a new, 3,000-seat gymnasium at 24th and Burt Streets to show off.

Tommy Mills took charge of Creighton's football program in 1915 after previously coaching at Omaha High, now Central, and took over basketball a year later. He later coached at Notre Dame under Knute Rockne and was head football coach at Georgetown. Eddie Mulholland and Charles Kearney, who played on the 1916-17 team, at right, later coached on the Hilltop. The tallest member of the team was 6-foot-1 Victor Spittler.

CREIGHTON BASKETBALL STARS

Eddie Mulholland, at the right, guard and captain of Tommy Mills' Blue and White floor quintet for this season as he appears ready for action. Mulholland's superior work not only on the gym floor but on the gridiron has won him a lasting name at Creighton.

Upper left, Ed Haley, and below him, Charlie Kearney, stellar forwards of the past season. Lower left hand corner, Vic Spittler, center, and ex-captain, and Howard Vandiver, guard, both prime factors in Creighton's 1916 basketball success.

Creighton overwhelmed Peru State 30-17 on Jan. 12, 1917, in the first official game.

The Blue and White went on to post a 13-3 record against a schedule that consisted largely of small Nebraska and Iowa schools with which Creighton had more in common at the time than bigger universities such as Indiana and Notre Dame that Mills had hoped to play.

Creighton claimed championships in two loosely organized conferences its first season. The team clinched the Nebraska Intercollegiate Conference title with a 33-14 win over York College at the new gym. It also claimed the championship of the Western Catholic College Conference, which included St. Ignatius of Chicago, Loyola of Chicago, St. Viateur's of Kankakee, Ill., Campion College of Prairie du Chien, Wis., and St. Joseph's of Dubuque, Iowa.

Mills' teams didn't lose a game the next two seasons, posting 21 straight wins, but he grew frustrated with the school's inability to schedule bigger-name schools. After the unbeaten 1918-19 campaign, he issued a call to bigger schools for games. He got his wish, guiding Creighton to a 15-3 record, with wins over Indiana and Michigan State in the 1919-20 season. But he then left for his alma mater, Beloit College, and eventually took a coaching position at Notre Dame, where he served on Knute Rockne's staff and also was the school's head baseball coach.

Eddie Mulholland, who had played for Mills, took over the Creighton program for the 1920-21 season but lasted just six games. He led the Blue and White to wins in the first five games before losing 24-19 at home to Des Moines University.

Creighton had waxed the gymnasium floor for a dance to be held after the Friday night game, causing slipping and sliding by the players. Mulholland argued unsuccessfully with school officials about future dances in the gym and resigned. The team was to play Des Moines again the next night, leaving no time to hire a new coach, so captain Charles Kearney took over. His teammates responded with a performance, according to The World-Herald, in which they "outplayed, outclassed, outguessed and out everythinged else that comes into play in a cage game." Creighton won 22-14.

CREIGHTON WINS BIG CAGE CHAMPIONSHIP

Blue and White Scores 457 Points in 17 Games Against Opponents' 317.

But One More Game Remains on Schedule, That With Trinity Thursday.

Creighton university basketball team, the first the Blue and White school has had that was of any consequence, has won the western Catholic college conference championship and scored a total of 457 points in the seventeen games played, against 317 for its opponents.

Added to the Catholic conference title, which the team won, is the state championship and the defeat of two strong Missouri Valley conference squads. Altogether this is an enviable record for the first year.

In the Catholic conference are the following teams: Creighton, St. Ignatius, Chicago; Loyola, Chicago; St. Viatures, Kankakee, Ill.; Campion, Prairie du Chien, Wis., and St. Joseph college, Dubuque, Ia.

Creighton has but one more game on its regular schedule, that with Trinity here Thursday night. Trinity will put up a game fight, but it is pretty certain the Blue and White will win this final contest. Captain Vic Spittler has his men well in hand now and they are working some of the greatest combinations on plays ever seen on a local floor.

1917: THE FIRST CONFERENCE TITLES

Creighton considers its 1916-17 team, which played games in the newly opened gym on campus, to be the school's entry into college basketball. Earlier teams weren't considered true college squads, as they played against opponents sponsored by the YMCA and local businesses. The Blue and White had only one close contest — a 4-point win at Nebraska Wesleyan — in eight games against Nebraska schools. The World-Herald said the 1916-17 season under Mills was "the first the Blue and White school has had that was of any consequence." While Creighton had vowed to schedule "big time" schools in Tommy Mills' first season, three years passed before the schedule began to include teams from outside the region. The biggest name on the schedule might have been Drake. Creighton split a pair of games with the Bulldogs from the Missouri Valley Conference in early 1917. Mills' teams won the next five matchups with Drake, boosting Hilltoppers' ambitions to join the prestigious conference. They would have to wait for an invitation.

Kearney stayed on as player-coach and 12 days later posted a 24-20 home win over Notre Dame before an overflow crowd that caused the ceiling under the gym's elevated track to loosen. Play was halted until spectators could move to safety. Creighton finished the year 15-6, and Kearney returned in 1921-22 to compile a 23-5 record, but his graduation left Creighton looking for a new coach.

To this point, Creighton's basketball teams had been led by students, recent graduates and the coach from a high school three blocks away from campus. Bigger ambitions meant casting the net wider.

1921: SETTING THE STANDARD FOR TEAM CAPTAINS

Team captain Charles Kearney, third from the left in the front row, led Creighton in scoring for four straight seasons from 1917-18 to 1920-21 and had a high game of 32 points against Yankton his senior year. He also stepped in to coach after Eddie Mulholland quit to protest the waxing of the gym floor for a dance. Forward Leonard "Jimmy" Lovely, to the right of Kearney, later captained the 1923 and 1924 teams. In Lovely's final game at the Creighton gym, a 32-12 victory over Marquette, CU center Ike Mahoney stopped play and told the crowd how he and the team felt about Lovely. "A deafening ovation was handed the blushing Blue pilot," The World-Herald reported. "Then the gallant Ike presented Lovely a platinum watch, the token of esteem from a great team to a great leader." Lovely, a two-time Helms Athletic Foundation All-American, is a member of the Helms Basketball Hall of Fame.

The Creighton Basketball Team.

Front Row, left to right—Howard Vandiver, r. g.; Harold Wise, r. f.; Captain Charles Kearney, c.; James Lovely, f.; Dick Giller, f.; Tom Berry, l. f.

Back row, Jason Dorwart, g.; James Condon, l. g.; Carem Camel, g.; Joe Mulholland, g.; Harold Linahan, student manager.

An architect for expanding the program

The school found its man in Arthur Schabinger, who had been recommended by former Creighton football coach Malcolm Baldrige — a lawyer and budding politician who would go on to serve in Congress. The two had met in 1921 at a Missouri Valley Conference meeting in Kansas City, and Baldrige had been impressed.

Creighton named Schabinger, the head of sports at Kansas State Normal, later Emporia State, to coach basketball and serve as the school's athletic director. His hiring "presages the entrance of Creighton into the Missouri Valley Conference," The World-Herald speculated, and the school did indeed head into the 1922-23 season as a member of a new conference.

However, that new league was the North Central Conference, after Blue and White officials were rebuffed in repeated attempts to hook up with the more prestigious MVC, of which Nebraska was a member.

"We have waited a decade for a chance in the Valley and have been ignored," a Creighton athletic board member said. "Present prospects for our entrance in the Missouri Valley Conference are no brighter than they were 10 years ago."

So Creighton cast its lot with the North Central, along with North Dakota, North Dakota State, South Dakota State, South Dakota, St. Thomas, Nebraska Wesleyan, Des Moines University and Morningside. Michigan State, Marquette and Detroit also were involved in talks at one time but in the end did not join.

The World-Herald applauded Creighton's move to the NCC: "The settlement of Creighton's stand on the new conference idea will be a relief for followers of the Hilltop teams. Creighton's repeated failure to land a place in the Missouri Valley Conference has been discouraging to Omaha gridiron and cage enthusiasts who have been watching the Hilltoppers' growing strength. Reliable sport prognosticators affirm that the new conference is the big hope for Creighton, and it seems that the local school has finally realized that."

April 18, 1922:

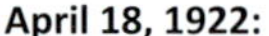

Emporia, Kas., April 17.—Arthur Schabinger, basketball and baseball coach at the Kansas State normal, has accepted an offer of basketball and track coach at Creighton university, Omaha, Neb.

Arthur Schabinger "suddenly and solidly established himself with Blue and White followers" when he scheduled a first-ever game against Nebraska, The World-Herald reported. Fans were no doubt even more pleased when Schabinger's team routed the Cornhuskers 46-24 at the Creighton gym. The 1922-23 schedule also included games with non-conference opponents Kansas and Marquette, along with 14 games against schools in the North Central Conference.

The 1926 NCC champion Bluejays were led by Albert Brown's 6.4 points a game. Brown later survived the Bataan death march during World War II.

Schabinger's first three teams captured NCC championships, winning 27 of 31 league games while posting an overall record of 39-9. The Bluejays also won the title in 1926-27 before leaving the conference in 1927.

A Roaring Twenties version of conference realignment provided the next turn in Creighton's athletic fortunes. In the spring of 1928, Nebraska, Missouri, Oklahoma, Kansas, Kansas State and Iowa State bolted from the Missouri Valley and formed the Big Six, partly because of the inferior competition they faced in football from the four other Valley schools — Oklahoma A&M, Grinnell, Drake and Washington University of St. Louis. Those schools, labeled "the little four," decided to play on in the Valley, and Creighton soon became the leading candidate for membership. The school accepted an invitation, and the Bluejay football team narrowly missed winning the conference championship that fall.

The World-Herald's sports editor, Fred Ware, conceded that while Creighton's move to the Valley did not excite him, it was one the school needed to make: "There is room for discussion as to whether Creighton's recent association with the staunch 'little four' was so much a step forward for Creighton as it was a step forward for Drake, Oklahoma and Washington. In basketball especially, Creighton is so far above its new associates in proficiency that unless there is marked improvement in every camp, the associates had best well grant Schabbie's kids the next five championships in advance."

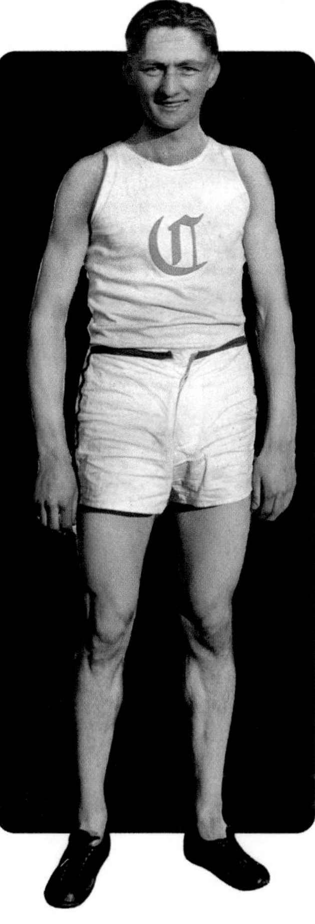

February 18, 1923:

CREIGHTON CONFERENCE CHAMPION

Blue Wins First Cage Pennant by Defeating State

The first North Central conference court championship gonfalon will be of sky bluee. "Creighton" will be blazoned across its length. And a mighty proud and lofty pennant pole on Omaha's Hilltop will sway with the weight of it this spring. All because Creighton's cage gladiators flayed South Dakota State at the Blue gym last night with a saber-like offense that slit the Rabbit wall for a 38 to 11 decision.

Creighton finishes at the top of the Big Nine pennant eligibles with a percentage of .909. The best that North Dakota university can do even though the Flickertails are awarded their disputed struggle with the Bunnies, is .000.

But the game. It was a heart-warming culmination of the Blue team's bitter conference fight—a battle that seemed lost last week when Captain Jim Lovley left the lineup with a wrecked knee. Creighton had to win without his last night.

The first ten minutes were nerve wreckers. No one could score. State broke the ice with a free throw. That was the invaders' only lead. Johnny Trautman stepped on the local throttle for a snappy follow through and the game was all over for State. The giant Rabbits never maneuvered past the Hilltop barricade and failed completely on the lengthy range.

Johnny Trautman scored 22 points in a 38-11 victory over the South Dakota State Jackrabbits that clinched the North Central Conference title in Creighton's first season in the league. "The Blue speedster played havoc with the Rabbit rear wall and battered the nets for 22 of the winners' total," The World-Herald reported. Trautman led Creighton in scoring in the 1922-23 and 1923-24 seasons. He also ran track, finishing third in the half-mile at the 1924 NCC meet.

1928: LEAVING THE NORTH CENTRAL CONFERENCE

Creighton compiled a 13-2 record in the 1927-28 season, competing as an associate member of the North Central Conference while waiting to join the Missouri Valley. The Bluejays were unbeaten against NCC members but didn't play enough games to claim the title. They also defeated Marquette and twice beat Oregon State, Colorado and Saint Louis. To Creighton, "the gaining of the North Central Conference championship in this sport would be somewhat analogous to hunting squirrels with a howitzer," The World-Herald's Fred Ware wrote. Front row, from left, are Manager J.V. "Duce" Belford, Jack Groat, C.E. Butterwick, Bart Corcoran, Leslie Strawhecker, Harry Binder and coach Arthur Schabinger. Back row, from left, are freshman coach Johnny Trautman, Hugh Fogarty, Joe Beha, Werner "Brud" Jensen, Fritz Kampf, Gordon Diesing and John Flynn. In front is Joe Schabinger, the coach's son, who served as a mascot. Six-foot-6 center Jensen dominated tip balls for Creighton, and Diesing led the Jays in scoring at 8.8 points a game. Ware later hired Fogarty at The World-Herald, where he eventually became managing editor.

Ware added, "Maybe domination of the Valley will profit the Hilltoppers more than an independent career, such as Notre Dame's, Marquette's, Butler's and Loyola's have profited them."

Schabinger's team played its first Valley basketball game on Jan. 15, 1929, and the Bluejays made a resounding debut against Grinnell. "An irresistible five-man offensive that zoomed up and down the floor in an azure wave to the confusion of the Grinnell College Pioneers gave the Creighton University Bluejays a 39-25 victory and thus enabled the men of Schabinger to make their entrance into Missouri Valley competition in the right column," a story reported the next day.

Creighton finished second in basketball in its first season of Valley play, but the Bluejays came back in 1929-30 to claim their first league championship. However, they made some of their biggest headlines that season outside conference play. In early January, the team pulled out a 28-27 win at Kentucky, which hadn't lost a home game in three years. The game was decided by William "Wee Willie" Worthing's three-quarter-court shot. Recalling the feat later, the 5-8 Worthing said, "The difference between an idiot and a hero is a very fine line." Creighton finished the 1929-30 season with a 24-point rout of Kansas, a game so lopsided, a story noted, that "all the wiles of (coach) Phog Allen failed to halt the Creighton parade."

Kentucky painted a mark on its home court to commemorate the long shot by Creighton's "Wee Willie" Worthing, who also starred in football and baseball.

The Bluejays' success under Schabinger was in part the result of the coach's innovative ways. Years later, The World-Herald's Bob Phipps assessed the man nicknamed "The Dutchman" in a column: "The Schabinger basket hunters more or less invented the fast break. An advanced thinker in the sport, Schabinger had a kind of baseball defense. Creighton players shifted constantly to intercept any pass by the opposition, then streaked downcourt ahead of the mob. The Blues won oodles of games with about 35 points. He used the short, the tall, the skinny and the bulky physiques without any discernible parts except those set by good basketball thinking, velvety ball handling and superb condition."

But Schabinger also was a fiery presence on the bench. "Those unfortunate ones seated next to him took a terrific beating," said an article describing his style. "Schabinger had a trick all his own with his knees. He played every minute of every game with those knees, slapping 'em from side to side as goals were made or missed. His hair took its share of abuse on every error by the Bluejays. Schabbie would run his fingers through his hair every time one of his lads made a mistake, and ruing the leaner years, when green performers were guilty of frequent misplays, he'd break par for the course, with 50 to 100 strokes."

January 16, 1929:

BLUEJAYS' DEBUT IN VALLEY LEAGUE BRINGS VICTORY

Hilltoppers Open Basket Barrage at Start of Game and Hold Iowans Without Goal for 15 Minutes.

L. TRAUTMAN LEADER

BY HOWARD WOLFF.

AN IRRISISTABLE five-man offensive, that zoomed up and down the floor in an azure wave to the confusion of the Grinnell college Pioneers, gave the Creighton university Bluejays a 39-25 victory and thus enabled the men of Schabinger to make their entrance into Missouri Valley competition in the right column Tuesday night.

That debut into Valley play found Schabie's lads playing a steady, heads-up game that kept the invading Pioneers ever out of range and it was not long until Creighton's first conference foemen were far in the rear.

That debut saw the Hilltoppers swing into a concerted attack right from the start, Jensen looping in a short one soon after Referee Browne's whistle started the skirmish and Louie Trautman following with a pair of side shots.

Lead, 19-8, at Half.

From there on out the Omahans were never in peril, scoring repeatedly to take a 19-8 lead at half time. After 12 minutes of the first period the Blues held a 17-to-3 lead and it was not until 15 minutes had passed that Grinnell's first field goal was realized.

Creighton Scores 39-32 Basket Ball Triumph Over Army

CREIGHTON BASKETEERS . . . . POSE FOR PICTURE . . . . WITH PRESIDENT

PRESIDENT met president Tuesday when Herbert Hoover, president of the United States, shook hands with A. A. Schabinger, president of the National Basket Ball Coaches' association. Mr. Hoover posed with the Creighton basket ball squad as the Bluejays were on their way from Morgantown, W. Va., where they defeated West Virginia, to West Point to play the Army. The meeting was arranged by Representative Malcolm Baldrige of Omaha, a former Creighton coach.

Left to right in the picture are Art Kiely, guard; Lester Kockrow, forward; Cornie Collin, forward; Tony Wiesner, center; Captain Van Ackeren, forward; Mr. Hoover; Coach Schabinger; Willard Schmidt, center; Mr. Baldrige; Assistant Coach Duce Belford; Bob Miller, guard, and Willie Worthing, guard.

1932: A VISIT TO THE WHITE HOUSE

The Jays closed out an undefeated 1931-32 Missouri Valley season with a 38-27 home win over Grinnell. The team also delivered major wins at Army and West Virginia on an Eastern trip, which included a meeting with President Herbert Hoover in Washington. The visit was arranged by Nebraska Rep. Malcolm Baldrige, who had coached Creighton football in the 1920s and been instrumental in hiring coach Arthur Schabinger. The 1931-32 team featured future Creighton Athletic Hall of Fame members Maurice Van Ackeren, William "Wee Willie" Worthing and Cornie Collin, along with future Olympian Willard Schmidt.

Schabinger dominated the Valley for seven seasons. He shared Valley titles in 1930 and 1931 and went unbeaten in the league in 1932 to win the championship outright. After two second-place finishes, Creighton again claimed a title in the 1935 season. That would turn out to be Schabinger's last Hilltop team.

While Creighton boosters found little fault with how he coached basketball, there was little consensus on Schabinger's performance as athletic director. The lack of big-time success on the football field led to conflicts that eventually cost Schabinger both jobs.

He resigned on July 1, 1935, with two years remaining on his contract. His basketball teams had compiled a .714 winning percentage in 13 seasons while claiming four NCC and four Valley championships.

"It is not without reluctance that we accept Mr. Schabinger's resignation," said the Rev. B.J. Quinn, Creighton's regent of athletics. "His record here includes many achievements, and he is a basketball coach who will be hard to replace."

To do so, Creighton turned to one of its own.

The basketball coach and athletic director, Arthur Schabinger, seated, with freshman coach J.V. "Duce" Belford. Schabinger resigned in 1935, and a World-Herald story acknowledged that "Creighton enjoyed a national reputation in basketball under 'Schabbie.'" However, sports editor Fred Ware wrote a day later, "People who surveyed the Bluejays' gridiron record with feelings of discontent were inclined to blame him ... for the failure of the 1934 squad and some of its predecessors to win more often." Creighton was 2-7 in football in 1934 and hadn't won a conference title in seven years. Ware added, "Only the future can determine the wisdom of the changes in personnel and policy, which have come to be known as the Creighton New Deal." Schabinger that fall became director of the U.S. Olympic Intercollegiate Basketball Tournament, which helped select players for the 1936 Olympics. He is a member of the Naismith Memorial Basketball Hall of Fame in Springfield, Mass.

'The Little General' leads the way

Eddie Hickey had played quarterback for Creighton and scored the first touchdown at the school's new on-campus football stadium in 1923. The 5-foot-5 Reynolds, Neb., native, who also played basketball for the Bluejays, graduated in 1927 with a law degree and planned to join his father's law firm after finishing school. But Hickey's father was killed in an automobile accident, and he chose instead to remain at Omaha Creighton Prep, the high school where he had taken a coaching job during his last year of law school.

It was at Prep where Hickey, nicknamed "The Little General," started refining the coaching skills that eventually would land him in basketball's hall of fame. Hickey coached football, basketball, baseball and track at the school while also serving as athletic director. His Prep football teams posted a 36-24-4 record, while he went 115-26 in basketball, winning 56 of 58 games in one stretch.

Schabinger hired Hickey in 1934 to become Creighton's head football coach, and the Bluejays went 2-7. When Schabinger resigned a year later, the school named Hickey its basketball coach while Marchie Schwartz took over football.

Like Schabinger, Hickey was considered a basketball innovator. He is credited with refining the three-lane fast break, which he once described as "not helter-skelter, but more like organized disorder."

But unlike Schabinger, Hickey was a cool, calculating coach. A 1936 article noted the difference between the two men's sideline styles: "Watching the antics of the former professor of the Hilltop court troops was often more entertaining than catching the play of the Blues and their rivals. Schabinger's lively capers on the bench, especially, were priceless. The bench was a red-hot griddle so far as Schabbie was concerned, from the opening tipoff to the final gun blast. But it's different now. Stoical Eddie Hickey, Schabinger's successor as the Hilltop head man, sits through it all quietly. While he may be seething inwardly, Hickey conceals his emotions."

While Hickey's first Creighton team won the Valley championship, the Bluejays failed to claim another in the following four seasons. But in 1940-41, the Bluejays began a three-season run that ranks as one of the finest in program history.

1936: A BLUEJAY IN THE OLYMPICS

Six-foot-7 Willard Schmidt walked slump-shouldered when he arrived on the Hilltop, because he was self-conscious of his height. Coach Arthur Schabinger told him to "stretch out, be proud of your size," and he also instructed the other players to encourage Schmidt by telling him he was lucky to be tall. The strategy apparently worked, as Schmidt helped the school to a Missouri Valley Conference championship in 1931-32 and was a three-time All-MVC selection. Schmidt was the tallest player on the gold medal-winning U.S. Olympic basketball team in 1936. As Schmidt and other U.S. Olympians headed off to Europe for the Games, a World-Herald editorial noted, "In Berlin, Nazism has already cast a minor curse upon the year's Olympics, yet it is good to stage a spectacle conceived in friendliness. Nebraska's representatives go in that spirit. Whatever degree of success attends their efforts in the contest arena, we know they will give their best." Weeks before the Games, Schmidt suffered a severe cut to his left heel that took eight stitches to close, but he was able to play in one of the Americans' five games and scored 8 points.

1935: BLUEJAYS GO TO WORK WITH A NEW COACH

Eddie Hickey's coaching career surely got a boost from Arthur Schabinger's resignation. Hickey had coached Creighton's losing football team the year before and inherited the Missouri Valley Conference's defending basketball champion. Among the holdovers was Emil "Box" Engelbretson, on the right, who led the Bluejays to another title in Hickey's first year. Engelbretson was Creighton's leading scorer for three straight seasons and was All-MVC his final two years.

Prof. Hickey and His First Creighton Court Class

Eddie Hickey, whose Creighton Prep teams of other years were notably successful, is the new head master of the Creighton university basket ball squad, succeeding A. A. Schabinger, whose resignation ended a 12-year term as Bluejay cage tutor.

Prof. Hickey is pictured above with five of his brightest scholars during a chalk talk. Behind Mickey, from left to right, are Bus Monteen, George Busch, Jack Lomax, Douglas Trish and Captain Emil Engelbretson.

Creighton's Dick Nolan (45) shoots against Ohio State, as Ed Beisser moves into position for a rebound in a 60-34 Bluejay win in December 1941. As the Bluejays began to pull away in the second half, the Creighton crowd chanted, "Double the score! Double the score!" The Jays heeded the call, extending their lead to 42-21 with seven minutes left before coach Hickey cleared the bench.

Creighton won the 1941 Valley championship while beating Marquette, Kentucky, Minnesota and Michigan State in nonconference games. The Bluejays advanced to the NCAA Western Regional in Kansas City, where they posted a 57-48 win over Big Six champion Iowa State in the opening round to move to the national quarterfinals, not yet known as the Elite Eight. Championship hopes were derailed in a 48-39 loss to Washington State, which made it to the national title game. Creighton closed out an 18-7 season with a 45-44 win over Wyoming in the regional consolation game.

"We face the toughest schedule in the middle west," Hickey warned before the 1941-42 season. The Bluejays opened with a 43-16 rout of Denver four days after the Japanese bombed Pearl Harbor to plunge the United States into World War II. They added home wins over UCLA and Ohio State in December and headed into Missouri Valley play with a 6-2 record. A 39-19 victory over Drake closed the regular season, with Creighton sharing the Valley championship with Henry Iba's Oklahoma A&M team.

Omaha Mayor Dan Butler hosted a salute to the Jays after their 1942 NIT success. "I know all Omaha joins me in paying well-deserved tribute to Hickey and this fine team that ranks with any in past Creighton history," he said.

The Bluejays then traveled to New York City for the National Invitation Tournament, which at the time was more prestigious than the NCAA tournament. Their opening assignment was a West Texas State team with a starting lineup averaging 6-foot-6 that had produced 28 wins in 30 games. The underdog Jays, playing before 16,585 at Madison Square Garden, led by 17 points in the second half before squeezing out a 59-58 victory.

Interviewed on the floor after the game ended, Hickey said, "I'm so proud of my boys, I could bust. They played like champions, didn't they?"

With West Texas and tournament favorite Long Island University losing in the first round, Hickey's team became the toast of New York. The World-Herald's Fred Ware wrote: "Never did a Creighton team perpetrate such a whacking upset."

The Bluejays didn't play their second NIT game for a week, and in the interim, spent time touring the city. The team visited Grant's Tomb and the top of the Empire State Building and sat in on a radio broadcast of Fred Waring's orchestra. The return to Madison Square Garden ended their time as toast of the town.

Creighton lost to Western Kentucky 49-36 in the semifinals, then claimed third place with a 48-46 win over Toledo. Stars Ed Beisser and Ralph Langer remained in New York to participate in a charity game involving collegiate players and the U.S. Army All-Stars. The rest of the team visited Niagara Falls before returning to Omaha, where proud alumni threw the Bluejays a victory banquet at the Hotel Paxton.

The next fall, Creighton's football team compiled a 5-4 record, closing the season with a 33-19 home loss to powerhouse Tulsa. It would turn out to be the last football game Creighton would ever play. A couple of weeks later, the Rev. David Shyne, Creighton's athletic director, announced that the school was suspending athletics for the duration of World War II.

Hickey's basketball team would be allowed to play its 1942-43 season, but Hickey and Maurice "Skip" Palrang, the school's football coach, were instructed not to schedule games for future seasons. Hickey's Bluejays opened in December with a five-point win over Kansas, the first of 16 straight victories over collegiate teams on the way to another Valley championship. Creighton also went 3-1 in exhibitions against powerful armed forces teams that featured former college stars.

1942: CREIGHTON'S LAST FOOTBALL TEAM

Maurice "Skip" Palrang, right, had been named football coach in 1939 after Marchie Schwartz's resignation. The Bluejays' last football game, played before a crowd of 9,000 at Creighton Stadium, was a 33-19 loss to Tulsa on Nov. 21, 1942. CU's Bill Brock (30) juggled a pass from quarterback Al DiMarco but gained control and carried it in for a 12-6 Bluejay lead in the second quarter. The Jays were still ahead of the unbeaten Golden Hurricane 19-12 in the third quarter before falling. Tulsa also had beaten Oklahoma and Arkansas and finished fourth in the Associated Press' final football ratings. Creighton ended varsity athletics in 1943 because of World War II. Basketball would later return, but not football. The end of Bluejay football eventually landed Palrang at Boys Town, where he produced some of the best high school football and basketball teams in Nebraska.

The season earned Creighton its only No. 1 ranking in program history. Sportswriter Dick Dunkel lifted the Jays to the top spot of the Dunkel Ratings, which were the pre-eminent college rankings until the Associated Press began its basketball poll in 1949. The Bluejays, who had already accepted another NIT invitation, made Dunkel look good when they posted a 20-point win in a rematch with Kansas that closed the regular season.

Creighton was made the NIT's No. 1 seed and drew Washington & Jefferson for a March 18 opening game. The Bluejays' journey to New York started badly, as all-conference guard Ward Gibson missed the team's train to Chicago. Gibson had been in Des Moines and was unable to get on the bus to Omaha because of wartime travel complications.

In Chicago, Hickey had arranged a scrimmage against Loyola University. "This throws our plans into a cocked hat," Hickey said, referring to Gibson's absence. "What a way to start the biggest trip of the season."

Gibson eventually caught up with his teammates, but misfortune dogged the Bluejays when they took the court against Washington & Jefferson.

The Bluejays led 28-19 at halftime and 38-26 with 10 minutes left before foul trouble — players were allowed only four personals in those days — claimed CU starters Beisser, Langer, Gibson and Donald "Pinky" Knowles. Washington & Jefferson closed the game on a 7-1 run to eliminate Creighton 43-42.

The opening paragraphs of the game report in the next day's World-Herald told the sad story.

"Creighton came to the end of the basketball trail Thursday night, a sorry ending triple distilled in misery," the story said. "Everything but the roof fell in on the hapless Blues before the finish. A wild, frenzied climax saw only Gene Lalley of the regulars remaining when the Presidents set the 16 thousand fans yammering with the late drive that brought victory."

In a follow-up story, The World-Herald's Howard Wolff wrote: "Bathed in the salty tears of recrimination, Creighton's deflated Bluejays turned to the lighter side of their ill-fated New York trip Friday with the bitter taste of that Washington & Jefferson nightmare still puckering up their mouths."

Hickey was still rehashing the game the next day. "It just doesn't seem possible," he said. "I guess all the good things that happened to us before came up in reverse. I can't see how we blew that big lead."

1943: AN EARLY RIVAL

Henry Iba became head basketball coach at Oklahoma A&M in 1934, a year before Hickey was hired at Creighton. Iba and Hickey dominated the Missouri Valley Conference, with the slow-paced Aggies and fast-breaking Bluejays either winning or sharing every Valley title between 1935 and 1943. During that stretch, A&M lost only three times in 72 games at Gallagher Hall in Stillwater, and two of the losses were to the Bluejays. Iba so respected Creighton's 1941-42 team that he admitted to attending one of their games. "It was the first time in eight years that I had scouted an opponent," he said. Hickey's unbeaten 1943 Valley champions swept Iba's team before Creighton suspended athletics during World War II. A&M, later renamed Oklahoma State, continued its basketball program during the war and won national championships in 1945 and 1946, the first school to take consecutive titles in basketball.

The team dispersed when it returned to Omaha's Burlington Station two days later. Hickey enlisted in the Navy but spent the duration of the war stateside, supervising physical training and coaching basketball. His players either enlisted or were drafted, and several saw combat.

January 16, 1943:

Dick Dunkel Places Jays Alone at Top

Oklahoma Ags' Sturdy Play Against K. U. Whetting Interest

By Howard Wolff

Creighton puts its No. 1 national ranking, plus a seven-game winning streak, in the path of Oklahoma Aggies' rowdy buckos at the Hilltop tonight at 8:30.

And an overflow assemblage will be there to see the fun with the gymnasium's capacity limit of 3,500 certain to be strained. Reserved seats were only a memory as far back as Wednesday, and the 1,500 general admission seats are expected to disappear long before Jays and Cowboys take their warmups.

General admission tickets will go on sale at 6:30. All reserved seat tickets must be picked up at the box office before 8 or they will be sold.

Many factors make this annual appearance of Hank Iba's crew a crowd puller.

First of all, the Jays are working on that victory string. And Friday Dick Dunkel's national rankings placed Eddie Hickey's crop as the No. 1 team in the nation with a 75.9 rating. Kansas is second at 75.1 and Duquesne third at 73.9. Creighton has beaten both Kansas and Duquesne.

Then the Cowboys' conduct in Wednesday's Kansas game at Lawrence puts a delicious edge on the Hilltop struggle. The hard-riding Cowboys committed 23 fouls, led to Dr. Phog Allen's letter to Iba suggesting a discontinuation of their cage rivalry because of the roughness of Aggie play.

Creighton Football Coach Skip Palrang, who scouted the Cowboys against Kansas, reported to Hickey he'd find Iba's crew "mean and rough."

To which Hickey replied: "We're big enough to take care of ourselves."

ON THE BIG STAGE

Coach Eddie Hickey, shown with Gene Haldeman, entered the 1942-43 season with confidence. "Because of the use of freshmen, I think we will have a little more reserve strength than last year," he said, referring to the previous year's team that had won the Missouri Valley and finished third in the prestigious National Invitation Tournament in New York. The Bluejays exceeded his expectations. They were a perfect 16-0 in the regular season and in January were ranked No. 1 in the Dunkel Ratings, a statistical system created by sportswriter Dick Dunkel. The Jays twice beat defending Big Six champion Kansas, which at one time had been No. 2 in the rankings, They also ended Duquesne's five-year home winning streak and defeated powerhouse Long Island at Madison Square Garden before a record crowd of 18,394. And they swept Missouri Valley rival Oklahoma A&M, coached by Henry Iba, to claim their third straight league crown. Creighton again accepted a bid to the NIT, rather than the fledgling NCAA tournament, and went to New York as the No. 1 seed. The Jays lost to Washington & Jefferson 43-42 in their tourney opener, a crushing blow after a great regular season. On the train ride home, The World-Herald's Howard Wolff reported, "Self-blame laid heavily on all squad members, as clicking wheels accompanied the oft-replayed nightmare." The Jays, despite their disappointment, ended up No. 5 in the Dunkel Ratings. Creighton professor Charles Bongardt, speaking at the school's athletic banquet, took note that the team earlier had been rated No. 1 and said, "There are those of us who strongly maintain that it still is, and during the entire season this team, like its two predecessors, brought new glory to the university, the community and the state."

RALPH "SWEDE" LANGER

Langer led the Jays in scoring in 1941-42 and 1942-43. The forward was named first-team All-American in 1943 by the National Editorial Association, a wire service at the time. He also was on the All-America team of Sir magazine, a men's publication, with an article by legendary coach Clair Bee saying he "hounds the ball like a whippet chasing the electric rabbit in a dog race." He was wounded in Italy in 1945 but recovered and played with the Denver Nuggets of the short-lived American Basketball League in 1946. He was back in Omaha in 1947 and played with the Omahawks of the similarly short-lived Professional Basket Ball League.

ED BEISSER

The 6-7 center finished second in scoring for the Jays, thanks to what The World-Herald called an "almost unstoppable swing pivot shot," or hook. "Big Ed" was named to three straight All-Missouri Valley Conference teams, the Helms All-America second team and the Sporting News third team. At a banquet after the season, Hickey surprised his senior center with a 21-jewel watch that came with his selection to PIC magazine's All-America first-team. After college, he played for the Phillips Oilers, which won three straight AAU titles. He earned an alternate spot with the 1948 Olympic team but didn't play with the U.S. team in London.

DONALD "PINKY" KNOWLES

Knowles played for Creighton as a freshman in 1942-43, earning the label of "a ball of fire" from The World-Herald. His scrappy play made him a crowd favorite. A story described how he "heeded the frantic yipping of the crowd" as he fired a last-second shot to end the first half of a big win over Oklahoma A&M: "Pinky dribbled just past the midcourt stripe, fired and the ball settled through the meshes without touching the rim." Knowles spent three years in the Navy, then returned for two seasons, leading the Jays in scoring in 1947-48 with 10.6 points a game. He took a year off from basketball as he started law school, then returned for a final varsity season at age 25.

WARD GIBSON

The 6-4, 205-pound sophomore was an All-Valley guard in 1943, known for his rugged defense and rebounding. His play in boxing out opponents and grabbing rebounds in the 1942-43 season opener earned a cry from the Creighton student section of, "Get it again, 'Iron Pants!' " The moniker "Old Iron Pants" stuck. Hickey preferred to call him "Automatic Ike," saying, "That boy's automatic. He does the right things at the right time." Gibson also was a clutch shooter, hitting two shots in the final minute to rally the Bluejays to the big victory over Long Island at Madison Square Garden. He came back after the war and led the 1946-47 team in scoring with 14.3 points a game. The Jays posted a 17-8 record that year, their only winning record between the end of the war and 1956-57, after the university had restored sports scholarships.

A downward spiral toward independence

The end of World War II brought a resumption of basketball competition for the Bluejays. The Rev. Thomas S. Bowdern announced on Oct. 18, 1945, that Creighton would field a team for the 1945-46 season.

J.V. "Duce" Belford, an assistant under Schabinger and Hickey who had served as Creighton's director of intramural and physical training programs during the war, was named coach. "We won't be able to match the records of former Creighton teams but it won't be because we won't try," said Belford, who had lost just one game in the previous eight seasons as the Bluejays' freshman coach. "We'll give the fans a lot of action in our first postwar season."

Eddie Hickey, left, congratulated Duce Belford on becoming Creighton's new coach after Hickey accepted the job at St. Louis in 1947. Hickey's career landed him in the Naismith Memorial Basketball Hall of Fame in Springfield, Mass.

The Bluejays took the court less than two months later, routing Omaha University 48-19 in the first game between the two schools since the time when Claus Delfs was coaching. Belford guided the team to a 9-10 record that season, going 3-7 against Valley teams, including 0-2 against new league member Wichita State.

Hickey returned the next season and, with 1942-43 stars Pinky Knowles and Gene Lalley back from the service, directed the Bluejays to a 17-8 record that included nine wins in the last 10 games. But six weeks after Creighton finished the season with a 51-43 win over Wichita State, Hickey resigned to become coach at Saint Louis University.

"The Little General" had posted a 126-71 record at Creighton, winning two Valley championships outright and sharing two others. "Naturally, I hate to leave Creighton," Hickey said. "I've been here as a student and coach since 1922. That's a long time. But this seems like the right move to make." His first Saint Louis team, with "Easy Ed" Macauley as the star, would win the NIT. Hickey would go on to win 436 games at Creighton, Saint Louis and Marquette, enjoying a career that would land him, like his predecessor Schabinger, in basketball's hall of fame.

Greater change was about to engulf the basketball program. Soon after Belford had guided the Bluejays through a 10-13 season in 1947-48, Creighton received an ultimatum from Missouri Valley officials: Either Creighton would resume playing football or the conference would ask the school to relinquish its membership.

Valley officials weren't the only ones clamoring for the school to get back into the business of football. In late April of 1948, Creighton students held an on-campus rally asking that football be restored and for a return to prewar basketball standards. World-Herald sports editor Floyd Olds wrote: "It's a matter which has two sides, of course. The loudest noises are being made by graduates and friends who want a Bluejay football team. But there are others ... who are satisfied with the present program, which has athletics on pretty much of an intramural basis."

In June 1948, the Rev. William H. McCabe, the school's president, informed Valley officials that Creighton intended to leave the conference. In a letter to the alumni, Father McCabe stated that "ascending costs of education will require all of Creighton's present resources as well as very substantial financial help from alumni and those who are interested in the service which Creighton has rendered."

Noting that football had not been restored after the war because of financial concerns, McCabe wrote: "Intercollegiate football has become even more costly in the past two years, and competition in football would involve an additional heavy burden that we could not reasonably ask our alumni and friends to bear." He indicated that Creighton would like to continue scheduling basketball contests against league members, but that it was prepared to go it alone as an independent.

Creighton wasn't the only private Midwestern school struggling with the growing financial demands of sports. Grinnell had dropped out of the Missouri Valley in 1939, and Washington University never returned to the conference after World War II. The two longtime league members would never compete again at as high a level.

Without a conference for its team and without scholarship aid for its players, Creighton struggled to find success on the court. Belford led Creighton to a 9-14 record in its first season of independent play but proclaimed that better days were on the horizon.

"We have ridden the crest of the basketball wave in the past," he said. "Right now we are in the trough. But we are firm believers that it takes two wave crests to make a trough."

1947: PINKY SINKS GONZAGA

"Little Pinky Knowles, the pepper pot from Iowa, made Duce Belford's full-time coaching debut a happy one," The World-Herald reported after Creighton defeated Gonzaga 32-29 in the 1947-48 season opener. Knowles (45) scored 11 points, including four in the final two minutes as the Jays put the game away. Gene Lalley (43) scored 8 points.

1948: LASTING CONNECTIONS TO CREIGHTON

Subby Salerno, left, Bob Gradoville and Jim Karabatsos continued to leave their marks on Creighton long after their playing days ended. Salerno coached the freshman basketball team after he graduated and the varsity from 1952 to 1955. The final team he coached included star sophomore Bob Gibson. Two of Gradoville's grandsons, Tim and Chris Gradoville, played baseball for Creighton. Brother Paul played basketball from 1950 to 1952, and Paul's daughter Pam Gradoville also played for the Jays. Karabatsos, who led the 1948-49 team in scoring at 7.7 points a game, taught English at Creighton for 30 years and was chairman of the English department from 1978 to 1981.

Creighton came back to finish 13-13 the next season, closing with a loss to St. Francis in the National Catholic Intercollegiate Tournament. The Rev. David Shyne, the athletic director, praised Belford and the players at a postseason banquet.

"For some reason difficult to explain, this Bluejay team captured the fancy of the fans," Shyne said. "This team created more school spirit on the Hilltop than we have had at any time since the war. And I can truthfully say that it was one of the most successful Creighton teams of all time, regardless of the won-and-lost record."

It was, The World-Herald's Olds noted, strictly an "amateur club."

"The boys played ball because they liked to," Olds wrote, "and for that reason they probably got more out of it than many of the more highly-rated teams."

But what Creighton wouldn't get during the next five years was a winning season. The Bluejays went 9-18 and 6-15 in Belford's final two seasons. Sebastian "Subby" Salerno, who played for Creighton from 1945 to 1949, took over in 1952 and went 11-14, 14-17 and 5-14 in his three seasons.

1949: JAYHAWKS FALL ON HILLTOP

Creighton upset Kansas 59-55 at the school gym with Bob Gradoville, second from left, scoring 12 points. The Jayhawks were led by All-America center Clyde Lovellette (16). Duce Belford's Jays earned a berth in the National Catholic Intercollegiate Tournament, where they lost 67-66 to St. Francis (N.Y.) to finish the season at 13-13.

1953: TESTING THE WATERS

The Creighton Alumni Association decided in 1953 to measure interest in restoring the basketball program to its stature prior to World War II. The Phillips 66 team of former college stars, considered the best amateur team in the country, came to the Hilltop for a game, and the school said it would weigh its future decision based on the turnout. "It could be the Jays are heading for a return to the big time," The World-Herald reported. The Jays did their part, trailing by just 1 point heading into the fourth quarter against the Phillips 66 powerhouse before losing 71-63. But only 1,038 turned out, and Creighton officials expressed disappointment. "Just what the Hilltop padres will do toward their announced goal of a return to the days of when Creighton was a national power in the roundball sport is questionable," Howard Wolff wrote.

Back on the 'big-time' path

By 1955, school officials had become convinced that their de-emphasis of athletics was not working out. The Rev. Carl Reinert, university president, hired Theron "Tommy" Thomsen as coach for the 1955-56 season and announced that Creighton was adopting an athletic policy "tailored to return the school to big-time basketball." The school would begin offering athletic scholarships again and look at possibly playing some games at Omaha's new Civic Auditorium, said Reinert, who had played basketball for Skip Palrang in high school. Reinert referred to the past policy of no scholarships as a "suicide code."

The Rev. Carl Reinert restored basketball scholarships.

Thomsen, who had previously coached at Coe College in Cedar Rapids, Iowa, said Reinert and other school officials assured him he would "have the horses to pull the Jays back up the basketball ladder."

The Bluejays played their first game at the Civic on Dec. 28, 1955, as part of the NAIA Tip-Off Classic. The tournament also drew Omaha University, Gustavus Adolphus, Regis, East Texas State, Texas Southern, Southeast Oklahoma and Western Illinois and had an opening-day clinic featuring all-time great George Mikan and Chuck Taylor, namesake of the shoes that many of the players wore.

Creighton lost its first game, dropping a 64-58 decision to East Texas State, with junior Bob Gibson scoring 25 points. Gibson, who had starred in baseball and basketball at Omaha Tech High School, had been recruited by Salerno but would become the featured player on Thomsen's first two teams.

Gibson led the team in both scoring and rebounding during his last two years. One of Gibson's favorite games at Creighton came in 1956, when he scored 20 points against No. 14 Holy Cross and Tom Heinsohn, who the next season was rookie of the year with the NBA's Boston Celtics.

Gibson, the first African-American to play basketball or baseball at Creighton, recalled confronting segregation on a road trip to Oklahoma City.

Chuck Taylor, described in The World-Herald as a "54-year-old former pro," appeared at a 1955 basketball clinic before the NAIA Tip-Off Classic at the Civic Auditorium. Here, Taylor gives instruction to Bob Moore of Clarkson High and Larry Fuerst of Midland College. Among his tips: "On defense, watch the other player's belt buckle."

"We were halfway to Oklahoma City, and our coach told me I had to stay somewhere else, that I couldn't stay with the team," Gibson said. "I was 18 years old, and that might have been the last time I cried.

"Luckily, we had another guy on the team from Omaha named Glen Sullivan. He told me, 'Don't worry about it, Gibby, wherever you stay, I'm going with you.' We went across town, and if the coach would have known how much fun we had, he wouldn't have liked it."

Gibson scored 1,272 points over his three seasons and was the school's third all-time leading scorer when his career ended in 1956-57. He said later he would have pursued a career in basketball had the old Minneapolis Lakers of the National Basketball Association offered him a contract.

Bob Gibson received a watch and a pen-and-pencil set in 1956 as the most valuable player from the Creighton alumni association's Jim Green. The theme of the year-end banquet, The World-Herald reported, "was pretty much a reiteration of Creighton's previously stated desire to return to basketball prominence." Coach Tommy Thomsen raised Creighton's record to 15-6 in the 1956-57 season, although the schedule featured games against Gannon, Western Ontario, St. Michael's of Vermont and Westmar of Le Mars, Iowa.

"If they had signed me, I would have never played baseball," said Gibson, who went on to become one of the greatest pitchers in major league history with the St Louis Cardinals. "That would have been a shame, I guess.

"I'm not as sure I would have been as good a basketball player. But I enjoyed the sport. It's always been my No. 1 sport."

Gibson did play one season with the Harlem Globetrotters before signing with the Cardinals.

Creighton posted a 15-6 record in Gibson's senior season — Thomsen's second as coach. The Bluejays played their first true home games at the Civic Auditorium in 1957-58, losing to South Dakota, DePaul, Marquette and Oklahoma City in the building.

Thomsen resigned after his 1958-59 team went 13-9. On Thomsen's watch, Creighton had made some baby steps in moving toward Reinert's goal of fielding a big-time basketball program.

His successor would take a pedal-to-the-metal approach to accelerate the process.

Bob Gibson splits Morningside defenders Don Poppen, left, and Jerry Kreykes in a 59-44 victory in Tommy Thomsen's first season as coach. Gibson led the Jays during the 1955-56 season with 22 points and 7.6 rebounds a game.

34
OFFICIAL
TIMEKEEPER

1959-1969

Reviving the dream

Creighton's previous rebuilding plan had been based on a good record against a weaker schedule. Red McManus drew up a new blueprint for raising the Bluejays' national stature. "You have to play the best teams in the country that you can schedule," he said. "And if you beat them, you're in."

Paul Silas grabs one of his 26 rebounds in a 1961 victory over Notre Dame in his second game for Creighton. In the season opener he had 29 rebounds, three more than the entire Colorado College team.

Anybody, anytime, anywhere

IN JOHN "RED" MCMANUS, Creighton found the perfect man to lead its attempts to move its basketball program to a bigger stage. The 34-year-old coach — hired on May 7, 1959, to take over for Tommy Thomsen — shared Creighton's desire for a big-time program. More importantly, McManus had contacts that could make it happen.

McManus came to Creighton after coaching Iowa's freshman team, which included future NBA star and later coach Don Nelson. Before his first game at CU, McManus appeared at St. Pius X grade school's newly built gym to deliver a speech titled "Watching Basketball and Enjoying It More."

"Red had spent a lot of time at coaching clinics on the East Coast," said Tom Apke, who played for McManus from 1962 to 1965. "He knew a lot of people, and it was through those contacts that he was able to put together schedules that had us playing a school like St. John's in New York. That was huge, huge, huge at the time."

McManus' scheduling philosophy during the decade in which he coached Creighton's program: Fear no one. That included powerful UCLA, with McManus squeezing John Wooden's Bruins into a window in Creighton's 1961-62 schedule.

"A tournament they were supposed to play in was canceled and that left them with a hole in their schedule," McManus recalled. "John Wooden called me and asked about a game with us that week. I checked our schedule and told him we were playing on Monday, Tuesday and Thursday. We had Wednesday open. I said, 'This will mean we'll play four games in a row, but we would play you even if we had to go 14 in a row.' "

McManus' team won all four games, including a 74-72 victory over the Bruins.

His teams won plenty of other games against big-name opponents. Lost their share, too. But true to the fiery nature of the man who led them, the Bluejays never backed away from a challenge.

McManus was a three-sport star in high school at St. Ambrose Academy in Davenport, Iowa. After graduating in 1943, he played two seasons of minor league baseball for the Brooklyn Dodgers, but his career ended when he was hit on the throwing arm by a pitched ball. He never completely regained use of the arm and returned to Davenport to attend St. Ambrose College, where he studied political science while coaching the school's baseball team and assisting in basketball. He later became head basketball coach at his old high school, winning 119 games and losing just 45 in eight years. In the fall of 1958, he enrolled at the University of Iowa to work on his master's degree and coach the Hawkeyes' freshman basketball team.

McManus' move to Creighton nine months later hardly created a stir around Omaha. The announcement was covered in a seven-paragraph story in The World-Herald, and the school held no on-campus ceremony to welcome its new coach. While the introduction might have been low-key, Creighton's initiation to the McManus era proved to be anything but.

McManus with starters from his first team, from left: Dick McMahon, Ed Hubbard, Dick Hartmann, Dick Harvey and Jack Chapman. McManus inherited a roster that was short on experience. He also lost one letterman who was informed by school officials, "You would be wasting your time coming back to school, because of your low grades in the past."

First, he set out to put some pizazz in the Bluejays' schedule, which had featured only a handful of games against big-name opponents in Thomsen's final season. In his first year, McManus lined up games against Saint Louis, Detroit and Loyola of Chicago, all national powers at the time. He also scheduled a four-game, six-day trip to the Northwest in late January and set up a stretch run that included road games at DePaul and Notre Dame and a home contest against Marquette.

Next, he began making public appearances in Omaha to drum up support for his program. At one press gathering, a Creighton faculty member remarked, "I imagine this will be a building season." When it was his turn to speak, McManus responded, "As far as I'm concerned, there is no such thing as a building season. We'll be playing to win every time out."

When practice started, McManus showed he would change the way the Bluejays played the game. His coaching philosophy was to get his players fundamentally strong in practice, then turn them loose on game night. The results were seen in his first game.

Jack Chapman takes a pass from teammate Dick Harvey (40) and heads for a layup against Colorado State College in 1959, while Jays Ed Hubbard (15) and Dick Hartmann (34) move into position. Creighton's 105 points broke the school record of 94, set against Drake in 1955.

Playing at the Hilltop gym, Creighton unleashed a withering attack on Colorado State College, later renamed Northern Colorado. In their first 40 seasons of basketball, the Bluejays had never scored 100 points in a game. In McManus' first game, they shattered the school record in the 105-54 victory. He was given "a hero's shoulder ride by a group of boosters after the contest," The World-Herald reported, and fans cut down the net on one of the baskets.

The Jays would not hit the century mark again in the 1959-60 season, but they did score 91 points against Northern Arizona and 97 against McManus' alma mater, St. Ambrose. After losing road games at DePaul and Notre Dame, Creighton closed its 13-11 season with a 69-66 victory over Marquette.

A trip worth the cost of the ticket

As important as that first campaign was in setting a tone on the court, there was an even greater development taking place behind the scenes. McManus was intent on upgrading the program by landing a talented high school player from Oakland, Calif., Paul Silas, as his first prized recruit. Recruiting was far less complicated in those days, with no summer AAU circuit or recruiting rankings. There also were no NCAA rules prohibiting third parties, boosters and alumni from being involved in the process.

Frank Walsh, a West Coast sports promoter and friend of McManus, had told the Creighton coach about the gifted 6-foot-7 Silas. Walsh often would stop by the car dealership at which Silas buffed cars and give his pitch about an unfamiliar school 1,600 miles away.

> "I went to Father Lemke and told him I would spend my own money, that here was a kid we had to get."
>
> **— McManus, on his effort to recruit Paul Silas**

Silas attended Oakland athletic superpower McClymonds High, the same school that had produced Boston Celtics star Bill Russell and major league baseball's Frank Robinson and Vada Pinson. Silas lived in a house his family shared with uncle Elton Pointer, across the street from a park where Russell used to play before leading the University of San Francisco to two national championships and the Celtics to 11 NBA titles.

"We were just little kids at the time, and Russ was awesome to us," Silas recalled years later. "We called him the 'Big Genie' because he was so huge."

Silas and his McClymonds High teammates went 69-0 during his three seasons on the varsity. He averaged more than 30 points a game as a senior and was named the state player of the year and a high school All-American. Others doubted McManus could get Silas to Omaha, but the coach decided to pay a recruiting visit.

The Rev. Norbert Lemke, who served as the faculty moderator between the athletic department and the university administration, tried to talk him out of making the trip.

"The plane ticket was on my desk, and I was ready to go," McManus recalled. "But there was this note from Father Lemke that said I should call off the trip, because we had no chance to get Paul. We talked it over, and the next morning, I went to Father Lemke and told him I would spend my own money, that here was a kid we had to get. He relented at the last minute."

The trip proved crucial. Silas was being recruited by a number of schools, including the University of San Francisco. To this day, he remembers the impact of seeing McManus show up on his doorstep.

"It was really strange," Silas said. "A lot of coaches, even ones in the San Francisco Bay Area, had not come around and talked to me. It was just great that he did that. He asked me if I would consider going to Omaha, Nebraska, to play basketball. I told him I would consider going anywhere. I just wanted to play and have some fun."

1962: HIGH HOPES ON THE HILLTOP

Chuck Officer, standing, and Paul Silas were photographed for a World-Herald article with the headline, "Creighton's climb back to big time." The story recounted the success of Eddie Hickey's teams in the 1940s, followed by nearly 20 years of struggles, and noted, "Now, during McManus' third season, hopes are burning luxuriantly."

Silas made a summer of 1960 recruiting visit to Omaha, where he stayed with Chuck Officer, who had been a freshman during McManus' first year at Creighton.

"School was out, and none of the guys were on campus except Chuck, so we had Paul stay with him," McManus recalled. "They stayed up until 3 or 4 in the morning talking. The next day, Chuck had this big smile on his face. I think Chuck was very responsible for getting him here."

But the deciding vote to get Silas to Creighton might have been cast by his father, Leon. He often had passed through Omaha while working as a railroad porter. "He knew there wasn't a heck of a lot to do in Omaha," Silas said. "He thought I would get a good education, and he was the one who made the decisions for me."

With no Silas — freshmen weren't eligible at the time — Creighton took its lumps in McManus' second year, going 8-17. The schedule included road games at Illinois, Iowa, Colorado, Xavier, Purdue, Marquette, St. John's, Providence, Duquesne, Dayton and Notre Dame, plus a home game against No. 5 North Carolina. Hopes for better days, though, were as close as the gym, where Silas practiced with the varsity squad.

"Red would let some of the freshmen practice with the sophomores, juniors and seniors," Silas said. "When I became a sophomore, I knew those guys. I had played with them and practiced with them, so it was really a good situation."

The freshmen occasionally would play intrasquad games against the varsity, and Silas recalled an angry McManus after one game the freshmen had won handily. "That's just the way he was," Silas said. "He wanted to win every game that he played."

By then, the Creighton community also knew that their coach was a fierce competitor. A gentleman off the court, McManus could turn into a monster once the ball was tipped off. His face would often turn beet-red as he patrolled the sidelines shaking his fist and yelling at the referees.

"People used to worry about my blood pressure," McManus recalled. "They were afraid I was going to have a stroke. Actually, my blood pressure was normal. I never had an ulcer."

Opponents could feel the heat, too. Pete McManamon, who played for McManus from 1960 to 1963, recalled a pregame incident at Marquette, which at the time was coached by former Creighton great Eddie Hickey.

"We were playing up there, the horn sounded, and we went out for the center jump," McManamon said. "Marquette doesn't come out. He (Hickey) would have you stand out there for 30 seconds or whatever, until he was good and ready. This infuriated Red.

"The next time we play at Marquette, the buzzer goes off and neither team comes out. The buzzer goes off again. Now Red and Hickey are screaming at each other, 'Get your team out there!' and 'No, you get your team out there!' Forgetting what happened the time before, we're all looking at each other like, 'What the heck's going on?' But Red remembered, and he wasn't going to let Hickey one-up him like that."

McManus' emotional sideline presence often earned him technical fouls. So did a sharp tongue. "What's the matter, you lose your guts?" he said to one official during a game. "You haven't called a foul on them the second half." The official immediately signaled a technical on the Creighton coach.

McManus' players also felt the heat. "He came after me," Silas said. "He came at everybody if, in his opinion, you weren't doing what he wanted you to do."

They also quickly learned about their coach's competitive streak. Apke, who joined the program in 1961, recalled a practice ritual in which McManus would work with an individual player at one of the side baskets in the school gym. "He would have somebody feeding the ball, and he would defend you and then you would defend him," Apke said. "Red used to cheat like hell. He would push and shove. He was trying to get us to play more physically and more aggressively. But, as a young player, the first time you went up against him, you're wondering if you're supposed to push back against your coach."

> "(McManus) came at everybody if, in his opinion, you weren't doing what he wanted you to do."
>
> **— Paul Silas**

With the addition of Silas, Creighton went into the 1961-62 season with high hopes and, for the first time in program history, all of its home games at the Civic Auditorium.

McManus, who previously had scheduled auditorium games only against big names like North Carolina, touted the seven-year-old facility as an aid in recruiting. "I don't have a beautiful campus to sell," he said. "I just have a good school which can offer a good education, a good place to play our games and a good schedule."

The home opener drew a crowd of 4,176, and the season's average crowd of 3,633 surpassed the Hilltop gym's capacity. In the second home game, 5,264 watched a victory that foretold a special season. The Bluejays knocked off Notre Dame 73-71 when Officer buried a 35-foot shot with five seconds to play. "I didn't know how much time was left," Officer said after the game. "I was trying to see the clock. I really don't know why I shot — I just did."

Silas contributed 22 points and 26 rebounds in the win, which prompted The World-Herald's Ralph Stewart to write, "Creighton University took a mighty stride back into the big-time basketball ranks."

Creighton would lose two of its next three games, dropping road contests at Illinois and Northwestern. The Bluejays then ran off seven straight wins, the first four coming in the brutal four-games-in-four-days stretch that McManus set up when he added Wooden's UCLA team to the schedule.

On Monday, Creighton posted an 82-77 home win over Gonzaga. On Tuesday, the Bluejays traveled to South Dakota, rolling to an 85-59 victory. On Wednesday, they were back home to take on UCLA, which, at the time, had yet to win the first of the 10 national championships with Wooden but still featured a backcourt of three-year starter John Green and future All-American Walt Hazzard.

Creighton didn't know much about the Bruins, as McManus had no scouting budget at the time. "I told the guys we'd start the game and then call time five minutes into it," McManus said. "Then, we'd go over the scouting report, and we'd come back and beat them." Creighton trailed 14-2 at the first timeout but eventually got things under control, pulling out a 74-72 victory.

On Thursday, the Bluejays finished the week with a 91-57 win over Rice.

They took a Christmas break and then added victories over Princeton, South Dakota and Wabash to their winning streak. The good times ended on the road with a 20-point loss at St. John's, followed two days later by an 86-80 loss at Seton Hall.

Herb Millard, 1961-62 Bluejay captain, leads team members past students as they prepare to board a bus for the NCAA regional in Manhattan, Kan. Creighton sports information director Harry Dolphin estimated that 2,000 Jays fans would make the trip. The school dismissed classes the day of the game.

The Bluejays regrouped to rattle off nine straight wins — six of them on the road — to earn the school's second trip to the NCAA tournament and its first since 1941. The players were elated. "We weren't a big school in college basketball," Silas said. "Nobody thought we'd be that good, and all of a sudden we're in the NCAA tournament. That was great."

1963: IMPRESSING THE NBA

Earl Lloyd, chief scout for the NBA's Detroit Pistons, was on hand for Silas' 24 points and 19 rebounds in an 89-79 win over Gonzaga. "Silas impressed me on two occasions when he took the rebound and went upcourt with the ball," Lloyd said. "We have trouble getting our big boys to do that." He noted that Silas played with an injured knee and added, "He would have killed those guys if he had two good legs."

At the time, the NCAA tournament consisted of just 25 teams. Creighton drew Memphis for a first-round game in Dallas, and the Bluejays pulled out an 87-83 win, as Silas scored 27 points and grabbed 22 rebounds. Creighton advanced to a Sweet 16 matchup against defending national champion Cincinnati in Manhattan, Kan., where the Bearcats held the Jays to 19 percent shooting in a 66-46 victory. Creighton closed the season with a 63-61 win over Texas Tech in a consolation game that was a part of the tournament in those days. "We were disappointed," McManus said, "but not ashamed."

A week after beating Creighton, Cincinnati defeated the UCLA team that the Bluejays had knocked off in December in the national semifinals, then won its second straight title with a 12-point win over Ohio State.

Creighton opened the 1962-63 season listed as a top 20 team in two preseason magazine rankings. Apke, a prep star from Cincinnati, was set to join the varsity after McManus had outrecruited home-state universities Cincinnati, Ohio State and Dayton for his services.

"We'll be in a postseason tournament again this season," McManus predicted before the season. He was right, but it would end up being the National Catholic Intercollegiate Tournament instead of the NCAA. McManus paid the price for an overly ambitious schedule, which featured road games at national powers Michigan, Notre Dame, Colorado, Ohio State and Arizona State and just 10 home games. The Bluejays finished 14-13, losing to Xavier in the Catholic tournament before closing the season with a 15-point win over Regis in a consolation game.

In spite of disappointment at not making the NCAA tournament, McManus' players reveled in the opportunity his scheduling presented.

"Red used to brag that as an independent, we played border to border and coast to coast," Apke said. "As a player, one of the cool things is that we played in so many states, in so many famous arenas and against so many powerhouse programs. This was the era before there was a thing as the so-called mid-majors, so traveling and playing against the big boys is the thing I'll always remember."

So does Silas.

"We played everywhere," he said. "You name it. The surprising thing was people did not know how good we were."

Steve Jansa, who played for McManus from 1966 to 1969, once joked about his coach's cavalier scheduling: "We just drove around in a bus and said, 'Anybody want to play us?' "

McManus' 1963-64 plan included home games against Arizona State, Notre Dame, Marquette, Memphis and Oklahoma City, which was in the midst of a four-year streak of NCAA tournament appearances. The road games included Iowa, Long Beach State, UCLA, Oklahoma City, Providence, St. John's and Miami. He also set up a season-closing trip to play New York University, the preseason No. 1 pick, in Madison Square Garden and a visit to Notre Dame. The Bluejays opened with nine straight victories, including an 84-83 win over fourth-ranked Arizona State. The next night, they found themselves in an even more memorable game.

1963: DOMINATING THE BOARDS
Chuck Officer (24) and Paul Silas helped Creighton to a 61-38 rebounding advantage in a 77-62 victory over La Salle. The National Athletic Bureau said Silas led the nation in "recovery percentage," a measure of the percentage of rebounds that went to one player. He grabbed an average of 22.5 percent of the rebounds by both teams in a game.

Junior college transfer Elton McGriff, back, and Paul Silas' cousin Fritz Pointer, with the ball, joined the 1963-64 starting lineup.

Creighton trailed Utah State by 6 points with less than a minute to play but closed the deficit to 78-76 with seven seconds left. Utah State had a chance to put the game away at the foul line but missed a free throw. Apke rebounded and fired the ball upcourt to Officer, who fell to one knee next to the foul line, his back to the basket. Without getting up, he threw up a 16-foot hook shot that swished to tie the game at the buzzer. Creighton went on to win 96-91 in double overtime, and Officer was carried off the court.

"It was a desperation shot," Officer said later. "There was no time to stand up. I saw the basket and just heaved the ball up. I never thought it would go in."

The 9-0 start occurred as McManus worked three newcomers — Elton McGriff, Charlie Brown and Fritz Pointer — into the starting lineup with Officer and Silas. It might not have been an accident that Pointer wound up playing alongside Silas, his cousin.

"I think there was some sort of deal cut with my uncle and my father when they were recruiting Paul," recalled Pointer, laughing heartily. "If they wanted Paul, they had to take me. I was riding Paul's coattails, and it turned out it was the best thing that ever happened to me. I made my contributions in other ways but not with the impact that Paul did."

At Creighton, Pointer got a chance to see the evolution of his cousin's game. McManus had molded a jump-shooting high school player into one of college basketball's great rebounders.

"In high school, he faced the basket," Pointer said. "Red recognized Paul's natural talent and timing and footwork. He remade Paul into a new player. You would never know by watching Paul in his college and professional lives that he was a jump shooter in high school. He had exceptional timing in terms of getting rebounds. He always played against bigger players, but his timing and his footwork gave him a chance to excel."

Silas not only earned All-America honors in college, he also would go on to play 16 seasons in the National Basketball Association and win three championship rings.

"I was not a good post-up guy when I came to Creighton," Silas said. "But Red was a very good inside coach. He ran that double-post offense, and he wanted me to be a post-up man. So I did it."

Silas said he adjusted quickly, thanks to his coach.

"He wouldn't tell you ... not to shoot. He gave you confidence. Once you knew he had confidence in you, you had confidence in yourself."

1963: A SOFT TOUCH ON HIS SHOT

Silas puts up a hook shot in Creighton's 84-83 upset of No. 4 Arizona State during his senior season. He finished with 19 points and 31 rebounds. Utah State coach LaDell Anderson, whose team would face the Jays the next night in Omaha, watched Silas play with his injured knee wrapped. "You know, it's amazing the way he does it — on one leg," Anderson said.

McManus congratulates Silas in 1964 as he leaves the floor in his last home game at the Civic Auditorium. There was a long standing ovation from his teammates and a crowd of 10,556. "Applause continued while (Oklahoma City's) Jim Ware scored two foul shots, Jay Tom Potter dribbled upcourt and hit a jumper and Oklahoma City returned the ball," The World-Herald reported.

Creighton's season-opening winning streak came to an end with a 16-point loss at No. 6 UCLA. The Bluejays bounced back to win six of their next seven games before back-to-back losses at Providence and St. John's left them 15-4 heading into February.

After splitting a pair of home contests, Creighton traveled to Miami for a memorable visit, in more ways than one.

The Hurricanes came into the game with future professional star Rick Barry leading the nation in scoring. Creighton held Barry to 4 points in the first half and 19 for the game — he averaged 32 per game that season — in a record-setting 124-94 victory.

"That was the greatest game we ever played," McManus said. "We did everything right."

The performance delighted the Bluejays' newest fan, a young heavyweight boxer by the name of Cassius Clay. Preparing for his first championship fight against Sonny Liston, Clay was working out at the arena when the Bluejays held their morning shoot-around. Borrowing a pair of basketball shoes from one of the Bluejays, the boxer who would go on to acclaim as Muhammad Ali showed he wasn't the greatest on the basketball court.

"He couldn't throw the ball into the ocean," McManus recalled. "If he were standing on the beach," Apke echoed years later.

Apke also remembered Silas and Ali taping a promotion for a Miami television station. "You have to remember that, at the time, no one was giving Ali a chance to beat Liston. Paul and Ali did this little publicity spot, with Ali playing one-on-one against Paul. One of our team jokes was that Paul Silas had a better chance of beating Sonny Liston than Ali had of scoring on Paul."

Ali couldn't attend the Bluejays' game but sent his chauffeur, who took some of the players to Ali's quarters after the game.

"We sat and talked to him, and we got a chance to meet Sugar Ray Robinson, too," said Pointer, who made the visit. "It was quite a thrill."

Creighton followed up the Miami win with a victory over Western Michigan in Chicago, then returned home to prepare for what would be Silas' final home game at the Civic Auditorium.

The morning of the game against Oklahoma City, McManus accepted an NCAA offer of an at-large spot in the tournament. The NIT called an hour later with its own bid, but McManus stuck by his commitment to the NCAA tourney, which by this time was the more prestigious.

"You look forward to a tourney from the first day of practice October 15," McManus said. "Especially if you're an independent."

> "You look forward to a tourney from the first day of practice October 15. Especially if you're an independent."
>
> **— Red McManus**

The Bluejays posted a 94-77 win over Oklahoma City, a team they had lost to by 16 points in early January, then took their act to Madison Square Garden, with Officer supplying another game-winning shot — this one from 20 feet at the buzzer — to beat NYU 88-86.

"For a basketball player, playing in the Garden is the heights," Pointer said. "That's mecca. It certainly beat playing in South Bend." That's where Creighton closed the regular season with an 84-71 win over the Fighting Irish. That left the Bluejays with a 21-5 record heading into a third matchup against Oklahoma City in the opening round of the NCAA tournament in Dallas.

Creighton rolled to an 89-78 victory, with McGriff scoring 25 points before fouling out. Silas added 15 points and a facility-record 27 rebounds. For the second time in three seasons, Creighton found itself one of the last 16 teams with a chance at the national championship.

"The fact that we were able to make it to the Sweet 16 was amazing to me," Pointer said. "And to think back on it, we were kind of unconscious to the whole thing. We just enjoyed playing the game so much that we just went about it as if we were just playing another game."

Fans at Eppley Airfield welcome home Silas and the Jays after their NCAA tourney win over Oklahoma City in Dallas. On the facing page, McManus is greeted by a sign of the times: The Beatles had appeared on "The Ed Sullivan Show" a month earlier.

Creighton's championship hopes ended in an 84-68 loss to fifth-ranked Wichita State on the Shockers' home court. Creighton trailed 57-54 midway through the second half before an 8-2 run put Wichita State in control. The next night, Silas ended his Creighton career by scoring 14 points and grabbing 13 rebounds in a 63-52 loss to Texas Western in the consolation game.

In his three seasons with the Bluejays, Silas grabbed 1,751 rebounds, sixth-most in NCAA history and the most ever by a three-year player. He is one of five players in NCAA history to average 20 points and 20 rebounds for his career. Silas' boyhood idol, Bill Russell, is one of the four others, along with Julius Erving, Artis Gilmore and Kermit Washington.

Silas was named the national Catholic player of the year and a third-team All-American by both the Associated Press and United Press International. He considered his greatest honor, though, to be leaving Creighton as a first-team Academic All-American.

"Before I came to Creighton, I didn't have the training that I necessarily should have had," said Silas, who also earned membership in Alpha Sigma Nu, the Jesuit academic honor society. "But I just learned what it took ... (and) it all fell into place. The main thing is I started asking questions from the professors, and they were very dedicated and wanted to help as much as possible."

Creighton's 22 victories established a school record. Three of its five regular-season losses came against teams that played in the NCAA tournament — eventual national champion UCLA, Oklahoma City and Providence.

Little did anyone know that McManus' glorious fifth season would be his high point.

WE LOVE YOU,
YEAH, YEAH, YEAH

ON THE BIG STAGE

Red McManus returned a solid corps of players and added Fritz Pointer, Charlie Brown and Elton McGriff to produce his best team. "A lot of guys came along as the season progressed," he said. Creighton posted home wins over Colorado, Notre Dame, Marquette and No. 4 Arizona State and won road games at Iowa, Miami, Notre Dame and NYU at Madison Square Garden. A victory over Oklahoma City in the NCAA tournament gave the 1963-64 Jays the school record for victories with 22, but losses to Wichita State and Texas Western at the regional ended the season on a sour note. McManus had to apologize later for calling an official in the final game "out-and-out crooked." He backtracked by saying the official "called a bad game, but he certainly wasn't crooked."

CHARLIE BROWN

Brown caught the eye of Jays fans in his first game, zipping two behind-the-back passes for assists in the 1963-64 season-opening win over defending Big Eight champion Colorado. At 5-9, the junior college transfer was "not much taller than the comic strip character," the World-Herald reported, and a bit of an oddity because he was married with a child, had a tattoo and liked sky diving. Brown's transition from junior college wasn't easy at first, he said, but passing to Silas helped. "He makes you look good — not like some big men – when you happen to throw a low pass, because he can still come up with it and score."

FRITZ POINTER

The 6-foot-4 sophomore, Silas' cousin and the brother of the musical Pointer Sisters, came on strong as the season unfolded. He came off the bench for part of the season but moved into the starting lineup after scoring 21 points and grabbing 14 rebounds in a loss at St. John's. He was a solid defender, holding Miami's Rick Barry to 4 points in the first half and 19 overall in a year in which Barry averaged 32 points a game. A New York reporter wrote after Creighton's victory over NYU: "No college team this season showed a better shooting punch than did Creighton with Fritz Pointer and Chuck Officer." Pointer finished third in scoring for the Jays at 12.6 points a game. He was eighth all time in scoring when his career ended in 1966.

CHUCK OFFICER

Officer first showed his magic touch by tossing in a 35-foot shot with five seconds left to beat Notre Dame 73-71 in December 1961, a big win on the way to a 1962 NCAA tournament bid. He did not enroll for the 1962-63 school year but returned for his senior year and helped get the season off to a fast start with one of the most memorable shots in school history, a 16-foot hook from his knees to send the Jays into overtime against Utah State in a game they won. Officer performed magic again two months later, scoring 18 second-half points, with the last two coming on a 20-footer at the buzzer, in a victory over preseason No. 1 NYU at Madison Square Garden. "Chuck Officer was the No. 1 single factor in this year's big advance over the 1962-63 showing," World-Herald sports editor Wally Provost wrote in 1964. Officer finished his career with 994 points, which was seventh all time at Creighton at the time.

PAUL SILAS

The 6-7 Silas led the Bluejays in scoring and rebounding for a third straight year, despite playing with a bad knee all season. His highest single-game scoring total was 37 in a home win over Notre Dame. "I've never seen anyone who was able to tip an offensive rebound on one side of the basket and — if it was a little strong — to react quickly enough to tip it a second time on the other side of the basket," said teammate Tom Apke. Silas' career rebounding totals were astounding: 22 games with 25 or more, more than 500 in each of the three seasons he played and an average of 21.6 per game for his career. He also finished with a career average of 20.5 points a game, best in school history at the time. "You sort of feel that such a player comes along once in a lifetime," McManus said. Silas retired from playing in 1980 and moved on to coaching jobs in the NBA. When he was inducted into the Creighton Athletic Hall of Fame, he said, "Here's a little boy from Oakland, Calif., who came to the Midwest not really knowing anything and not having real good study habits and so forth that went on to become an Academic All-American and have a successful pro career. I look at this as where it really all began for me."

Talented rosters with torturous schedules

McManus continued to play meat-grinding schedules and never won more than 14 games in his final five seasons on the bench.

The Bluejays needed to win six of the final seven games just to finish 13-10 in 1964-65, with a schedule that included road games at No. 7 St. John's, No. 8 Kansas State, Iowa, Northwestern, Memphis, La Salle, Marquette and Notre Dame. Added to that was a holiday tournament with games against Brigham Young, Florida State and LSU.

1966: MCMANUS MILESTONE

Star forward Tim Powers presented Red McManus with a trophy in 1966 in honor of his 100th coaching victory at Creighton. "We're just going for 100 more," McManus said. Powers led the 1965-66 team in scoring at 21.5 points a game and had 45 points against Idaho State that season, the school's fourth-best all-time single-game total.

Optimism returned the next year, however, with a lineup featuring seniors Fritz Pointer, Tim Powers and Neil Johnson, plus promising sophomore Wally Anderzunas. Creighton business manager Gene Duffy reported "the finest advance ticket sale in Creighton history."

"We really believe we're going to get a (postseason) bid," McManus told boosters. And perhaps feeling pressure from scheduling as an independent, he also disclosed that Creighton had applied for re-entry into the Missouri Valley. He said there was little chance of approval, however, because the school didn't have a football team.

The Bluejays opened the 1965-66 season by upsetting 10th-ranked Kansas State, the first of three straight wins. But five straight losses followed, including at home against No. 9 Bradley and on the road at No. 6 Minnesota. The Jays failed to get any traction after that and finished at 14-12 with a season-ending victory at Notre Dame.

World-Herald sports editor Wally Provost pointed out after the season that the Jays had split four games with Top 25 teams. "The Bluejays' mode of play was colorful, exciting, even though it was frustrating at times," he wrote, then added, "Coach Red McManus was put under fierce pressure by an element of critical fans."

Bob Portman joined the varsity for the 1966-67 season, again raising hopes for a breakout season. Portman, a 6-foot-5 forward, was another San Francisco-area prep star whom McManus had lured to Omaha with the promise of a big-time schedule.

"Red told me when he was recruiting me that he'd go anywhere to play anybody," Portman said. "We played some really great teams. It was fun, and it turned out to be truly what Red told me it was going to be."

One of Portman's biggest games came near the end of his sophomore season when the Bluejays welcomed Houston to the Civic Auditorium. The Cougars' lineup featured future hall of famer Elvin "The Big E" Hayes and Don Chaney. Hayes was a dominant scorer — he would average 31 points a game during his collegiate career — while Chaney was a defensive wizard who later was named to NBA all-defensive teams when he played for the Boston Celtics.

Portman wound up scoring 35 points in the 87-80 loss.

"We had a smaller team that year," Portman said. "But I remember our crowd really got into the game."

Portman gave them something to be excited about, as he found early success against Houston's 1-3-1 zone defense.

"Chaney was a tremendous player, and he was out there on top running back and forth, but Portman was breaking in behind him and getting that reverse jump shot off real quickly," McManus recalled. "I once told him, 'Every time you play, you're going to have to prove you're the fastest gun in the West because everybody's going to throw every defense at you.' "

Portman wound up averaging 18.3 points per game in 1966-67, but the Bluejays finished with a 12-13 record.

The Bluejays would win just eight times in 1967-68, their roster depleted by Anderzunas' suspension and injuries to guards Dave Hickey and Jack "Jocko" Ilcisin. Portman was a one-man show, setting school records by averaging 29.5 points per game and scoring 738 points. He also set the single-game scoring record when he hit Wisconsin-Milwaukee with a 51-point barrage on Dec. 16, 1967.

1966: ANOTHER JAY TO THE NBA

Neil Johnson led Creighton in rebounds in 1965-66 with 12.1 per game and was a second-round 1966 NBA draft selection. He spent four years in the league with the New York Knicks and the Phoenix Suns, where he was reunited with former Jay Paul Silas during the 1969-70 season. Johnson also played three seasons with the Virginia Squires of the American Basketball Association.

1967: RECRUITING ASSIST FROM THE JESUITS
Bob Portman had 32 points in an 82-65 win over Minnesota, one of 12 games in which he scored 30 or more points during the 1967-68 season. Portman had been set to attend Washington but made his last recruiting visit to Creighton. "I liked the Jesuits and the coaching staff here," he said.

"I was fortunate that I always had the green light (to shoot) with Red," Portman said. "Even when I would start off a game kind of shaky, he would keep encouraging me to shoot."

McManus often said that Portman's school-record game wasn't his best. He remembered a 43-point game Portman had at Kansas State in February of 1968, when he came within a point of tying Wilt Chamberlain for the all-time scoring record at K-State's old Ahearn Fieldhouse.

Then there was the 42-point game at La Salle in January of 1968. Portman made 16 of his first 19 attempts against Explorers star Larry Cannon. "He was hitting everything," McManus said. "Their guy looked over to their bench and threw up his hands like, 'What do I do with this guy?' "

1968: FAVORABLE COMPARISON
Bob Portman scored 35 points with 18 rebounds in a victory over Portland, moving into 10th in Creighton career scoring after just a season and a half. Portland coach Bill Turner, who mixed zone defenses and double teams without success against Portman, was asked after the game if he had seen a better player that season. "Alcindor!" he exclaimed, referring to UCLA center Lew, later Kareem Abdul-Jabbar. Other Jays pictured are Dave Hickey (31) and Jerry Babcock (45).

It was evident by the start of the 1968-69 season that McManus was on shaky ground. The school's athletic board offered him a one-year contract for the 1968-69 season, denying a man with three small children the security of a longer deal.

Apke, then an assistant coach, said a segment of Creighton's fans and administration was growing tired of McManus' behavior during games.

1969: GREAT CAREER OVERSHADOWED BY A GREATER ONE
Creighton Prep grad Wally Anderzunas scored 1,267 points in three years on the Hilltop, averaging 21.5 points a game his senior year and 17.2 points a game over his career. Those numbers would normally earn the loudest ovation on Senior Night, but Anderzunas played beside Bob Portman, who scored 609 more points and averaged 24.6 points over three years. Anderzunas was a sixth-round draft pick of the Detroit Pistons.

"He would say things and act out his emotions, and he received a lot of criticism for that," Apke said. "Some people at Creighton got tired of that being the public image. When Red got mad, he would stand up and give the choke sign to officials. He would, on the road, respond to a heckler in the crowd. His temper often got the best of him."

Years later, McManus admitted he could be hard on officials but said it was partly because he was protecting his team.

"I always felt that you had to let them know you were in the game," he said. "We were playing on the road a lot, and if you didn't say anything, they would carry you right out of the gym with some bad calls."

McManus accused referees of "stealing" more than a few games from his team. He liked to say that some referees were bad, while the rest were brutal.

Entering the 1968-69 season, McManus said, "The handwriting was on the wall." He had opened a formal-wear business as a hedge in case things didn't work out at Creighton, which was paying him only $11,300. Plus, he said, the university wasn't trying to improve the program. "We weren't going to get much more support, and I didn't want to be there under those circumstances," he said.

He offered his resignation during the season, calling it "kind of a mutual thing."

His team responded with a five-game winning streak late in the season that put it in position for consideration for an NIT invitation. The Bluejays went into the regular-season finale — which not only would be McManus' last game but the final home appearance for Portman and his high-scoring teammate Anderzunas — needing to beat St. Bonaventure to possibly wrap up a postseason berth. The Bonnies were led by 6-11, 265-pound All-American Bob Lanier, who came into the game averaging 28.3 points and 16.1 rebounds.

The evening started off well enough, with Portman, Anderzunas, Jansa, Hickey and Ilcisin honored on Senior Night. But then things turned strange.

The much-heralded Lanier was ejected a little more than eight minutes into the game for a flagrant foul. He left after scoring just three points and grabbing three rebounds, and the Jays led 42-37 at halftime. During the break, three players from McManus' 1959-60 team presented the retiring coach with a trophy that listed the names of the players on his inaugural squad, with one of the names misspelled. Things went downhill from there.

The Bluejays lost the lead in the second half, battled back to tie and then frittered away a chance to win in the final 31 seconds with a costly turnover and a charging call that erased an Anderzunas basket that would have put Creighton ahead.
The Red McManus era officially ended with a 74-72 loss. Portman finished with 29 points, pushing his career total to a school-record 1,876. He averaged 26.2 points as a senior, giving him the two highest season scoring averages in program history. Anderzunas had 24 points in his final game and ended up sixth on the scoring chart at the time. McManus finished with a 138-118 record. His final victory had come two days before the St. Bonaventure game when the Bluejays scored a hard-fought 79-74 win at Notre Dame.

Creighton had beaten more than its share of big-name opponents in McManus' 10 seasons. In the final analysis, the man who was unafraid to play anybody might have been done in by his own desire to compete with the best. He would never again coach a college basketball game.

Creighton students showed their disapproval after a 74-48 loss to Notre Dame in 1962. The sign on the dummy said, "McManus and the Jays."

"Red was too stubborn to accept that we couldn't shoot for the big time," Apke said.

McManus acknowledged that his lofty goals might have created expectations for fans that he couldn't fulfill.

"We would knock off some big guys, and they would get the idea we ought to do that every week," he said. "They seemed to think we had the best players in the country. While I was coaching, we played Notre Dame 14 times, and we broke even with them, seven wins and seven losses. We beat them at South Bend four times, and that's hard to do. But when we came home after one of the seven losses, I found myself hanged in effigy."

McManus added that it was the first such hanging on the Creighton campus since several years earlier when a cafeteria worker suffered the same indignity. Her alleged offense: She made lousy coffee.

Normally, this part of the story would end here. Sports divorces can become messy business. This one would turn out to be a love affair.

1969-1994

Peaks and valleys

Tom Apke was asked about joining a conference when he was hired in 1974 to replace Eddie Sutton as Creighton's basketball coach. "There is a lot of merit to being in a conference, since it relieves much schedule pressure which an independent faces," Apke said. "We're interested." The Bluejays would win the Missouri Valley Conference the first year they returned to the league. Five years later, they would finish dead last.

Creighton's Rick Apke (44) and Randy Eccker celebrate the 1978 Missouri Valley Conference title game victory over Indiana State and Larry Bird.

A vision on a shoestring budget

RED MCMANUS GOT A NEW GENERATION to believe that the school could be a player on the national stage. In an attempt to take the next step, the Bluejays turned to an unlikely choice: a Kansas native with no Division I coaching experience. Creighton announced on March 10, 1969 — five days after McManus coached his final game — that Eddie Sutton had been selected as the school's new coach.

Eddie Sutton began a "Bluejay Barnstorm" after being hired, trouping to communities in Nebraska and western Iowa to drum up support for Creighton basketball. "We want the folks in Omaha's shopping area to be fully acquainted with the Bluejays."

Sutton had spent the previous three seasons coaching at the College of Southern Idaho, a junior college located in Twin Falls, Idaho. Prior to that, Sutton had coached seven seasons at an Oklahoma high school following his graduation from Oklahoma State.

At his introductory press conference, the 33-year-old Sutton promised there would be no lowering of expectations or "watering down of the schedule" on his watch.

He also indicated that his coaching style might be more low-key than what Creighton fans had grown accustomed to with the firebrand McManus. In other words, the days of a Creighton coach giving a referee the choke sign had probably come to an end.

But while he pledged to be different on the outside, Sutton's innards blazed with the same competitiveness that fueled McManus' quest to elevate Creighton in the college basketball world.

"I think Red took the first steps in playing a great national schedule and moving the games down to the Civic Auditorium," said Tom Apke, who had returned to Creighton as an assistant coach in McManus' final season and was retained by Sutton. "Eddie took Creighton on the next step. He had a vision, and maybe we needed an outsider to come in and show us what we could become."

Sutton came on board at a time when the Creighton athletic department was wrestling with the university's financial commitment to the program. While other schools were starting to pump cash into their programs, Creighton was trying to operate on nickels and dimes.

Apke took a $1,200 pay cut from his job as a teacher and coach at a Cincinnati parochial school to return to Creighton to join McManus' staff as a $7,800-a-year assistant coach. The man Apke replaced — Herb Millard — had not only assisted McManus in basketball but also coached baseball, ran the intramural program and taught physical education courses.

"Each of those became full-time positions," Apke recalled, "but at the time, Creighton athletics were really run on a shoestring budget. There wasn't a lot of money."

Sutton said when he took the CU job that he had made $13,000 annually at his junior-college position. Asked whether taking over the Creighton program would represent a raise in pay, Sutton smiled and replied, "Not necessarily."

Meanwhile, his predecessor was starting to adjust to private business. McManus and his wife, the former Mary Jean Timmerman, had three children, and he turned down several coaching opportunities to concentrate on the formal-wear store in west Omaha he had opened two years earlier.

When it came to the business of coaching basketball, Sutton was a disciple of Henry Iba, the legendary Oklahoma State coach and former Creighton rival for whom Sutton had played. Sutton promised to play the same kind of hard-nosed defense that Iba espoused but that his offense would "be somewhat more liberal."

Red McManus still had time to talk basketball as he measured customers at his Mr. Tuxedo shop in July 1969. He pointed out to a reporter that six of his former players were in professional basketball: Paul Silas, Neil Johnson, Elton McGriff, Bob Portman and Wally Anderzunas from Creighton and Don Nelson from his Iowa freshman team.

A crowd of 6,028 turned out Dec. 1, 1969, to watch the beginning of the Sutton era of Creighton basketball. The Bluejays, getting 24 points and 17 rebounds from Cyril Baptiste, rolled to an 84-62 victory over Wisconsin-Oshkosh. Baptiste's debut had been eagerly awaited, as McManus had called him the "most talented player" he had ever signed. As a high school senior, Baptiste averaged 25.2 points and 16.4 rebounds per game, and the Miami Herald named him its athlete of the year in 1968.

"I thought Cyril was going to be the next Elvin Hayes," Apke said. "He was big and strong and physical. He was extremely talented."

Baptiste arrived in Omaha in 1968 and played on the freshman team during McManus' final season. One of his freshman teammates, Tom Garvey, recalled playing pickup games with Baptiste against Creighton's senior stars, Bob Portman and Wally Anderzunas.

"Wally was a very good player, but Cyril would just kick his butt," Garvey said. "He was the greatest athlete I've ever seen."

Unfortunately, Baptiste spent much of his adult life battling demons. Garvey said it was common knowledge around the Creighton team at the time that Baptiste was using drugs, but schools normally did not test for drugs in those days.

"We always heard stories about it, and we wondered about it," Apke said. "But we never had any direct knowledge of those kind of things." Years later, Baptiste told the Miami Herald that he was using drugs when he played at Creighton.

Compounding Baptiste's problems, Apke said, was that the player became extremely homesick. "He was just out of place. He was very talented but unfortunately was never the fit for Omaha or Creighton that we wish he had been."

The 6-foot-10 Baptiste would lead the Bluejays in scoring in 17 of Creighton's 25 games in 1969-70. He had back-to-back games of 34 and 33 points early in the season, and he scored 18 points and grabbed 12 rebounds in a matchup with New Mexico State's Sam Lacey, later a first-round NBA draft pick, in a late December loss in Las Cruces.

Ralph Bobik had 16 points and 12 assists while going against South Carolina guard Mike Dunleavy, who later played and coached in the NBA. Bobik, who held Dunleavy to 11 points on 5-of-15 shooting, averaged 5.2 assists a game as a sophomore. On the facing page, Cyril Baptiste rides on fans' shoulders after Creighton's upset of No. 5 New Mexico State in 1970.

The teams met in a rematch a month later at the Civic Auditorium. The Aggies came into the game ranked fifth nationally, and a crowd of 11,214 that included Boston Celtics General Manager Red Auerbach somehow jammed into a building that seated just less than 10,000 for basketball. With Joe Bergman scoring 18 points and Baptiste adding 15, Creighton pulled off a 72-68 victory. Creighton fans stormed the court after the win, which raised the Bluejays' record to 11-5, and Baptiste and his teammates cut down the nets. Sutton, in an understatement, called it the "biggest win we've had here. I thought the kids showed a great deal of poise."

Auerbach, who was in town to scout Lacey and Jimmy Collins of the Aggies, came away with another prospect's name on his list.

"He is one of the most agile big guys I've seen all year," Auerbach said of Baptiste. "He has very good presence for a sophomore."

The Jays gained little traction from the win. They lost their next game at Southern Illinois and closed a 15-10 season with losses to No. 8 Marquette and No. 13 Houston.

Sutton hit the recruiting trail, signing three players who would play key roles later in their career. One was 6-foot-7 point guard Ralph Bobik.

Ted Wuebben had 18 points and eight rebounds against Oklahoma center Alvan Adams, a future NBA rookie of the year with the Phoenix Suns. Wuebben, who led the Jays in rebounding three straight seasons, said he liked to play on the back side of the basket when opponents shot, because "that's where the ball comes" on misses.

"His nickname was 'Crazy Ralph' because he was flamboyant,'' Sutton recalled. "He'd try all these crazy passes. He was the first player I had who tried to throw the ball behind his back."

Sutton also landed a versatile player out of Dayton, Ohio, in Ted Wuebben, and persuaded a Nebraska high school star from Schuyler to concentrate on basketball.

"I had made a decision to go to a smaller school and play multiple sports," Gene Harmon said. "I had informed everybody of my decision. Coach Sutton asked to meet with me again, and he presented a challenge to me that made a lot of sense. I changed my mind."

But with those three not yet on the varsity, Sutton's second team produced results similar to his first. The 1970-71 Bluejays opened the season by winning seven of their first eight games, with the only loss coming against North Carolina. The Bluejays beat Georgetown in a tournament in late December but struggled with consistency once the calendar turned.

They lost five of their last six games — one of the defeats was a 66-61 home setback to a Marquette team ranked No. 2 in the country — and finished the season with a 14-11 record. Baptiste again was the leader, averaging 20.2 points and 11.2 rebounds a game, but a March 6 victory over Cleveland State would prove to be the last game he played. He dropped out of school.

"It was something I up and did," he said. "I just didn't like the environment. I didn't like the change from Miami."

Baptiste scored 939 points and grabbed 551 rebounds in his two seasons at Creighton. After he left, he had a chance to make the Golden State Warriors but failed the physical after testing positive for drugs.

Bobik, Harmon and Wuebben joined the varsity for the 1971-72 season after playing on the best freshman team (17-2) in school history. While the Bluejays would score a home win over 17th-ranked Jacksonville, the season ended a disappointing 15-11.

They matched that record the next season, with their biggest win coming when Harmon made a 35-foot shot at the buzzer to beat seventh-ranked Houston.

In need of a breakout season, Creighton got it in 1973-74. The Bluejays, who had never won more than 15 games in Sutton's first four seasons, picked up No. 16 in early February by beating Duquesne at the auditorium. A week later, they defeated No. 6 Marquette 75-69 in Milwaukee, where it had lost only once in the previous 100 games.

The Jays were at the midpoint of a 10-game winning streak that pushed their record to 21-4 in late February. The players figured they had a good shot of returning to the NCAA tournament for the first time in a decade, even though they were getting little attention nationally.

"There was truly a lack of respect for what we were able to do and what we were able to accomplish our senior year," Harmon said. "We were ranked consistently, but we were never able to crack the top 10. Maybe we didn't have enough star power, or maybe it was because we were an independent."

The latter continued to have its advantages. Sports Illustrated featured the "Travelin' Jays" in its Feb. 25, 1974, edition. By the time Harmon and the other seniors would finish their careers, the magazine noted, they would have played in 20 states and have made a 10-city exhibition trip to South America between their junior and senior seasons.

Gene Harmon scored the Jays' first 11 points against Wisconsin-Oshkosh in his varsity debut in 1971. He finished with a team-high 21. "The mighty blond from Schuyler was the standout of the cast," The World-Herald's Don Lee wrote.

Harmon (44) jumps for joy after his long jump shot beat No. 7 Houston at the Civic Auditorium in 1973. "Well, I'd have to say it's the biggest shot I ever had," Harmon said.

"It was a lot more fun traveling around the country than just going to Lincoln or Lawrence or Norman," said Harmon, referring to three Big Eight outposts at the time. "It was a lot more fun going to the West Coast and the East Coast on a consistent basis than being limited by a conference."

The Bluejays' last road trip of the 1973-74 season was to Hawaii, where they won the first game to boost their winning streak to 10 games. Creighton saw its streak end in a 61-60 loss the next night, and the Bluejays returned home to close out the regular season with a 78-69 loss to No. 14 South Carolina.

The two losses didn't prevent the NCAA from issuing an at-large invitation to Creighton and assigning the Bluejays to a first-round game against Texas at Denton, Texas. The tournament consisted of 25 teams that season, and Creighton found its way back to the Sweet 16 by ending the Longhorns' season with a 77-61 win.

The Bluejays traveled to Tulsa to face No. 14 Kansas with a spot in the Elite Eight on the line. The Bluejays took a 33-30 lead at intermission, with junior center Doug Brookins scoring all 10 of his points in the first half. Creighton still led 54-53 with less than two minutes to play after Harmon scored, but the Jayhawks got the winning basket with 1:21 left to produce a 55-54 win. Kansas went on to defeat Oral Roberts to advance to the Final Four, while Creighton beat No. 16 Louisville 80-71 in the consolation game to finish the season at 23-7. The wins passed the total from Paul Silas' senior year.

"That was a difficult loss," said Harmon, referring to the one that got away against Kansas. "We honestly believed that we could have made the Final Four that year. We had beaten Marquette in Milwaukee earlier that year, and they ended up making the Final Four. We came close but didn't quite get it pulled off like we thought we could."

Harmon, who had led Creighton in scoring in each of his three seasons, finished with 1,369 points, at the time the fourth-best total in school history. To this day, he cherishes the chance to play for Sutton.

> "Coach Sutton was definitely one of the best coaches in the United States."
>
> **— Gene Harmon**

"Coach Sutton was definitely one of the best coaches in the United States," Harmon said. "When I was coming out, I had an NBA scout tell me that in his estimation, he was one of the top five college coaches in the nation."

Creighton would soon find out that others shared that view. Sutton left the NCAA regional at Tulsa saying that he would investigate some job opportunities that, in the wake of the Bluejays' record-setting season, had come his way.

Twelve days later, he was being introduced as the new coach at Arkansas. He inherited a program that had posted losing records in eight of the previous 11 seasons and had not won the Southwest Conference title since 1958 . Sutton got the Razorbacks to the FInal Four in his fourth season. Terms of Sutton's five-year contract at Arkansas were not disclosed, but it was believed he would receive a base salary of between $33,000 and $37,000, plus benefits. He reportedly made $24,000 in his final season at Creighton.

Sutton left Omaha without a farewell press conference. The World-Herald reported he had told Dan Offenburger, the school's sports information director, that if anyone called asking for him, to say: "Tell them the last time you saw me I was heading for the golf course with a smile on my face."

A TEAM TO REMEMBER: 1973-74

ON THE BIG STAGE

Eddie Sutton took his team to Brazil for 12 games during the summer of 1973 to prepare it for the season. Guard Ralph Bobik, who returned with an Amazon blowgun, said, "The trip should really help us play better on the road." The senior-led Jays proceeded to go 8-3 on the road, highlighted by a 75-69 win against sixth-ranked Marquette in Milwaukee, where the then-Warriors had won 99 of their previous 100 games. The Jays rallied from 12 points down, then pulled away from a team that would finish the season as the national runner-up. "All season long we've been living for this game," said Jays junior guard Charles Butler. Losing coach Al McGuire, who would win a national championship in 1977, said, "They're a better ballclub than we are. Well-disciplined, well-coached." The Marquette win came during a 10-game winning streak that put Creighton in position for its first NCAA tournament bid in 10 years. Creighton opened NCAA play with a 77-61 win over Texas but lost 55-54 to Kansas in the Midwest Regional in Tulsa. An 80-71 victory over Louisville in a consolation game gave the team a school-record 23 wins. "It's most gratifying to be on the greatest team in Creighton history," said forward Gene Harmon, who with Ted Wuebben and Bobik had started three years. The underclassmen were a talented group as well, carrying the Jays to 20 wins and another NCAA bid in the 1974-75 season. Sutton joined the National Collegiate Basketball Hall of Fame in 2011.

DOUG BROOKINS

Brookins (52), a 6-8 center, led the Jays in the upset of Marquette, scoring 25 points. He finished with 1,115 points in three seasons, averaging 13.6 points and 6.3 rebounds for his career. Brookins was drafted by the NBA's Washington Bullets in 1975.

CHARLES BUTLER

Butler (21) at 6-foot-4 was the Jays' smallest starter. He missed the beginning of the 1973-74 season with a thigh injury but returned in January and averaged 6.3 points a game. The guard was considered a defensive specialist with "an uncanny knack of anticipating an opponent's next move," according to The World-Herald. He and Brookins shared the team MVP award in 1975.

GENE HARMON

Harmon led the team in scoring for three seasons and finished his career with 1,369 points. The 6-6 forward was a high school star at Schuyler, Neb. "Hopefully, I've been some inspiration to small-town kids in Nebraska," he said. An outstanding shooter, his long jumper at the buzzer beat No. 7 Houston at the Civic Auditorium in one of the greatest finishes in school history. Harmon was drafted in the sixth round by the Boston Celtics and inducted into the Creighton Athletic Hall of Fame.

TED WUEBBEN

The 6-6 Wuebben led Creighton in rebounding for all three seasons he played. He also had the most rebounds in a single game by any Jay not named Silas, grabbing 24 against Cleveland State in 1973. He was in the hospital with back spasms the week before the NCAA regional game against Kansas. "Oh, I'm going to play," he said. "I've been waiting four years for this, and a little pain isn't going to keep me out." He did play, and coach Eddie Sutton noted, "He got a little tired, but he played well."

RALPH BOBIK

Bobik, a 6-7 guard, averaged 6.7 assists a game during his career, leading the team each year he played. World-Herald writer Don Lee referred to him as the "crazy-legged master ball-handler" during his senior year, when he set the school record with 252 assists. Bobik had a sense of humor about his passing skills. "The way I shoot ... I figure I'd better be giving the ball up," he said. Bobik finished his career with 549 assists, the highest total for a three-year player. He was drafted in the fifth round by the Phoenix Suns and inducted into the Creighton Athletic Hall of Fame.

On the road to the Valley

Speculation about Eddie Sutton's replacement quickly turned to assistants Tom Apke and Tom Brosnihan, both Creighton graduates. The Creighton Athletic Board selected the 30-year-old Apke, who was relieved by the vote. He had applied for at least two head coaching jobs at smaller schools but had been turned down.

The World-Herald asked Tom Apke about fan support when he was hired in 1974. "One reason crowds have fallen off is that expectations of recent years seldom have materialized," he said, then added, "A coach owes it to his fans to play an exciting brand of basketball."

"I felt like I was a good college coach, but I was wondering if I'd ever get a chance," Apke said. "When I was hired, it was literally a dream come true. It was great for me, and I thought it was good for Creighton to have one of their own at the helm."

Brosnihan, a successful high school coach at Omaha Creighton Prep before joining Sutton's staff, remained as the No. 1 assistant.

Apke knew there was a segment of the Creighton fan base that wondered whether he was the right man for the job. But he felt that Sutton had laid the groundwork for success.

"I thought Eddie, coming in as an outsider, was able to give some direction and show people that we could dream bigger dreams," Apke said. "That we didn't have to be content with being poor, tiny Creighton, as we sometimes thought about ourselves."

Apke was tested early in his first year. He had entered the season banking on 7-foot-1 Mike Heck, a Papillion High School product and the program's first 7-footer. Heck, who had picked Creighton over a reported 150 schools, had played in 30 games as a sophomore in 1973-74, averaging 8.4 points and 4.3 rebounds.

"I think he's going to be a great player someday," Apke said before the season. "The only thing that keeps him from being a great player right now is his physical development — strength and endurance — but he has been working hard on this. All he needs to score more is to play more. He's not a pretty player, but very few big guys look good when they play. They just get the job done." The week before Creighton opened Apke's first season, The World-Herald ran a lengthy feature story on Heck's prospects for a breakout season.

Heck scored 24 points and grabbed nine rebounds in the opening game against North Dakota. He left the floor in the final minute to a standing ovation for playing a key role in the 74-68 victory.

The next night, Heck called his mother around midnight and then headed for bed. He never awoke. On Dec. 5, 1974, the 20-year-old was found dead in his seventh-floor dorm room in Swanson Hall.

Dr. Lee Bevilacqua, who had been Creighton's team physician since 1959 and served as a father figure to many of the players, broke the news to the team.

Apke then talked to the players. "I did all the talking, and then asked for comments from the players, but no one could say a word," Apke said afterward. "I think you can tell by the looks on the players' faces he will be missed as an athlete and as an individual. He was such a fine person."

Donald Knowles, the former Bluejay great who had dropped the nickname "Pinky" in his job as Douglas Country attorney, announced after an autopsy that Heck had died of a heart disorder.

Creighton's next games were to be in a four-team tournament the Bluejays had scheduled for the Civic Auditorium. Apke was uncertain what to do — the opposing teams already were on their way or had arrived in Omaha — until he received a call from Heck's father saying that Mike would have wanted them to play.

"I think there were some people that worried whether I was right for the job," Apke said. "It was like, 'Tom was a nice player, a nice young kid and a good-looking assistant coach, but can he cut it?' If that was going to be a problem, the Mike Heck tragedy pushed that all to the back. It rallied a lot of people around the university, its athletic programs and our basketball team."

Apke had been enthusiastic about Mike Heck (54) heading into the 1974-75 season. "He's added some weight this year, and he should have more endurance," Apke said a week before the first game. "We're shooting for 30 to 35 minutes of playing time and 17 to 18 points a game." The news of Heck's death hit the team hard. "Everyone was stunned," said senior Tom Anderson of Arlington, Neb.

1975: DISTINGUISHED ALUM

Bluejay fans welcomed back Paul Silas at a 62-53 victory over the University of Nebraska at Omaha. Silas was in town with the Boston Celtics to play the Kansas City-Omaha Kings, Omaha's short-lived NBA franchise.

The Bluejays won their first game in the tournament before losing to Texas-El Paso. They lost three more times in December — one of the defeats coming at No. 2 Indiana — and took a 6-4 record into the new year. But Apke sensed his team was beginning to come together. The Bluejays started 1975 with a 71-70 win over Drake when Charles Butler made a 40-foot shot at the buzzer. That triggered a 14-game winning streak that helped carry Creighton back to the NCAA tournament, the first time in school history that the Bluejays had earned back-to-back berths.

The Bluejays drew fourth-ranked Maryland in the tournament, which had been expanded to 32 teams. Creighton fell behind by 12 points at the half, rallied in the final 20 minutes but saw its season end in an 83-79 loss.

The expansion of the tournament might have been overlooked at the time with the focus on the Jays' game against Maryland. But the move from 25 to 32 teams turned out to be significant in that it increased pressure on independents such as Creighton to start exploring ties to a conference.

"When the NCAA changed the basketball tournament rules to include more than one team per conference, life as an independent wasn't as attractive," Apke said. At-large bids in the tournament that had been available only to independents began to go to conference teams that previously weren't eligible. Conference teams had less incentive to play independents — other than teams like Notre Dame or Marquette that would draw big crowds — that would be competing for spots in the tournament. "That made for some real trouble in scheduling as the lesser-known independent," Apke said. "That's when we started to look around, and we looked at a number of possibilities."

Apke headed into the 1975-76 season having to replace scoring leaders Butler and Doug Brookins, so he turned to the budding star he had plucked out of his hometown of Cincinnati.

Apke had set out to recruit his brother, Rick, shortly after replacing Sutton as coach. At the time, Rick Apke also was being courted by a number of bigger schools, including Michigan.

"When Rick was a junior and his team won a state championship, Steve Grote was the senior star on the team," Tom Apke said. "Grote went to the University of Michigan, and when Rick was a senior, Michigan came after him hard.

"I sat Rick down, and we put two columns on a piece of paper. We wrote down everything that was advantageous to Michigan and everything that was advantageous to Creighton. Fortunately, I knew more about Creighton than he knew about Michigan, so at the end of the day we had more pluses on the Creighton side. We got him to sign."

Dan Offenburger, the Creighton sports information director, decided to have a little fun with the brother-signing-brother story. Offenburger had worked with NCAA officials each spring as part of Creighton's role as host school for the College World Series in Omaha.

Tom Apke said Offenburger sent a letter to the NCAA and, without mentioning the recruit's name, detailed several recruiting "violations" that the Creighton coach had committed during the recruiting process. Offenburger wrote that Apke had purchased several meals for the recruit's family and had paid for a round of golf for the recruit's father.

Worst of all, Apke had his own father sleeping with the recruit's mother.

Warren Brown, the NCAA director of enforcement, inquired about the "irregularities." When the joke was explained to Brown, he fired off a one-word response on official NCAA stationery: "Shameful."

Rick Apke as a freshman finished as the fourth-leading scorer on Creighton's 1975 NCAA tournament team, while coming off the bench in each of the 27 games.

Freshman Rick Apke (44) joined his brother's team and averaged 6.4 points as a reserve.

"Rick was undersized and not physically mature, because he was a year young for his class," Tom Apke recalled. "I used to tell everybody that I thought it was best for him to be coming off the bench.

"My mother once was quoted as saying that was OK for his (Rick's) freshman year, but that she was going to have to have a talk with the coach about next year. We were able to make light of those kind of pressures, because we were winning and Rick was such a good player."

1975: GETTING IN ON THE ACT
Robert Scrutchens (standing) and Cornell Smith (kneeling) photographed teammates, from left, Tim McConnell, Daryl Heeke and Rick Apke on press day.

Rick Apke averaged 16.8 points a game as a sophomore. He was joined in the 1975-76 starting lineup by sophomore point guard Randy Eccker, who averaged four assists a game.

Apke came back the next season to average 19.8 during the 1976-77 campaign, Creighton's last as an independent. The Bluejays went 21-6 during the 1976-77 regular season to earn the school's first trip to the National Invitation Tournament since Eddie Hickey's team played in the 1943 tournament. But the bid didn't cause a celebration on the Hilltop.

Creighton entered the NIT having lost its previous three games, including a 72-60 decision to No. 19 Marquette that might have cost the Bluejays a trip to the NCAA tournament.

"At one point that season, we were ranked," Eccker recalled. "We had a great team, but two of our last three games (in the regular season) were against North Carolina-Charlotte and Marquette. They both made the Final Four that year, and Marquette wound up winning the national championship.

"Everyone — the fans and the players — was deflated going into the NIT. We were playing Illinois State at home, and (it seemed like) they had more fans at the auditorium than we did. They had a great team, ended up winning, and they got to go to New York. That's a four-game stretch that I'd like to have back."

After a 29-year absence, Creighton returned to the rigors of conference play during the 1977-78 season.

"As I look back on it, I think the one thing I did that helped grow our athletic department was being the guy that got us back into the Missouri Valley," Tom Apke said.

The Valley, once one of the premier conferences in the nation, was starting to lose its luster, as teams such as Louisville, Cincinnati and Memphis State had dropped out to join other leagues and been replaced by West Texas State and New Mexico State, lesser programs that meant long road trips for the other schools.

1977: HANDS-ON INSTRUCTION FROM BIRD

More than 2,000 people attended a Missouri Valley Conference preseason clinic at Creighton's Kiewit Fitness Center. Among the players who took part was Indiana State star Larry Bird. Each of the league's nine schools sent its head coach and two of its players to the event, which coincided with Creighton's return to the MVC. "I'm in hog heaven," said Dan Offenburger, who had been promoted to assistant athletic director, as he surveyed the crowd.

The Valley finally ended its requirement that schools play football and in March 1976 invited Creighton to rejoin the league, effective at the start of the 1977-78 season. This conference announcement hardly left Creighton fans crying tears of joy.

"The public sentiment and the sentiment within the Creighton family was, 'Oh, that's nice,'" Apke said. "I don't know if too many of our fans thought it was that big a deal that we were rejoining the Valley."

CRASH LANDING

Billy Bluejay, played by Dan Krzemien, made his 1979 entrance by sliding down a rope from the ceiling of the Civic Auditorium. The crowd enjoyed the stunt, even though he landed on his feathers.

STILL GOING STRONG

The Jaybackers booster group started in 1966 with 20 members and was steered by an executive committee of Red McManus, Joe Vinardi, Harry Hess, William Jurgensen and Bernie Conway. "It's experimental, but I think it will work out real well," McManus said at the time. By the mid-'70s, the group was holding events at the cavernous Anthony's restaurant in Omaha. From left are Vinardi, Howard Poepsel, Hess and Philip Maschka in 1974.

AN EXTRA COACH

Irma Trumbauer for years was a familiar sight behind the Bluejay bench. She first started following the Jays when she managed Creighton dining halls and later began making road trips with the teams. Ted Wuebben, who played for Eddie Sutton, said the Bluejays always knew where she was sitting and could hear her calling the number of the next point when they shot free throws. If Creighton had 42 points, for example, she would yell, "43, 43, 43."

Even Apke's players were lukewarm about the news. They had just finished 19-7 with a schedule that had included, as usual, games from coast to coast and border to border.

"Most of us loved being an independent," Eccker said. "We played a great schedule — our schedule was as good as Marquette or DePaul or any of the other top independents. We traveled, and we traveled first class.

"We never thought of ourselves as anything but equal to any of the teams we were playing," Eccker said. "But we also knew the tide was changing. We played on the road because people weren't coming back to Omaha to play us. Everything in those days was going toward conference."

Eccker said college basketball was less compartmentalized in those days, with no "major" and "mid-major" labels. "We never thought of ourselves as being anything but one of the top teams," he said. "We were big time back then."

Changes were coming, though, as Apke was putting together a bid to join the Valley. About the same time, the NCAA was moving ahead with legislation that would tighten restrictions for membership in Division I, its highest level of play. The new rules would require some schools to compete in more varsity sports with athletic scholarships than they had been. Title IX legislation, meanwhile, was compelling athletic departments to add sports for women to match men's. The combination meant more sports and more scholarships.

1978: TOP-NOTCH DEFENSIVE EFFORT

Creighton's John C. Johnson (25) got the better of West Texas State guard Maurice Cheeks (11) in the Jays' 72-51 win. Cheeks, a two-time all-Missouri Valley selection and future NBA All-Star and coach, came into the game at the Civic Auditorium averaging 16 points a game. Johnson's defense, mixed with a matchup zone, held Cheeks scoreless. Johnson scored 17 for the Jays.

The added pressure on college budgets eventually forced some schools, especially ones without financially successful football programs, to drop down from the top level of competition. Oklahoma City, once the Jays' independent rival, had qualified for five NCAA tournaments from 1963 to 1973. By 1984, the school was in the National Association of Intercollegiate Athletics, along with Doane College and Peru State in Nebraska.

Kevin McKenna makes certain Marquette's Artie Green doesn't get away from him. "It doesn't look like obscurity will be one of Kevin McKenna's problems in college," The World-Herald's Steve Sinclair wrote of the freshman's contributions.

The Bluejays' first Valley game came on the road at Wichita State, with Creighton winning 71-70 when the Shockers' last shot bounced off the rim. Rick Apke scored 29 points in outdueling Wichita State star Lynbert "Cheese" Johnson, who had 26 before fouling out with four minutes to play.

Creighton's first conference home game came 11 days later, with freshman Kevin McKenna scoring 15 points in a 78-58 victory over Tulsa. Seven of McKenna's 15 points came from the free-throw line. "I was getting fouled a lot, which is a change," McKenna said. "Usually, I'm the one doing the fouling."

McKenna added not only some firepower to Creighton's lineup but also some spice to the locker room. One of his teammates tagged him with the nickname "Eddie," after the rascally character Eddie Haskell on the "Leave It to Beaver" television show.

"No question about it," McKenna said when asked whether he deserved the nickname. "I always felt that I was complimentary and nice around my elders, but behind the scenes, I probably wasn't the best person to be around. I had a mischievous streak in me, kind of like Eddie Haskell."

Creighton lost three of its next five league games, leaving the Bluejays 4-3 heading into a game at No. 13 Indiana State. The Sycamores, also new to the league, were led by junior sharpshooter Larry Bird.

"We played a lot of really good players when I was at Creighton," Eccker said. "The first time we played Bird, we had never seen any film on him. He's averaging 30-some points a game, and we thought he was probably pretty good. But we had played against some pretty good guys.

"The first shot he takes, he catches the ball ... turns and nails about a 35-footer. Kevin Kuehl, who was guarding Larry, looked at me and we were both like, 'He must be pretty good.' "

Creighton fell behind by 14 points in the first half, and the arena's scoreboard malfunctioned.

"Our players kept asking about the score, and I said, 'Don't worry about the score, just play,' " Tom Apke said. "We fought our way back into it and, with the score tied with about eight minutes to go, the scoreboard suddenly came back on."

Former CU coach Eddie Hickey was an early proponent of the matchup zone defense. "We called it a zone pickup with free switching," Hickey explained in 1978. "We used some adjustments in what areas of the court we could cover against a particular team."

In spite of 32 points by Bird, Creighton pulled out a 72-64 victory to hand the Sycamores their first loss in 30 home games. After the game, Apke credited Eddie Hickey, the former Bluejays coach, with an assist.

Hickey was living in Terre Haute, Ind., and had written Apke a letter before the game offering some suggestions, including the use of the matchup zone, which he helped pioneer. Apke said Creighton's use of the zone helped turn around the game.

Three weeks later, the teams met again in Omaha. Bird, slowed by the flu, scored only 11 points in an 89-57 loss.

"Larry was not himself," Eccker said of the second meeting. "And it was our senior night, and it meant a lot to us to be playing in our last home game, whether Larry was healthy or not. We played about as well as we could play."

Creighton lost its next league game, at Tulsa, but rebounded to win the conference title by closing the regular season with a 62-56 win at Southern Illinois. Apke had his players eat and sleep off campus before the trip to Carbondale, because more than 500 cases of the flu had been reported among Creighton students.

Unaccustomed to league play, the Bluejays headed for their locker room after beating the Salukis. They were in there for about five minutes when Apke said, "Hey, guys, what about the nets?" They returned to the court and went through the championship ritual.

The regular-season title earned the Bluejays the No. 1 seed in the 1978 Valley tournament and a bye into the championship game to be played on the Jays' home floor in Omaha. Indiana State won its way into the championship contest, but Bird arrived in town nursing a sore back.

The Indiana State staff contacted Dr. Lee Bevilacqua, the Bluejays' team physician, to provide some treatment for the Sycamores' star player. The next day, Bevilacqua approached Apke and told the Creighton coach about what he had done.

Dr. Lee Bevilacqua tends to the injured John C. Johnson while teammate Kevin Kuehl looks on. Bevilacqua had started helping with the team in 1959 as a senior in medical school. "When I got here, it was almost like having another dad on campus," Kevin McKenna said. "He just treated us like one of his own kids."

"Doc apologized for working on Larry's back," Apke said. "I told him that the Hippocratic Oath must be a little stronger than the school fight song."

Creighton's strategy that day was to deny Bird the basketball.

"We didn't want him to have many touches," Apke said. "We held him to 12 field-goal attempts. He made 11 and tipped in the miss."

Bird scored 18 straight points to give his team a 52-44 lead with 6:20 remaining. Creighton began its comeback by unleashing its "monster" press, which caused two turnovers and two 10-second calls. Creighton tied the game with 4:41 to play and got the ball back after another Indiana State turnover.

Apke ordered his team into its stall, which the Bluejays called the "5 game," and ran the clock down to 23 seconds.

"We called timeout and tried to run a special play, but I probably made one pass too many before getting into the play," Eccker said. "They were double-teaming me, and I thought, 'I have to get this to Rick.' I shoveled the ball to Rick, and he hits a big-time shot."

Rick Apke's 18-foot shot swished through the net with three seconds left and capped the 54-52 victory. In winning, Creighton became the only team in the nation that season to win both the regular-season and tournament championships in its conference.

Tom Apke gives instructions to Rick during the Bluejays' final timeout before Rick's game-winning shot against Indiana State. Apke's "5 game" would spread the floor and use a series of passes and cuts to free a player for an easy basket. "We are trying to score," Apke said. "We don't use the word 'stall.' We call it a 'control game' in which we no longer take the outside jumpers and play for a higher-percentage shot." He credited Henry Iba with the offense, which Iba passed on to Eddie Sutton. Apke liked it as an assistant to Sutton and retained it.

On the facing page, the crowd erupted after Rick Apke's shot dropped through the net. "The noise near the end of the game was of another world," The World-Herald's Michael Kelly wrote. "It was off the decibel scale. The roar was along that fine line between heavenly and demonic."

GO
JAYS!

The victory put the Bluejays back into the NCAA tournament, and the Bluejays headed to Wichita, Kan., to face fourth-ranked DePaul. The Blue Demons had posted a dramatic, 85-82 triple-overtime victory over Creighton in Omaha on Feb. 1.

The Bluejays jumped out to a 20-point lead 17 minutes into the NCAA game and led by 14 at the half. DePaul rallied, shooting 77 percent from the field in the second half, to pull out an 80-78 win that brought a disappointing end to a 19-9 season.

"The Valley was such a great conference that year, with guys like Bird and Roger Phegley and Mo Cheeks and Slab Jones," Eccker said. "To win the regular season and the tournament, and to be the only team in the country to do that, was pretty phenomenal."

Creighton finished tied for third in its second season in the league and tied for second in 1979-80. Of the Bluejays' 12 losses that season, four were by a point and a fifth was by four points.

That, along with the pressure Creighton was getting from Valley officials to upgrade its other sports, led Apke to give up his position as athletic director prior to the 1980-81 season. Offenburger, once the school's sports information director, was promoted to the head of the department.

"Losing all those close games bothered me," Apke said. "I just felt like I never had the time that year to get close to that team and revisit some of the things that were causing us to make mistakes at crucial times. I knew I couldn't continue to be athletic director and head basketball coach."

1981: THE ICEMAN COMETH UP WITH THE BALL

Daryl Stovall (40) outraces Tulsa's Paul Pressey and David Brown for the ball in Creighton's 66-64 win in the semifinals of the Missouri Valley tournament. Stovall made two free throws with one second left to secure the win. Dr. Lee Bevilacqua, seated at left, had provided Stovall with his nickname during the season. "Doc started calling me 'Iceman,' and it has kind of hung with me," Stovall said. Teammate Kevin McKenna endorsed the label, saying, "He iced the game for us." Stovall scored 1,115 points in his CU career.

Creighton started the 1980-81 season with victories in 11 of its first 13 games, winning four of the games by 5 points or fewer. The Bluejays finished second in the regular-season race and opened the conference tournament with wins over Indiana State and Tulsa to earn a trip to Wichita to play the Shockers for the automatic berth in the NCAA tournament.

Wichita State featured a front line of future NBA stars Antoine Carr and Cliff Levingston, but the Bluejays pulled out a 70-64 win to clinch their third trip to the NCAA tournament in Apke's seven seasons.

Creighton's George Morrow splits Wichita State's Cliff Levingston (54) and Karl Papke (45) in an attempt to grab a loose ball in the Shockers' victory in Omaha in January 1981. Morrow was an eighth-round selection of the Boston Celtics.

Facing St. Joseph's in a first-round game at Dayton, Ohio, Creighton led 50-44 with 7:42 left but went 6½ minutes without scoring a field goal. The Bluejays' season ended in a 59-57 loss. Shortly after returning to Omaha, Apke fielded a call from the University of Colorado to inquire about whether he would be interested in the Buffaloes' vacant head coaching job. Normally, Apke said, he would have turned down the opportunity.

"I had said no to previous offers that I had received," Apke said. "But that last year, my relationship with Dan Offenburger, which had always been good, became strained at times as we adjusted to our new roles. That strain between Dan and me probably contributed to me listening to Colorado and ultimately taking their offer."

The departure of Apke left many Creighton fans upset and frustrated. They had lost a rising star in the coaching ranks when Sutton bolted for Arkansas seven years earlier. Now they had to confront the reality that the Creighton coaching job wasn't even good enough to keep a true-blue Bluejay from flying away. Little did those fans know that their frustrations were about to mount.

A TEAM TO REMEMBER: 1977-78

ON THE BIG STAGE

Tom Apke's team wrote the perfect script for Creighton's return to the Missouri Valley Conference. The Jays won their MVC opener at Wichita State and defeated Tulsa in their first conference home game. The regular-season title came down to the final game against Southern Illinois. The Jays won 62-56 before a regional television audience and a raucous Saluki crowd of 9,950, claiming the league with a 12-4 record. The Bluejays faced Indiana State and star forward Larry Bird in the MVC tournament final at the Civic Auditorium. Rick Apke's shot fell through the net with three seconds left to give Creighton a 54-52 victory that is considered among the school's greatest. It also was the school's first basketball tournament championship. Creighton advanced to the NCAA tournament for a matchup with No. 4 DePaul in Wichita. The Jays led by 20 points with three minutes left in the first half and by 14 at halftime. But the Blue Demons rallied for an 80-78 win, as Rick Apke's rushed shot missed at the buzzer to end Creighton's season at 19-9. Tom Apke knew at the time that the 1977-78 team was special. "You never get everything out of a group of kids that is possible," he said. "But we've come close to getting maximum efficiency out of this group."

RANDY ECCKER

The 6-foot point guard averaged 5.4 assists per game in his senior season and led the team in assists for three straight seasons. "Most passes are just kind of simple," he said. "If there's a man open, I feel it's my job to get them the ball." Eccker also quarterbacked Tom Apke's "5 game" stall that made a late-game lead difficult for opponents to overcome. He is a member of the Creighton Athletic Hall of Fame.

RICK APKE

The coach's brother (44) finished his career with 1,682 points, which at the time trailed only Bob Portman. Apke could play inside at 6-8, averaging 7.8 rebounds a game his senior year, but he was also a deadly outside shooter. "I'm happy Rick has achieved some individual acclaim, but more significant is the fact he's been a key player in a golden era for Creighton basketball," said brother Tom. "He played on two NCAA tournament teams and an NIT team in four years, and helped us win a conference championship." Rick Apke was a third-round NBA selection but instead went to medical school.

KEVIN MCKENNA

McKenna (30) was a key contributor on a veteran team as a freshman. "He has been a great catalyst in some of our comebacks because of the way he plays with reckless abandon," coach Tom Apke said during McKenna's freshman season. He finished his career with 1,500 points. He was a fourth-round draft choice of the Los Angeles Lakers and played on the 1982 NBA championship team.

JOHN C. JOHNSON

The 6-3 Omaha Central grad was the team's second-leading scorer and a reliable rebounder. His two free throws in the last minute helped secure the MVC regular-season title at Southern Illinois. Johnson said the raucous crowd bothered him a little on the first one, "but the second one, I shook it off. I knew it was for the Missouri Valley Conference championship."

DAVE WESELY

At 6-7, the junior battled taller centers but made up the difference in strength. He averaged 12 points a game and 7 rebounds and ranked second on the team in minutes played. Kansas City Kings General Manager Joe Axelson, in Omaha to scout Larry Bird, was impressed by the way Wesely ripped the ball away on rebounds. "He did it with authority — like he really meant business," Axelson said.

Reaching for the stars, but coming up empty

Every athletic director would like to hit a home run on the first big coaching hire. Dan Offenburger swung for a grand slam and struck out.

He considered four men to replace Tom Apke: former Creighton great Paul Silas, longtime Creighton assistant Tom Brosnihan, former Creighton player Mike Caruso and Willis Reed, who as a player had led the New York Knicks to two championships.

The first three were logical candidates, but Reed? He had had little connection with college basketball since his playing days in the mid-1960s at Grambling State. His only previous head coaching job, with the Knicks, ended in a firing in 1978 after little more than a season on the bench. But his name popped up during a conversation with Eddie Donovan, the Knicks' general manager.

"Eddie told me to hire Willis Reed, because he thought Willis Reed could become one of the all-time greats in college coaching," Offenburger said. "My first reaction was here was a big name, and the Knicks were just trying to help him out. But Eddie said he was one of the greatest human beings you'd want to meet, he had contacts, he knew the game, and he knew how to handle the players. Then he said to find out for myself."

Offenburger did, checking with a number of people, including Silas, then the coach of the NBA's San Diego Clippers. The responses were glowing, and Reed came for an interview.

The job was first offered to Silas, who declined. "Paul told me he was very set in the pros," Offenburger said. He then offered it to Reed, and on April 12, 1981, Creighton announced that the 38-year-old Reed would be Creighton's new coach.

The Reed hiring was not a resounding hit with some segments of the Creighton fan base. Some fans were angered that Brosnihan, the loyal soldier, had been passed over again. Offenburger admitted that it was difficult to pass over Brosnihan for the job many outside the program thought he deserved.

"He was a classmate of mine," Offenburger said. "I'm godfather to one of his children. It's just that we were trying to do something totally different."

November 15, 1981:

Dan Offenburger bristled at suggestions that Willis Reed would use the Creighton job as a stepping-stone to the NBA. "Hey, this is the kind of business where you look to improve yourself," he said. "Willis and I have talked about what he wants to do here. He says it should take four to six years to do it. Five years is a long time for a basketball coach to stay at a school." Offenburger also pointed out that Reed's son, who was not a basketball player, had transferred from Tulane to Creighton to be with his father.

But in many ways, Reed's hiring wasn't a new turn: It marked the continuation of Creighton's long quest to put its basketball program among the nation's elite.

Offenburger admitted that one of the reasons he went after Silas and Reed was to land a big-name coach who could bring some flash to the program and attract big-time recruits.

"He gives us the opportunity for a dimension that we've never had in Creighton basketball," Offenburger said of Reed. "Which is to compete among the very top teams in the country in recruiting. Given our location and our resources, we have limitations in reaching to the talent pools on the East Coast, South and Southern California. A nearby example would be Nebraska football — to capitalize on local talent and supplement it with talent across the nation."

Creighton finished eighth in the Missouri Valley Conference in Willis Reed's first season in 1981-82. The Bluejays had the best record in the Missouri Valley during Tom Apke's last four years, winning one more game over that period than Indiana State, which had a 16-0 league record in Larry Bird's senior year.

As it turned out, the Bluejays took a couple of steps in the wrong direction in Reed's first two seasons. He lost his first game to Wisconsin-Stevens Point, at the time an NAIA school that offered little athletic aid. Reed's first team won just seven games, and just two after the first week of January. Creighton ended its 1981-82 season by losing 13 of its final 15 games, and its 7-20 record was the worst in program history.

While times were tough for Reed, another Offenburger hire was slowly starting to get the Bluejays' women's basketball program turned around. Offenburger had plucked Bruce Rasmussen out of the Iowa high school ranks, and the young coach, with his own dreams of glory, was getting traction after a rough start.

He already had a solid player on campus in Connie Yori and thought he had found another difference-maker in Jackie Glosson, who had wowed him with her athleticism while on a recruiting trip to Milwaukee. "I saw Jackie Glosson goal-tend in high school," Rasmussen said.

Glosson signed and was set to enroll at Creighton in the fall of 1981, but a late ACT score was too low for her to qualify. Not wanting to lose her, Rasmussen steered her to Moberly Junior College, where a buddy, Dick Halterman, coached the women's basketball team. Rasmussen believed Halterman would keep other coaches from moving in on Glosson, and she could eventually find her way back to Creighton after two seasons at the Missouri school.

On one of his frequent trips to Moberly to check on Glosson's progress, Rasmussen came away impressed with the young coach of the team that played in the game after the women. Dana Altman, in his first and only year as coach of Southeast Community College in Fairbury, was coaching against Moberly in the men's game.

"He was 23, 24 years old, but looked like he was 15," Rasmussen recalled. "He was running up and down the sideline. His team was pressing."

Rasmussen liked what he saw in Altman.

He also continued to like what he saw in Glosson. As a freshman at Moberly, she was a first-team junior-college All-American. She won national player of the year honors as a sophomore, as she and another Creighton recruit, 6-foot-1 Kathy Schulz, led Moberly to a national championship.

"With those two," said Rasmussen, "we'd have a chance to win the national championship."

But Oklahoma State hired Halterman, and he took Glosson and Schulz with him to Stillwater, where they helped the school win a pair of Big Eight championships. Glosson was named All-American as a senior.

Bruce Rasmussen with Connie Yori after she passed Bob Portman's career scoring record. She finished with 2,010 points.

While Rasmussen's prized recruit got away, Reed landed his in center Benoit Benjamin.

The 7-foot Benjamin was from Monroe, La., about 45 miles from where Reed had grown up in Bernice. Reed traveled to Monroe during the summer of 1981 to watch Benjamin — who had averaged 29 points, 19.5 rebounds and six blocked shots as a junior — play in some pickup games.

"I liked what I saw immediately," Reed said.

Reed was battling top schools for Benjamin and made the three visits to Monroe that were allowed under NCAA rules. There were stories that Reed, who was single, dated Benjamin's mother, Carolyn, whose husband died in an automobile accident in 1973. Reed dismissed the talk, saying: "One of the best experiences of recruiting — and it's a hard job — is that you get to meet a lot of real nice folks." Benjamin, who claimed that recruiters illegally offered new houses, cars and boats, eventually signed with Creighton, spurning a last-second push by his home-state university, LSU.

Benjamin turned in an impressive freshman season, leading the team in scoring (14.9 points per game), rebounding (9.6) and blocked shots (3.4). His play supplied Creighton fans with some hope on a 1982-83 team that won just eight games and finished 10th in the Valley.

The Bluejays, with Benjamin again leading the way, made a giant step forward in the 1983-84 season, Reed's third. They won 17 games, finished fourth in the Missouri Valley regular-season race, advanced to the league tournament championship game and played in the postseason. Creighton faced Nebraska in a first-round NIT game that drew a crowd of 9,158 to the Civic Auditorium and led 54-52 with 1:30 remaining. But Nebraska scored the last four points, the final two coming after Benjamin drew a technical foul with 10 seconds remaining.

Benjamin earned first-team All-Valley honors by averaging 16.2 points, 9.8 rebounds and 5.2 blocked shots per game, and teammate Vernon Moore was a second-team selection. After the season, Creighton extended Reed's contract for another three years.

Benoit Benjamin took trips to Kentucky and LSU before committing to Creighton. "I feel like a kid on the night before Christmas," Willis Reed said after Benjamin made his decision. Red McManus chimed in: "It's the best news I've heard since we signed Paul Silas."

The Bluejays carted some heavy expectations into the 1984-85 campaign, which they opened by outgunning the University of Nebraska at Kearney in a 103-95 shootout at the auditorium. By mid-February, fans were talking about a return to the NCAA tournament after a 72-64 victory over Wichita State put the Jays at 9-3 in the MVC and 20-6 overall.

But things were about to unravel quickly for Reed's team. The Bluejays lost by 15 in their final home game of the season, a battle for first place against 15th-ranked Tulsa.

They then dropped Valley road games at Southern Illinois, Illinois State and Drake to fall into a fourth-place tie in the league. The Drake defeat was by a 103-54 score to a last-place team that had lost five games in a row by an average of 20.4 points.

"It seems to me the attitude is that we've given up," George Morrow, an assistant coach who had played for Tom Apke, said afterward. "We're saying to hell with it. How did we beat Marquette? How did we beat Notre Dame? How did we beat so many great teams? We're capable, but right now, it's a matter of believing."

Creighton finished off the regular season with a 5-point defeat at Dayton, then punctuated the collapse with a 66-59 loss to Bradley in the Missouri Valley tournament. The Jays were one of only eight 20-win teams that weren't selected to play in a postseason tournament. An NIT official pointed to the Drake loss as a factor.

Fifty-eight days after the final game of that 20-12 train wreck, Reed resigned with two years remaining on the contract. In the next six days, Benjamin announced that he was leaving Creighton early to turn professional — the two-time All-American would wind up being the third player picked in that year's draft — and Offenburger followed Reed in resigning.

How did a team that once seemed destined to be a lock for the NCAA tournament disintegrate? World-Herald staff writer Steve Sinclair painted a picture of a team and athletic department in turmoil.

1983: A SECOND SCORING THREAT FOR JAYS

Creighton guard Vernon Moore rises up against Marquette defenders, including future NBA star and coach Glenn "Doc" Rivers (31) and Kerry Trotter (32), a Creighton Prep grad who had faced Benoit Benjamin in the McDonald's High School All-American game. Marquette won 64-52. Moore finished his career with 1,654 points.

1985: BEN AT HIS BEST

Benoit Benjamin had 43 points, 16 rebounds and 10 blocked shots in a 96-90 win over Southern Illinois. It was one of three triple-double performances he had at Creighton.

The problems included player discontent over alleged double standards involving Benjamin, disputes between Reed and Offenburger, a trip that Creighton Vice President Robert Gerraughty made with the team that upset Reed, and Reed's telling team members during the season of a possible law enforcement investigation into drugs.

No Creighton player was ever charged with any drug offense, but possible drug use by players was one of the reasons Gerraughty had traveled with the team to Southern Illinois and Illinois State.

Moore, the Bluejays' senior guard, said Gerraughty didn't ask the players whether they used drugs. "He just said he mainly heard a couple of players were unhappy and thinking about leaving," Moore said. "Since I've been here, everybody has been pretty straight. I've never seen anybody take drugs or heard about it."

But Gerraughty's visits with the players reportedly upset Reed because of the timing on a crucial road trip near the end of the season. Sinclair's report also told of internal conflict between Reed and the man who brought him to Creighton.

Reed said his main reason for resigning was his frustrations over recruiting violations by other schools. Supporters of the coach and the athletic director pointed to a growing rift between the two men as the actual reason, although neither would confirm that.

In leaving, Reed said he enjoyed his years at Creighton.

"I really liked Creighton," he said at the time. "I had a great relationship with a lot of the administration and the priests. My son graduated from there, and my daughter is going to graduate. It's too bad the job didn't work out. But it gave me an opportunity I needed at that time of my life. And I appreciate that they stuck with me through some hard times."

Offenburger's resignation ended a 17-year association with Creighton, including five years as athletic director. Offenburger urged any estranged fans to "come home to Creighton" at a farewell press conference.

"At times in my career, I've had to be a part of difficult decisions," he said. "Some people have been upset with me. It has been difficult to have good friends stay upset. As I leave Creighton, I apologize to anyone I may have offended."

> "At times in my career, I've had to be a part of difficult decisions. ... As I leave Creighton, I apologize to anyone I may have offended."
>
> **— Dan Offenburger**

Offenburger referred specifically to former longtime team physician Lee Bevilacqua, a friend who once had helped the Offenburger family through the tough decision about unplugging the machines that kept 9-year-old Nancy Offenburger alive. She died in 1974 of Reye's syndrome.

Offenburger had been part of a decision to dismiss Bevilacqua as team physician in 1982 after Bevilacqua disagreed with decisions in the athletic department. The move upset many former players and fans, and Bevilacqua quit attending games. Offenburger also mentioned Brosnihan, the former assistant he passed over to hire Reed.

As for the reason for his resignation, Offenburger said merely, "It's just time."

Once again, Creighton was beginning a search for the next coach to lead it to the big time.

Bringing passion back to the program

Tony Barone knew little about Creighton when he visited the campus in the spring of 1985. He knew even less about Athletic Director Don Leahy.

"I couldn't have picked him out of a lineup," Barone said. But after spending time with Leahy, Barone became convinced of one thing: He wanted to come work for Leahy as Creighton's new basketball coach.

"When I came in to interview for the job, I just became totally sold on Don Leahy," Barone said. "The thing that impressed me about Don was how enthusiastic he was, and how he felt that the university had to have a quality basketball program."

Don Leahy sought assurance of CU's strong commitment to its basketball program before he applied to be athletic director. Among the boosters who spoke up was Red McManus, who said basketball success helped the university raise money and enhance its national reputation. "It's the one thing that really holds the school together," McManus said.

Creighton had turned to Leahy to get the program back on track in the aftermath of the ugly ending to Willis Reed's four seasons as coach. Leahy, a Nebraska high school coaching legend at Omaha Creighton Prep, came to Creighton after spending the 11 previous years as the athletic director at the University of Nebraska at Omaha. His first priority was to find someone to replace Reed, and he didn't lack candidates. Former Creighton basketball star Paul Silas, who had turned down the job in 1981, indicated that he was interested in returning to his alma mater. And among the 59 other applicants for the job was an up-and-coming head coach by the name of Lon Kruger, the former Kansas State star.

Eight men interviewed for the job with the university's search committee, which named three finalists: Barone, DePaul assistant coach Jim Molinari and former University of Illinois-Chicago head coach Tom Meyer.

"We had excellent candidates," Leahy said.

Leahy, Creighton President Michael Morrison and university Vice President Robert Gerraughty selected the 37-year-old Barone, a Chicago native who had grown up across the street from Wrigley Field and been a batboy for the Chicago Cubs. Although he stood just 5-foot-8, Barone earned a basketball scholarship to Duke University, where he lettered three seasons and earned Academic All-America honors.

Barone started his coaching career as a high school assistant coach. He then sandwiched a stint as a Duke assistant coach in between head-coaching jobs at two Chicago-area high schools. In 1978, he joined Dick Versace's staff at Bradley and soon was named the associate head coach. The Versace-Barone team directed Bradley to two Valley championships and one NIT title.

"He's impeccably prepared," Versace said when Barone was named Creighton's head coach. "He's a terrific teacher and coach, and a wonderful family man. He will be great for Creighton."

While Barone's specific knowledge of the university itself was limited, he was well aware of the basketball talent he was about to inherit after having coached against the Bluejays the previous seven seasons. "There were a couple of players that had the ability, but they hadn't really performed at a high level in the Valley," Barone said. "We knew Benoit was leaving. When you go into that kind of situation, you better get a realistic view from the administration, especially the athletic director, as to what are the expectations.

"I'm going to change a lot of things," Tony Barone said when he arrived at Creighton. "That's simply because I think the team has to represent my personality on the court. Our effort is not going to be questioned."

"Don was upfront. He said it was going to take time, that it wasn't going to be 'hop on board,' and in two years you're winning. We were going to have to redo and restructure the program."

Kevin Sarver, who had grown up in western Illinois, enrolled at Creighton a few months after Barone took the job. He was familiar with Barone's work at Bradley and wondered how the new coach would do, given the level of talent the Bluejays had on their roster.

"I didn't know about what had happened here in the Willis era, or what Tony had to do to pick up the pieces," Sarver said. "That's Tony. He finds ways to get things done."

1985: DEALING WITH FRUSTRATION

Barone showed the growing pains of his first season during a 56-53 loss to NCAA-bound Xavier. "I'm not big on moral victories," he said. "We still lost the basketball game, and if we're satisfied because we lost by three, that would be a major mistake as far as I'm concerned."

Barone credits Leahy for helping set the foundation on which he would build his program.

"Don assured me that we were going to get the time it took to get this done," Barone said. "There were a lot of things that we had to work against. People around here were still reeling from the Kevin Ross situation."

The 6-foot-9 Ross had been recruited years earlier by Tom Apke. With his eligibility expired after four years of play, Ross dropped out of school and was found to have a second-grade reading level. He could not write a check or read a menu.

Creighton agreed to pay $6,500 to send Ross to Westside Preparatory School, a private elementary school in Chicago. He graduated from Westside, at the age of 24. National news reports about Ross surfaced as Barone took charge.

Two years into Barone's tenure, Ross sued Creighton for breach of contract, alleging that the university's educators had failed to teach him adequately. "Kevin Ross was a good guy," Barone said. "He just got caught in a situation that wasn't good for him based on his background." Creighton admitted no liability and eventualy settled the suit for $30,000 in 1992.

The backlash from the Kevin Ross affair wasn't the only burden Barone sensed as he set out to build his program. Five months after taking the job, Barone told The World-Herald that he was "totally disappointed" with the attitude that Omaha had toward Creighton basketball. "I've got no unrealistic belief in what we can or can't do," he said. "But it bothers me for people to tell me we can't do something. This town is really negative in its approach. I'm going to change that, if I can."

Barone recalled stopping at the Eppley Airfield gift shop when his team was preparing to leave Omaha. He said he pointed to the Nebraska apparel for sale and asked the clerk why there wasn't Creighton gear. "I felt that a Creighton fan, even in his own mind, was a little bit of a second-class citizen when compared to a Nebraska fan," he said.

If Omaha's expectations were low at the time, Sports Illustrated's were scraping the bottom. The national sports magazine, in its annual college basketball edition, listed Barone's 1985-86 team as one of "six teams to pity" and predicted that Creighton would finish last in the Valley.

"I appreciate the publicity from Sports Illustrated," Barone said when asked for his reaction. "We got two paragraphs. I think it proves how intelligent Sports Illustrated's writers are. I wonder in my own mind how many basketball games those people have seen."

The Bluejays came into Barone's first season having lost players that accounted for 67 percent of the scoring and 73 percent of the rebounding the previous season. Barone managed to squeeze 12 wins out of that team, and the Jays finished tied for fifth in the Valley with a 7-9 record.

Creighton took a step backward in Barone's second season, as the Bluejays compiled a 9-19 record. They finished tied for seventh in the league (4-10) in the 1986-87 season, but a wave of reinforcements provided Creighton with a glimmer of hope.

Leading the charge was a former soccer goalkeeper from Loveland, Colo., and a highly recruited big man from Rockford, Ill.

1986: BIG WIN IN A DOWN YEAR

Junior college transfer Rod Mason (24) got his first start in an 80-65 upset of Iowa State, which returned three starters from a team that had advanced to the NCAA Sweet 16 the previous season. "I've never been more proud of a group for a first game," Tony Barone said of his team, which would finish 9-19. The game drew nearly 9,000 to the Civic Auditorium.

1986: PROMISING START FADES

Creighton's Gary Swain led the Jays with 17 points in a 63-57 loss to Marquette at home. The Jays had beaten Iowa State, Nebraska and Xavier in the three previous weeks, but the loss to Marquette began an eight-game skid. Creighton lost five of its first six Valley games in the 1986-87 season and finished 4-10 in the league.

Bob Harstad and Chad Gallagher were the anchors of Barone's second full recruiting class. They also provided Barone with a lasting example that hard work and thorough preparation are just part of the equation for basketball success.

Sometimes, you also need to get lucky in recruiting. Barone's assistant, Dick Fick, came across Harstad when the two coaches were digging for prospects at a basketball camp in Rensselaer, Ind. At the time, the camp was a magnet for college coaches.

Bluejay assistant Dick Fick pointed out Bob Harstad to Barone.

"If you thought you were a player," Barone said, "you went to Rensselaer."

Harstad did, but he wasn't high on the pecking order. That meant he played most of his summer games on the outdoor courts, while the more highly coveted players got to play indoors.

"It was 105, and the courts were terrible," Barone said. "Most coaches never spent time out there. Because we felt we were just beginning our program, we felt like that's what we had to do. We were trying to unearth anybody."

Fick watched Harstad play a game, reporting to Barone that he had to check out the player that seemed to get every rebound. Barone then watched Harstad and liked him enough to put him on Creighton's recruiting list for the coming season.

Barone traveled to Loveland in the fall to watch Harstad play soccer, then returned to watch him practice with his high school basketball team.

"When he came out to play, he had these high-cut basketball shoes on with low-cut socks, and a mohawk," Barone said. "When I got back, I told Fick, 'He's a guy that looks like he doesn't have any socks on, he has a mohawk, and we have to sign him tomorrow.' "

The Bluejays eventually did and also picked up a commitment from Gallagher, a 6-foot-10 prize that many other schools had sought.

"He was one of the top players in Illinois at the time," Barone said. "But he was a borderline student. He wasn't a bad student, but he was definitely borderline. We put a lot of effort into trying to figure out if he could make it academically at Creighton. We signed him based on the belief that he could.

"Those two guys started us off."

Bob Harstad started as a freshman in the season opener of the 1987-88 season and finished second in the Missouri Valley Conference in rebounding.

Harstad was in the starting lineup when Creighton opened its 1987-88 season with a 21-point loss at California, and Gallagher soon would be. The Bluejays' early-season schedule tested Barone's young players, with games against Kansas State, Nebraska and Iowa State before back-to-back tournament appearances in Las Vegas and Hawaii.

The Bluejays were 3-3 when they headed to Las Vegas. They won a close game against Alaska before Jerry Tarkanian's UNLV team spanked them 90-59. From there, it was off to Hawaii, where Creighton opened the Rainbow Classic with an 86-55 loss to Jim Valvano's North Carolina State team. After dropping the second game of the tournament 88-51 to Southern Methodist, Barone held a team meeting in his hotel room.

Junior college transfer James Farr, left, and freshman Chad Gallagher joined Bob Harstad as starters in their first season at Creighton.

"It lasted about 2½ hours," Harstad recalled. "He got into your personal life. He used all kinds of analogies, like if we were in a foxhole, we'd stab him in the back. It was a rampage like I'd never experienced before.

"No one was safe from the verbal abuse. You don't want to laugh, but it was kind of funny. But you couldn't laugh, because you knew he was pissed off."

The travel plans called for the Bluejays to spend a couple of days in Hawaii after their final game. Barone issued his players an ultimatum: If they lost to Hawaii the next night, they'd head straight to the airport and spend the rest of the trip there waiting for their flight home.

Creighton appeared headed for a couple of days of walking the concourses when they fell behind Hawaii 19 points at the half. Harstad remembered pulling Rod Mason aside and asking the senior guard to do anything he could to reverse the direction of the game. "I'm not spending two days at the airport with him," said Harstad, referring to Barone.

Fortunately for the Bluejays, Mason and Mike Johnson got hot in the second half to lead a rally that produced an 81-69 victory. By then, Harstad had come to realize that Barone was anything but the coach who had recruited him.

Asked for his first impression of Barone when they met during the recruiting process, Harstad replied, "I thought he was a sweet man."

How long did it take for that to change? "About 10 seconds into our first practice," Harstad replied, laughing. Still, he knew there was a method to Barone's madness.

"At the time, when he went off on us in Hawaii, I thought he was being an ass," Harstad said. "But looking back, I think it was all planned. He did it for a purpose. After that, we started to bond as players. All the guys in that room started to come together as a team out of fear and necessity."

The Creighton community, too, had come to realize that it had a bit of a loose cannon on its hands. Barone never hesitated to speak his mind. His sideline demeanor conjured up memories of the days when the fiery Red McManus directed the program.

Like most coaches, Barone would come out for the start of the game neatly dressed in a coat and tie. It wouldn't take long before the coat was gone. Then the tie. It wasn't uncommon for him to finish a game with a shirttail hanging out, his face flushed, his hair rumpled.

Barone's act offended some fans, but that's what it was, Barone said years later. An act.

"It was part of the shtick, I guess," Barone said. "I was trying to generate some enthusiasm. Me running up and down the sidelines or taking my coat off was part of trying to do that. I probably said some things I shouldn't have said or acted on the sidelines less mature than I should have. But initially, we had to be a little over the edge."

The Bluejays ended Barone's third season with a 16-16 record. They tied for fourth place in the league, but their coach came away feeling encouraged about the direction the program was headed.

Barone had thrown his young players into the fire, and they had responded. Gallagher ended up the team's third-leading scorer behind senior Mason and junior James Farr. Harstad had averaged 9.0 points and 8.5 rebounds while starting every game. Other young players such as Johnson, Matt Roggenburk and Duan Cole had made important contributions.

"This is a great group of kids," Barone said during a rough patch of the 1987-88 season. "We're going to challenge for the Valley title the next two years with this group of kids, unless I lose my mind before then."

Barone tells an exhausted Harstad to "explode up" each time he jumps during a workout.

"We weren't in the mold that we were going to let our young guys develop as freshmen, give them some time as sophomores and maybe by their junior years they'd be good players," Barone said. "We just threw them into the lineup, and if we got our brains beat in, so be it. Fortunately, we got lucky in that we had identified some guys that turned out not only to be good players, but good people. They all meshed, and we were able to hit a home run with them because they figured me out and they figured out that if they played together, we could win."

The growing pains Creighton experienced that season, Harstad said, would prove beneficial.

"When you're a freshman, you're just happy to be out there," Harstad said. "I remember playing North Carolina State in Hawaii and looking over and seeing 'Coach V' (Jim Valvano) on the bench and thinking, 'What in God's name am I doing here?' But toward the end of that season, we beat Marquette and we won a close game against Southern Illinois in the Valley tournament. At that point, you're not saying, 'Man, we could be good.' I think it was more like we knew we had the right to be out there."

Creighton turned the corner in the 1988-89 season in spite of being picked seventh in the Valley's preseason poll. After an inconsistent nonconference season that included a 30-point loss to Iowa State, the Bluejays opened league play with wins in eight of their first nine games. They followed mid-February stumbles against Tulsa and Wichita State with three league wins down the stretch to produce the school's first Valley regular-season championship since 1978.

They tacked on three wins at the conference tournament to clinch the school's first trip to the NCAA tournament since 1981.

"That was a heck of an accomplishment for those guys," Barone recalled. "Back then, the Valley was a one-bid league. You had to win the tournament."

Duan Cole was among the freshmen who accounted for 49.1 percent of the minutes played during the 1987-88 season. He started three games but played mostly as a backup to point guard James Farr. "Duan had the most difficult adjustment, because we moved him from another position to point guard," Barone said.

The Bluejays headed for Dallas, where they had drawn a first-round assignment against sixth-ranked Missouri. The Tigers were playing without coach Norm Stewart, who had missed the final month of the season after undergoing cancer surgery. Creighton came out red hot, shooting 57.7 percent from the field in taking a 2-point lead into halftime. Twenty minutes later, the Bluejays' 20-11 season was over, as Missouri used a 24-7 run to fuel the rally that produced an 85-69 win.

With all the key contributors returning, Barone had high expectations for his 1989-90 team. Voters in the Valley's preseason poll agreed, tagging Creighton as the favorite in the title race.

Creighton struggled from the get-go, losing its opener to Coppin State and then dropping its third game of the season at fifth-ranked Missouri. An early January win over Notre Dame started Creighton on a streak in which it won seven of eight games, but late road losses at Drake and Illinois State left Creighton tied for second in the Valley.

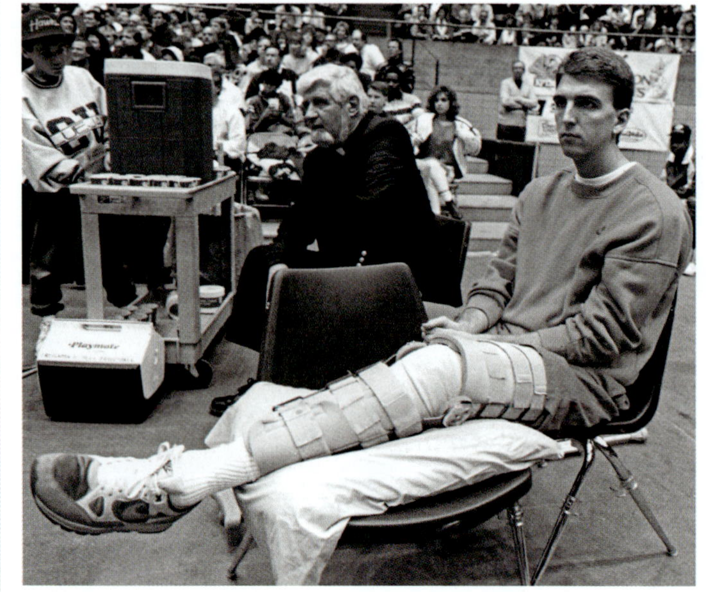

1990: ANOTHER SETBACK

Todd Eisner took a seat at the end of the Creighton bench next to the Rev. Robert Hart, the team chaplain, midway through the 1989-90 season. Eisner had major surgery on his right knee as a freshman and on his left knee as a junior. "I've never really heard of anybody that's blown out both knees in a three-year period," said Eisner, who was leading the team with 5.1 assists per game at the time of his second injury. Tony Barone said the team wasn't the same without Eisner. "You might replace some of his skills but not his mental approach to the game," he said. Eisner returned for his senior season.

A home victory over Wichita State — the Valley still played its conference tournament at campus sites — advanced Creighton into the final at Illinois State, where the Redbirds claimed the league's automatic NCAA berth with a 69-64 victory. Harstad said afterward that the Bluejays still had hopes of landing an at-large berth in the tournament. "I think we have an outside chance," he said. "We've had a good year. Every year we seem to improve our wins. We can just keep our fingers crossed and hope."

It was just the second time in program history that Creighton had won 20 games in back-to-back seasons. But it wasn't enough to impress the NCAA basketball committee, which passed over the Bluejays. The school settled for the consolation prize, a berth in the NIT. Creighton's season came to an end in Chicago as old rival DePaul pulled out an 89-72 win.

"They're an excellent team, and they showed it," DePaul coach Joey Meyer said. "It took so long to shake them because Harstad and Gallagher are excellent players."

By then, Harstad and Gallagher — who finished one-two in the league's player of the year voting — had come to be known as the "Dynamic Duo." They set out the next season to bring a pair of illustrious careers to a close with an exclamation point.

Harstad, the Valley player of the year as a junior, made five of 11 3-point shots as a member of a summer NIT all-star team that toured Europe. Barone said Harstad would again play inside for his senior year. "I would be real reluctant to take a kid who is going to be the fourth player in the history of the conference to get 2,000 points and 1,000 rebounds and change his position this year," Barone said. "I'm pretty slow, but I'm not that slow."

"There is no limit to how far we can go," Gallagher said before the season.

Harstad said the Bluejays were shooting for a spot in the national rankings, an accomplishment that had eluded them in spite of their success the previous two seasons.

Coaches normally downplay rankings, but Barone said the recognition they bring would be fitting for this group. "It's almost an acceptance thing," he said. "You're accepted as a program when you get ranked. We would like to appear in those ratings sometime in March. That would be wonderful."

The season got off to another up-and-down start, with a mid-January loss leaving Creighton 8-6. The Bluejays then rattled off eight straight wins, lost at Tulsa, and strung together four more wins to capture their second Valley regular-season title in three seasons.

The Jays routed Drake in the opening game of the 1991 MVC tournament, played at neutral-site St. Louis for the first time. They followed with a win over Southern Illinois in the semifinals and advanced to the championship game against Southwest Missouri State, later known as Missouri State.

25
SHOCKERS

Gallagher, on the facing page, finished second to teammate Harstad in the 1990 Missouri Valley Conference player of the year voting. The order was reversed the next season, with Gallagher claiming the award.

One of the stars of the tournament was junior guard Latrell Wrightsell, who scored 12 points against Southern Illinois and had a tournament-record eight steals against Drake.

The morning of the final, Wrightsell learned that his father, Henry Stewart, had died of cancer at age of 51. Wrightsell went out and scored a season-high 16 points in a hard-fought 68-52 victory over the Bears to wrap up the tournament title and advance to the NCAA tournament.

"I can't even explain how I feel," said Wrightsell, wiping tears from his eyes while being hugged by teammates and fans after the game. "I'm just so happy we won. My family was all at home watching me."

Teammate Todd Eisner called Wrightsell the MVP of the game. "It was absolutely amazing how he could block out the tragedy that he had earlier in the day and come and play with the amount of enthusiasm and courage that he had," Eisner said. "Everybody on the team would say his inspiration today and in the last six or seven games have been absolutely paramount to us capturing the conference championship this season."

Barone praised Latrell Wrightsell's aggressive play in the 1991 Illinois State game. The coach said he needed his guards to drive the ball at the basket to pull defenders away from Harstad and Gallagher. "Hopefully, we'll get some penetration from him," Barone said of Wrightsell's growing role.

Omaha youngsters Chris McLaughlin, Bubba Klement and Kevin McLaughlin react to the announcement that Creighton would play New Mexico State in the NCAA tournament. About 700 watched the televised coverage of the announcement at the old gym. Duan Cole said his only disappointment was the Bluejays' seeding. "With the year we had, it seemed like we deserved a little better than 11th," he said.

The win, the 15th in 16 games, improved Creighton to 23-7. Barone and the Jays waited a week to learn that their opening game of the NCAA tournament would come against 15th-ranked New Mexico State in Salt Lake City.

With Gallagher, the Valley player of the year, scoring 18 points and grabbing 14 rebounds, Creighton upset the sixth-seeded Aggies 64-56 to pick up its first NCAA tournament win since 1974 and secure a school-record 24th win.

"There's absolutely no question that this is the biggest win since I've been at Creighton," Barone said after the game. "It's the biggest because of what we did. It gets us to the record, and it gets us to the final 32."

Creighton, a No. 11 seed, advanced to a second-round game against Seton Hall, a No. 3 seed, and led at halftime. "I thought we were going to win," Barone said.

The Pirates had other ideas. They turned up the defensive heat and hit Creighton with a second-half scoring explosion to win 81-69. Seton Hall had runs of 7-0, 9-0 and 12-0 in a decisive 29-9 run in the first nine minutes and 14 seconds of the second half. The loss brought an end to the careers of Creighton seniors Harstad, Gallagher, Eisner, Darin Plautz and Bill O'Dowd. Harstad, who started all 128 games of his career, finished as Creighton's all-time scoring leader with 2,110 points. Gallagher was second with 1,983.

And Creighton, which had started the season with the slogan "20-20-20 Vision," for the first time in program history had won at least 20 games three seasons in a row.

More than two decades later, Harstad remembers with crystal clarity the day the team arrived back in Omaha.

"It was March 17," he said. "As a player, there are moments that stick in your mind because of a great win or you played particularly well. But I'll never forget that day, when everything came into perspective. You've dedicated four years and almost 100 percent of your life to the university and basketball. You realize that this incredibly wonderful and painful and emotional journey is over. Basketball was everything I was, it was my identity. I remember thinking, 'What do I do now?' You realize that you're never going to play another college basketball game in your life."

In six seasons, Barone had guided Creighton to a 102-82 record and three postseason appearances. That made him a hot commodity on the coaching market, and three weeks after the season ended, he accepted an offer to become Texas A&M's new coach.

In six seasons at Creighton, Barone was alternately charming, infuriating, funny, moody, inspiring, critical, jovial, sullen, sensitive, insensitive, sentimental, volatile, supportive and impatient.

"He was a different guy to know," said Sarver, a Creighton student when the coach arrived and the school's sports information director by the time he left. "He was demanding. He was a micromanager. He wanted to know everything that was happening about his program."

Sarver recalled that Barone could be a guy that would tell you jokes in your office at 8:30 in the morning, chew you out like you've never been chewed out before 15 minutes later, and then chat with you about the Chicago Cubs 45 minutes later.

"It was tough to know which Tony you were going to get at any particular moment. But the one thing I will always remember about Tony is that he was unbelievably loyal and a good guy."

> "It wasn't a good decision. ... I learned you can't sell out your beliefs just because you're making a lot of money."
>
> **— Tony Barone, on leaving for Texas A&M**

Barone was inheriting a train wreck at Texas A&M — the previous coach had gotten the Aggies in hot water with the NCAA, and the school was facing probation. But the Aggies were willing to pay him a lot of money — they doubled his Creighton salary — and he jumped at the opportunity.

More than 20 years later, he summed up the move in two words: "Bad idea."

"My bride told me it was going to be a bad decision, and it was," Barone said. "They doubled my salary, and most people say that if they're going to double your salary, you have to go. But it wasn't a good decision. The problem was I really didn't fit in at Texas A&M because of my particular approach to basketball.

"I felt like I could fit in because they were going on probation, they had no players, I could fix this thing and I was making a lot of money. I learned you can't sell out your beliefs just because you're making a lot of money."

Money would also figure into Creighton's search for a successor to Barone. The school didn't have a lot of it to throw at a proven head coach to lure him to Omaha. Instead, Creighton decided to give the job to one of Barone's assistants.

It was essentially the same strategy Creighton had employed 18 years earlier when it selected Tom Apke over Tom Brosnihan to replace Eddie Sutton. This time, the results would be drastically different.

ON THE BIG STAGE

Creighton swept the Missouri Valley Conference regular-season and tournament championships for the second time in three years. The "Dynamic Duo" led the way. Chad Gallagher was the league's player of the year, following Bob Harstad's selection the previous season. The NCAA tournament bid was the second in three years, with an NIT berth in between. The Bluejays beat No. 15 New Mexico State in the first round — their school-record 24th win and first NCAA tournament victory in 17 years — but were eliminated by No. 13 Seton Hall. Barone had the highest praise for the senior class of his final CU team: Harstad, Gallagher, Todd Eisner, Darin Plautz and Bill O'Dowd. "I don't think there will be another group to go through that university to match those kids."

DUAN COLE

Junior guard Cole made opponents pay if they focused too closely on Harstad and Gallagher. The 5-10 Cole averaged 13.8 points a game during the season, shooting 47 percent on 3-point shots, one of the best single-season percentages in school history. He came back his final year to average 19.2 points a game and finished his career with 1,361 points.

LATRELL WRIGHTSELL

Wrightsell, a 6-1 guard, came on strong at the end of the year as the Jays won 12 of their final 13 regular-season games. He scored a season-high 16 points in a 68-52 victory over Southwest Missouri State in the Missouri Valley Conference Tournament final and was named to the MVC all-tournament team. While never a big scorer during his career, he was a steady point guard, logging 13 assists in one game and 12 in another, and twice had eight steals in a game.

TODD EISNER

Eisner, a 6-foot-7 forward, had undergone two major knee surgeries by his senior season and wore a brace while playing. He led the Valley in 3-point shooting in his sophomore year, when he made one of the biggest shots in program history, a 3-pointer with 2 seconds left to send the Jays into overtime against Southern Illinois, an eventual victory that helped propel them to a Valley regular-season title. Heading into the 1991 MVC tourney, Indiana State coach Tates Locke summed up one of Creighton's strengths: "They have a courageous player who comes off the bench, and he's really been a thorn in our side. He's got a leg that looks like it needs to be surgically removed, and he keeps playing and playing and playing."

CHAD GALLAGHER

Gallagher's 19.4 points a game led the Jays in scoring during the 1990-91 season. Gallagher scored a season-high 36 points on 16-of-23 shooting against Siena and had 27 points in a win at Indiana State. Creighton was the only league team to beat the Sycamores on their home court. Gallagher also made 15 of 18 shots and scored 32 points to lead CU's 90-67 win at Notre Dame. Harstad said his teammate deserved the MVC player of the year award. "I don't think there's a team that's stopped him," he said. "There's not enough you can say about how much he's improved."

BOB HARSTAD

As a high school senior, Harstad received little interest from college coaches. "The reason we signed him," Barone said, "was probably the purest reason for signing a kid — he played so hard." His success as a freshman caught opponents' attention, and he was frequently double-teamed his final three years. "Every time he touches the ball, he is attacked," Barone said. The 6-6 forward finished his career with more than 2,000 points and 1,000 rebounds, numbers matched at the time by only three Missouri Valley players: Oscar Robertson, Larry Bird and Xavier McDaniel. When Harstad broke Bob Portman's career scoring record, the Civic Auditorium crowd of 9,500 gave him a 90-second standing ovation.

Gambling on youth, and losing

With Tony Barone gone to Texas A&M, the school considered two of his assistants — Dick Fick and Rick Johnson — as his successor. Fick had thought he would get the job. But on the morning of April 15, 1991, Fick was summoned to a meeting with Dick Myers, the school's new athletic director. The conversation was short. Myers informed Fick that Johnson would be the head coach.

"I learned what the word devastating is all about," Fick said.

The 31-year-old Johnson was seven years younger than Fick. He also had been a member of Barone's staff for six years but had been a part-time assistant the first four seasons. Myers acknowledged that the selection of Johnson over Fick might surprise some in the Creighton community, but he declined to say why Johnson was selected. "We did not want to be swayed by the sentiment and maybe the pre-appointment of the obvious candidate," Myers said.

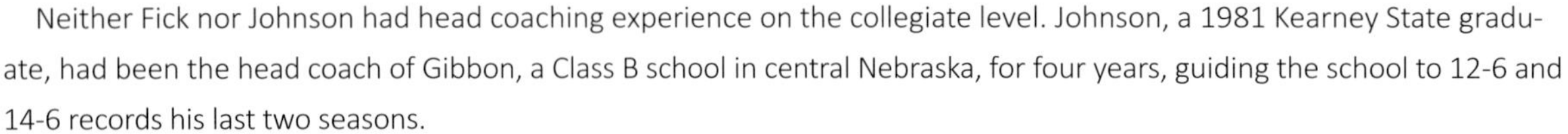

Neither Fick nor Johnson had head coaching experience on the collegiate level. Johnson, a 1981 Kearney State graduate, had been the head coach of Gibbon, a Class B school in central Nebraska, for four years, guiding the school to 12-6 and 14-6 records his last two seasons.

Jim Hendry in 1991 led Creighton to its only appearance in the College World Series in Omaha.

"It was the same kind of gamble Creighton University took years ago when they hired a young baseball coach at the age of 27," Johnson said. "I just hope that I can achieve the same type of accomplishments as Jim Hendry." Hendry had developed a nationally ranked program in his seven seasons at Creighton. Two months after Johnson's selection, Hendry would lead the Bluejays to their only appearance in the College World Series.

Barone had taken over a program that was reeling in the wake of the Willis Reed years and led Creighton back onto the big stage of the NCAA tournament twice in his final three seasons. But Johnson was going to have to head into his first season as coach without five key players, including stars Bob Harstad and Chad Gallagher, who had helped produce a school-record 24 wins in the 1990-91 season.

"We've been the best team in the Missouri Valley Conference the last four years," Johnson said. "That's the same commitment that we're going to continue to have."

Johnson inherited three talented guards — Duan Cole, Latrell Wrightsell and Matt Petty — but faced having to rebuild the Bluejays' front line with the departure of Harstad, Gallagher and Darin Plautz.

The Bluejays opened Johnson's first season with a 17-point loss at Iowa State but bounced back to defeat Colorado State. Up next was the annual meeting with Nebraska. The Huskers that season featured sophomore sharpshooter Eric Piatkowski, who would go on to be a first-round NBA draft pick by the time his career ended. Johnson's team battled Nebraska until the end before dropping a 90-85 decision, but the performance raised glimmers of hope in some segments of the CU fan base.

The Bluejays won Johnson's first Valley game a little more than a week later, beating Bradley 55-53, to improve to 2-2. But then the bottom dropped out on the 1991-92 season. Creighton would lose 10 of its next 12 games and eventually seven of its last eight to end the season at 9-19. That would be Johnson's highest win total.

The Bluejays opened the 1992-93 season with losses in six of their first seven games, and their only winning streak of the season came when they won a pair of home games over Southern Illinois and Southwest Missouri State at midseason. They finished the season at 8-18 — 10th in the league — and failed to make the conference tournament, which at the time took only the top eight of the 10 teams. In the span of two seasons, Creighton had gone from first to worst in the league.

"I was upset that we didn't fire Rick after that second year," said Bruce Rasmussen, who had moved from coaching women's basketball to the athletic-director-in-waiting chair.

Myers, the man who hired Johnson, left after one year on the job. The school brought in Tom Moore, a Creighton graduate and retired banker, to serve as athletic director and made Rasmussen his assistant. Moore had no experience in intercollegiate athletics.

"With his business background, Tom was supposed to teach me about business," Rasmussen said. "The idea was that if I didn't do anything to mess it up, I was going to become the athletic director in about a year and a half. Even though I didn't have the title, I was in charge of the day-to-day operation of the department."

Rasmussen said he went to the Rev. Michael Morrison, Creighton's president, after Johnson's second season and suggested that the coach be let go. Morrison opposed the move, Rasmussen said, because Johnson still had two years left on his contract.

"Father said we're not paying a buyout," Rasmussen said. "So I spent a lot of time the next year putting together data to show what not firing him cost us in terms of ticket sales and corporate sponsorships and Jaybacker donations."

In spite of the success Creighton had under Barone, the school had never sold out the Civic Auditorium in his tenure. The Bluejays averaged a Barone-era high of 6,337 for the 1990-91 season. The attendance had slipped to an average of 3,654 per game in Johnson's second season, but that was for tickets sold. The actual body count at games might have been half of that average.

In spite of the last-place finish in the 1992-93 season, there were some positives. Of Creighton's six Valley wins, one came over league champion Illinois State, one was over second-place Southern Illinois and a third came against third-place Southwest Missouri State. Of Creighton's 12 league losses, half were by margins of 7 points or fewer.

"You always think you know how you'll handle game situations, how you'll handle your personnel, how you will make a decision," Rick Johnson said after his first season. "But until you have to make those decisions, whether it's a play or playing time or any number of things, it's a whole different story." At left is Chris Rodgers, who was in the same recruiting class as Bob Harstad and Chad Gallagher but sat out one year with an injury.

1991: VINARDI CENTER OPENS

Margaret Vinardi, widow of longtime booster Joe Vinardi, and the Rev. Michael Morrison, Creighton's president, raise the banner at the dedication of the Joseph J. Vinardi Athletic Center. The $2.4 million addition to Creighton's old gym provided new offices for the athletic department, a weight room and a court for the women's basketball team. Joe Vinardi was one of the founders of the Jaybackers booster group.

Creighton returned four starters for Johnson's third season as coach. In addition, junior-college transfer Nate King was eligible after sitting out the previous season to resolve academic shortcomings.

King had averaged 13.7 points and 9.7 rebounds in his final season of junior college play in 1991-92. His signing with Creighton helped elevate the recruiting class to first in the Valley and 50th nationally in the eyes of one national analyst. He was picked as the 1993-94 preseason newcomer of the year in the league poll, but his presence wasn't enough to lift Creighton out of the bottom spot in the poll.

Losses in nine of the season's first 12 games defined the path on which the Bluejays were headed, and by the end of January, Creighton had won just five games. It was about that time, Rasmussen said, that the decision was made that Johnson would not return the next season.

"The only right way to treat him was to do everything we could to support him until the end of the year," Rasmussen said. "But we knew we were going to be looking for a basketball coach."

A 70-49 loss to Bradley in the final game put an ugly exclamation point on the season, as well as Johnson's coaching career. He resigned the next day, citing differences with school officials on the direction the program was headed. Asked whether he had submitted his resignation after learning he had no other available options, Johnson replied, "I can't comment on that, but you could possibly conclude that."

Johnson's teams lost 59 of the 83 games in which they played. The three-season total of 24 victories were the fewest over that span in program history.

Rasmussen looked back almost two decades later to ponder what might have happened had Creighton given the job to Fick instead of Johnson. "In hindsight, whichever one was picked was not going to be successful," Rasmussen said.

At the time Barone left, Rasmussen said, Creighton's administration was struggling with its commitment to the athletic program. The NCAA had raised the number of sports a school had to offer to maintain Division I status from 10 to 12. The cost of scholarships was rising.

"The university basically said they weren't going to spend more money," Rasmussen said. "They hired Rick Johnson because they could get him for $75,000 and save $100,000 from what Tony was making.

"I know a lot of people wanted to hire Dick Fick. He was a very knowledgeable men's basketball coach, but Dick had skeletons in his closet. And Dick's skeletons had skeletons. You couldn't hire Dick Fick, so Dick Myers took the easy way out and hired Rick."

When he was passed over for the Creighton job, Fick hinted that rumors of a drinking problem might have been one of the reasons. He would go on to become a head college coach at Morehead State, where he compiled a 64-101 record in six seasons. He died in 2003 at the age of 50 after a long battle with alcoholism.

In some ways, Rasmussen said, Johnson was as much a victim of circumstances as he was of bad coaching. The Bluejays' home arena, opened in 1954, was starting to show its age. The school's on-campus practice facilities were substandard. Barone had simply overcome hurdles that Johnson could not.

"We had no commitment to basketball at the time, and the university was trying to lessen its commitment," Rasmussen said. "I came along at a time when we had been embarrassed, and it was either we raise our commitment, or we don't have athletics."

With little to sell, Rasmussen hit the road to find his school a new basketball coach. He took along a cryptic warning from his boss.

"Father Morrison had told me, 'If this doesn't work, you're done.' "

Rasmussen, new to the world of athletic administration, took that to mean it wasn't just him who would pay the price. Creighton's basketball program, and perhaps the entire athletic program, could be on the brink of elimination.

1993: EMPTY SEATS

Creighton basketball attendance fell during the 1992-93 season to its lowest level since 1967-68. Athletic Director Tom Moore said Creighton was considering scheduling a regular-season game at the 5,400-seat Ak-Sar-Ben Coliseum. "It might not be realistic to think that Creighton can get 7,000 to 9,000 a game at the auditorium all the time," said Bruce Rasmussen, then the assistant athletic director. "There are a lot of options in Omaha that we can't control. We have to do a better job of taking care of the ones we can control."

2003
VALLEY
CHAMPIONS
NIT

1994-2010

Taking it to another level

Dana Altman's arrival ended the boom-and-bust cycle of Creighton basketball. He built a framework that would remain even after he left. "One of Dana's goals was for Creighton to become Omaha's team and not just that Catholic school where lawyers and doctors went to games," Athletic Director Bruce Rasmussen said.

Kyle Korver was on top of the world after the Bluejays wrapped up the 2003 Missouri Valley Conference tournament title with an 80-56 drubbing of Southern Illinois.

Finding your way in the dark

AS BRUCE RASMUSSEN BEGAN HIS SECRET SEARCH for Rick Johnson's successor in early 1994, he thought back to a trip to Moberly, Mo., a dozen years earlier.

"I remembered watching Dana Altman coach his ass off that night," Rasmussen said.

Rasmussen was athletic director in waiting in 1994 when he started the process of finding a new head basketball coach.

Altman had been Southeast Community College's coach at the time, but he left the Fairbury, Neb., school after the 1982-83 season to become Moberly Junior College's head coach. The Wilber, Neb., native took Moberly to the national junior college tournament in two of his three seasons before becoming an assistant coach at Kansas State. After three seasons of working for Lon Kruger — who had expressed interest in becoming Creighton's coach in 1985 — Altman was named head coach at Marshall University. He guided the Thundering Herd to a 15-13 record in his one season there, then returned to Kansas State in 1990 to replace Kruger.

Altman's second Kansas State team made it to the National Invitation Tournament. His third finished 19-11 after earning a spot in the NCAA tournament, and he was named the 1993 Big Eight coach of the year. With his 1993-94 Kansas State team poised for another postseason run, it appeared on the surface that Altman was on a roll in Manhattan.

"But I had heard through the grapevine that he was frustrated at Kansas State," Rasmussen said. "So I decided to call." Rasmussen knew the call was a long shot.

The Bluejays were wrapping up their worst three-season stretch in school history: Johnson's first team won nine games, his second won eight, and his third won seven. Equally troubling was the state of the program off the court. Creighton's funding for both men's basketball and the athletic department ranked near the bottom of the Missouri Valley. Little money was available to market the program or to provide the kind of academic support other schools were giving their student-athletes.

Then there were the facilities. Kansas State played in a state-of-the-art arena that had opened in 1988. Creighton held its practices on campus in a structure built before the United States entered World War I and played its games at Omaha's drab Civic Auditorium, which was four decades old and in dire need of renovation. Metal folding chairs made up the courtside seating, and the locker rooms were dingy and depressing. The arena's walls were painted battleship gray, which only added to the oppressive setting.

Darian DeVries, who played for Northern Iowa from 1993 to 1998, recalled the Panthers' home games at the UNI-Dome, an air-inflated football stadium that featured a curtained-off playing court for basketball. "Back then, I thought the Civic was the only place we played that was worse than the UNI-Dome," DeVries said. "They still had those metal folding chairs, and there weren't a lot of fans coming to the games at the time."

As daunting as the situation appeared, Rasmussen faced a less visible threat that was even bigger. "There were people that wanted us to drop basketball, or to drop out of Division I," he said. "As a university, we were trying to decide what to do with athletics."

Still, Rasmussen decided that he would not limit the scope of his search for a new coach. He thought back to 1991, when school officials debated whether to give the job to assistants Johnson or Dick Fick after Tony Barone left for Texas A&M. "People asked me whether I thought we should hire Rick or Dick Fick," Rasmussen said. "My answer was we shouldn't hire either one of them. I thought we should go out on a national search and find out what's out there."

So while Rasmussen's gut told him Altman probably wouldn't be interested in Creighton, he made the call anyway. Altman initially expressed no interest but later accepted a second invitation to talk to Rasmussen. The two men agreed to meet at the home of Altman's parents in Wilber. "He said if anybody finds out," Rasmussen recalled, "I'm out."

Rasmussen left Omaha on the day of the meeting, telling no one — not even wife Jill — where he was headed. "She asked me where I was going," Rasmussen said. "I said, 'I can't tell you.' She asked me when I would be home. I said, 'I don't know.' "

He made the 90-minute drive to Wilber, to an address Altman had provided.

"He told me to pull into the garage," Rasmussen said. "He said the door would be up, and I was to pull it down after arriving. He told me to go to the house and knock."

Altman arrived later, and the two men talked for hours, finally ending the meeting about 2 a.m.

"It was obvious to me an hour into the conversation that it was like talking to a brother," Rasmussen said. "What he thought about the game of basketball and what I thought about it was a lot alike."

One of the key issues discussed that night was what Creighton was willing to do for its basketball program.

"I was surprised by the level of commitment he was willing to make," Altman recalled. "I told him I couldn't ask my assistants to come to Omaha for less than what they're making now. I wasn't interested in taking a pay cut. I told him that if he could show me that they're willing to do the things I felt necessary to build the program, I'd consider it."

One thought stayed on Altman's mind as he made the two-hour drive back to Manhattan: "There is no way Creighton is going to be able to pull this off."

The next day, Rasmussen called.

"He said, 'Coach, we can do it all,' " Altman said. "He told me that he would get us everything we needed to be competitive."

Altman said Creighton officials stressed their desire to rebuild the basketball program when they hired him. "It's everything from tidying up the locker room to increasing the recruiting budget, the travel budget," he said. "It would put them comparable to figures that we had at Kansas State and, in some cases, surpassing them."

Altman still wanted to check out Creighton's facilities, but that required another clandestine meeting.

Rasmussen acquired a key to the Civic Auditorium and gave Altman, wife Reva and daughter Audra a late-night tour of the facility. "We got there around midnight," Rasmussen said. "The place was a dump."

They headed next to the Creighton gym. "Back then, even in the light, this place looked bad. At midnight in the dark, it looked awful. I remember Reva was carrying Audra, and she had this look like, 'What are we doing here?' "

Mike Thibault coached the Omaha Racers throughout the team's eight years in the Continental Basketball Association, from 1989 to 1997, leading them to the 1993 CBA title and the 1994 finals.

Altman eventually said he would accept an offer to become Creighton's next head coach, but with one condition. "He said if anyone finds out, it's over," recalled Rasmussen. "So I didn't tell my AD. I didn't tell my president. I didn't tell anybody." That included the 11-member search committee that was appointed to find a new coach after Johnson resigned.

"They didn't know it," Rasmussen said, "but I already had someone verbally committed to the job."

The committee wanted Rasmussen to conduct interviews with prospective candidates. Among those he talked to were Mike Thibault, the coach of Omaha's franchise in the Continental Basketball Association, and former Creighton player Kevin McKenna, also a CBA coach.

But mostly Rasmussen stalled for time, as Kansas State's season continued. The Wildcats lost their last three regular-season games and dropped a 21-point decision to archrival Kansas in the Big Eight tournament. But they received an invitation to play in the NIT and extended their season by defeating Mississippi State and Gonzaga. They then pounded Fresno State in the quarterfinals to earn a trip to New York.

Complicating matters further, Altman's name began to surface in reports about other openings. "I was starting to get pressure from the committee," Rasmussen said, "and I was thinking, 'I don't have anything to go on except Dana's word.' "

Finally on March 28, Vanderbilt ended Kansas State's bid for an NIT title with an 82-76 win. Afterward, Altman told the Manhattan (Kan.) Mercury newspaper that he had been contacted "indirectly" about the Creighton job. Rasmussen told The World-Herald that Altman had not been offered the job, but he confirmed that Creighton had an interest in Altman.

"But has Dana Altman expressed an interest in us?" Rasmussen said. "I've talked with Dana Altman, but I've also talked to 53 head coaches at some of the top schools in the country. Have I talked with Mike Krzyzewski? Yes. Have I talked with Dean Smith? Yes.

Have I talked with Eddie Sutton and Charlie Spoonhour? Yes." Rasmussen said those conversations had been to discuss people who had applied for the job.

On March 30 — four weeks after Johnson resigned — Kansas State ended its season with a 92-79 loss to Siena in the NIT consolation game. Altman told reporters after the game that he intended to talk with Creighton officials, but he down-played any significance to the meeting, saying, "Coaches talk to people all the time." In Omaha, Rasmussen said any offer would have to come from the Rev. Michael Morrison, CU's president.

The Rev. Michael Morrison, Creighton's president, first met Altman on the day the coach was hired.

Altman arrived in Omaha the next morning to meet with Creighton's search committee. Rasmussen picked him up at the airport and thought he "looked like he had been up all night."

"He had met with his coaches and players and some key boosters (at Kansas State), who had tried to talk him out of possibly leaving," Rasmussen said. "He was looking like he was going to back out."

Rasmussen took him to meet what he mistakenly thought would be an excited Creighton search committee. "There were three or four people on the committee that didn't want to hire him. I remember Dana looking at me like, 'What have you gotten us into here?' "

Altman eventually did receive the committee's approval and then met with Morrison, whom Rasmussen had briefed the previous week about his desire to hire Altman. Morrison expressed initial reservations about the move, but Rasmussen convinced him, with help from CU administrator Mike Leighton, that it was the right one to make.

"Father finally said OK," Rasmussen said, "but he then looked at Mike and me and said, 'If this doesn't work, you're both fired.' "

At a press conference that evening, Altman was asked why a coach from a Big Eight program would take what appeared to be a step backward to come to Creighton.

"Family. I'm from Nebraska, and my wife is from Nebraska," Altman said. "She's got two brothers and sisters who live in Omaha. ... Creighton says it's willing to make a great commitment to the program and the coaching staff. They talked about building a program and giving us the time to put it together the way we want to."

Rasmussen declined to detail the school's financial commitment to the basketball program but said Morrison had agreed to increase funding.

Almost two decades later, Rasmussen can't help chuckling about the process that brought Altman to Omaha.

"At the time, the Creighton job was a bad job," he said. "I would call Dana, because I got nervous several times during the process that something would go wrong. He would just say, 'I gave you my word.' No one on this campus knew that we were going to hire him. His assistant coaches didn't know he was leaving. All I had was his word, but his word was gold."

Altman recalled that his five-year contract contained one important clause.

"I would be Creighton's coach as long as the school remained Division I," he said. "I knew there were some serious thoughts about that, and Ras was honest with me about it. He said, 'We have to get this going or else.' "

A little recruiting luck goes a long way

Altman set out to reshape the program. Of the players returning, only 6-foot-8 Nate King had performed with any measure of distinction during the 1993-94 season. King led the team in scoring and rebounding while earning second-team All-Missouri Valley honors.

Altman's first recruits included guard Tad Ackerman (40), who made 82 3-pointers in his first season at Creighton.

Two other seniors — Jason Bey and Donald Davenport — also returned, as did sophomores Randall Crutcher and Troy Wharton and redshirt freshman Adam Reid. Johnson's staff had signed three players the previous fall in freshmen Jimmy Sexton, Jermond Remmer and Joel Templeman.

Altman immediately hit the recruiting trail to look for some additional help.

"We've got to get some players," he said. "Other things can wait. Recruiting can't wait. We have to do as much as we possibly can before the signing period to get some people interested in coming here."

Altman's first recruits were junior-college players Tad Ackerman, Marcus Lockett and Adrian Grinnon. He also tried to drum up support for his program, making countless appearances throughout the area to preach a gospel of hard work and patience.

"There's no doubt people want us to get this thing turned around, and they want it to happen overnight," Altman said before his team prepared to open practice in the fall. "But we have a long way to go. I knew that on April 1. I know that now."

Never flashy or flamboyant, Altman made sure not to make any promises he couldn't keep.

"I think you have to be consistent with your personality," he said. "I'm not going to trick our fans or our players. I'm not going to paint a rosy picture that's not true. I'm a plodder. I know what's ahead of us, and I know what it's going to take to get us there. We're going to bounce back, but I don't know how quickly."

While guarded in discussing first-year expectations with those outside the program, Altman made sure his players knew exactly what would be expected from them.

"He's pretty straight with us," Bey said before the season. "He tells us what we have to work on and what he expects. We don't want to come in with the idea of being a .500 team. His message to us hasn't been, 'Let's rebuild.' It's been, 'Let's win, let's turn some heads, let's get some respect.' "

As it turned out, Altman's first Creighton team wasn't even a .500 team. The Bluejays matched the previous season's victory total of seven, and they won two games in a row just once. They lost 11 of their last 12 to finish 7-19 overall and tied for ninth in the Valley (4-14), missing out on the conference tournament for the third straight season.

Still, Altman's first team provided fans with a glimmer of hope. The Bluejays might not have played well that season, but they played hard.

"I'll never figure out how Dana won seven games that first year with what he had to work with," said Kevin Sarver, who was the school's sports information director at the time. "Then to get close to .500 in his second year, I think our fans were getting it. Here was a guy from the Big Eight, a guy that had been there and done that, and he knows what he's doing."

The Bluejays finished with a 14-15 record in Altman's second season and made a return to the Valley tournament by finishing in a fifth-place tie in the conference. The team featured a flashy freshman from Milwaukee in Rodney Buford, the first of several difference-making recruits that Altman and his staff would lure to Creighton.

Altman had signed Buford on the final day of the spring signing period in 1995.

"We had missed on another kid," Altman said, "and we brought Rodney in and signed him at the last minute."

"Rodney has a tremendous amount of potential," said Tom Diener, who coached Buford at Vincent High School in Milwaukee, after he signed with Creighton. "I don't have any problem in saying that I think he has the most potential of any high school player coming out of Wisconsin this year."

In spite of starting just 11 of 29 games, Buford led the team with a 14.5-point scoring average. The next fall, Altman signed another Wisconsin high school player, a boot-tough guard named Ben Walker who had been recruited by seven Big Ten schools as a running back in football.

The Bluejays finished 15-15 in 1996-97, as an academic problem forced Walker to delay his arrival at Creighton until the next season. That allowed him to join forces with Ryan Sears, who picked Creighton after the four Division I schools in his home state of Iowa passed on him.

Rasmussen considers Buford, Walker and Sears examples of how luck figures into recruiting success almost as much as hard work and due diligence.

Rasmussen had told Altman about a point guard from Ankeny, whom he had watched outplay a five-star recruit who wound up at Iowa.

Altman asked about his height.

"I told him I saw him play as a freshman, so he was probably 5-10 or 5-11 by then," said Rasmussen, who had tried unsuccessfully to persuade Johnson to recruit Sears' older brother, Todd, who played baseball at Nebraska. "He asked me how much Ryan weighed. I said probably a buck-fifty (150 pounds).

"I said, 'Please go take a look at him,'" Rasmussen said, and Altman did. "Dana came back and asked, 'Why isn't anyone else recruiting him?'"

Ben Walker missed the first 12 days of practice his freshman year because of an eligibility question. He permanently joined the starting lineup four games into the 1997-98 season.

Altman pursued Sears, even though Iowa, Iowa State, Drake and Northern Iowa were showing little interest in him.

Sears wasn't impressed. "I remember Coach coming to watch games when I was in high school," he said. "I thought I was better than what I probably was, and Creighton wasn't on the map yet."

Altman recalled that the recruitment of Sears underscored the overall state of Creighton's program at the time.

"Ryan Sears was a kid that nobody in the Midwest wanted," Altman said. "It came down to us and Pacific. It was frustrating that we couldn't get him to commit. At that time, we were having a hard time beating 'nobody.'" Sears eventually signed and would start the first game of his freshman season, as well as the 123 that followed. He combined with Walker and Buford to help Creighton break through in Altman's fourth year.

The Jays won 18 of their first 24 games in the 1997-98 season, with one of the victories snapping a seven-game losing skid to in-state rival Nebraska, but back-to-back losses to Illinois State and Bradley closed the regular season. Creighton, which finished second in the Valley standings, then dropped an eight-point decision to Bradley in the league tournament.

"When we recruited him, we thought he might be able to help us as a freshman," Altman said of Ryan Sears. "But we had no idea that he'd be able to do what he's done. He comes to play hard every game."

The three straight losses at the end didn't sour the NIT on Creighton, and the Bluejays found themselves in the postseason for the first time since 1991.

Buford got a chance to go home to Milwaukee to face Marquette, and he put on a show with 24 points. The Jays led by seven points in the second half, but Marquette used a 17-2 run over the final 4:12 to pull out an 80-68 victory. The loss finished off an 18-10 season for the Bluejays that had their leader encouraged.

"The NIT year was big," Altman recalled, "because it got guys feeling like we have a chance. It changed how our guys felt about themselves. None of those guys had been to the postseason."

Altman's program was starting to gain some traction off the court, too. Omaha had renovated the Civic, remodeling the locker rooms and slapping a coat of white paint on the arena that brightened the venue.

"They changed the appearance of the place," Altman said. "Until the renovation, we never took kids there on recruiting visits."

Creighton also had fixed up the Vinardi Center on campus, remodeling office space and locker rooms, building a learning center where players could study and revamping the practice area. "We had people step up and help us out," Altman said. "Father Morrison stepped up, too. Getting the money raised was important. Compared to now, it was really a small amount, but it at least showed the guys we were bringing in that we were trying to be competitive."

Altman wasn't ashamed to take recruits to the Civic Auditorium after the renovation. The athletic department began "priority seating" to take advantage of improvements on the court and in the facility.

Creighton couldn't have done that, Rasmussen said, without the support of outsiders who believed in what was happening on the Hilltop.

"When Tony Barone was here, we went through a period of excellence, but we still weren't drawing that well," Rasmussen said. "It was Tony's feeling that Creighton would never draw well, and I think so many other people had that same perception.

"Nebraska was Nebraska's team," Rasmussen said, while the perception was that "Creighton was a university for doctors and lawyers, and it wasn't a community program. If you looked around the country, when Marquette was good, they were Milwaukee's team. When DePaul was good, they were Chicago's team. Dana and I felt that if we were ever going to be good, we had to be Omaha's team. Fortunately, we were able to convince others to buy into that vision."

The players also were buying into Altman's vision.

"One of the things Coach Altman always talked about before games was being the tougher team, of fighting and scratching and clawing," Sears said. "That was the way I wanted to play. That was the kind of team I wanted to be a part of, and I think it was a feeling that a lot of the other guys in the locker room shared."

To prepare for the 1998-99 season, Altman took his team on a two-week spring exhibition tour of Italy and France. The Bluejays went 5-1, playing some games against professional teams.

"That was a huge trip for us," Altman said. "We played some good teams, and we had to play really hard. We got a lot out of that."

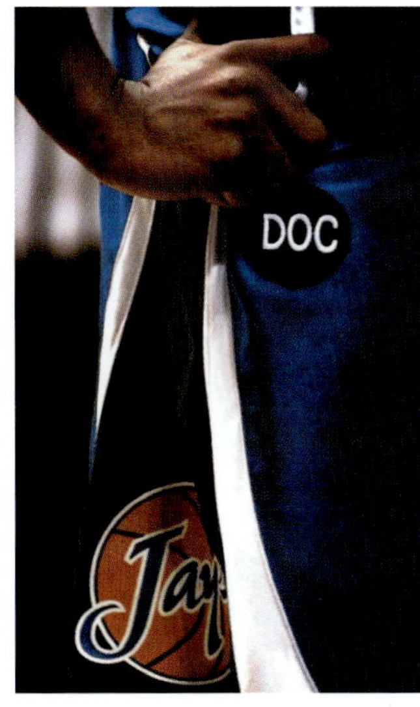

1998: BLUEJAYS LOSE 'DOC'

Creighton canceled the first practice of the 1998-99 season after learning of the death of Dr. Lee Bevilacqua. "Doc" began his role as volunteer medical counsel for the athletic program in 1959. The players wore a stitched tribute to Bevilacqua on their uniforms. "For me, being so far from home, I felt he was part of my family," said Doug Swenson, a senior from North Dakota. "This gives us something else to play our hearts out for." Rasmussen said Bevilacqua's legacy would be the hundreds of lives he touched. "Sometimes you wonder how much impact just one person can have," he said. "That impact can be huge if the person cares a lot. And Doc cared more than anybody." Bevilacqua died after suffering a heart attack at a Creighton soccer game in Nashville, Tenn.

Sears tries to slip past Oklahoma State's Joe Adkins in the Jays' win. Sears' 3-pointer with 58 seconds left broke a 60-60 tie and helped end a 25-year stretch between home wins over a ranked opponent. Doc Bevilacqua had helped persuade OSU coach Eddie Sutton to play the Jays.

The Bluejays opened the next season by winning 10 of their first 12 games, with one of the wins coming against an Oklahoma State team ranked 18th nationally. Creighton used a 12-2 closing run to pull out a 66-60 win that ruined Eddie Sutton's return to Omaha.

The Bluejays were picked to win the Valley but struggled in league play. An early February loss to Wichita State left them 7-6 in the Valley, but wins in four of their final five regular-season games pushed the Jays into a tie for second place.

Creighton avenged that loss to the Shockers with a 76-65 win in Buford's final appearance at home.

The day of the game, The World-Herald's Tom Shatel sized up the impact that the high-flying Buford had on the program: "Buford was a human-highlight film. His career is an endless string of eye-popping moves, breathtaking dunks and electrifying one-handed alley-oops. But the magic in Buford's game was the reaction of the crowd. Smiles. Huge smiles. Folks hugging and high-fiving from the electric jolt. Buford put a smile on Creighton's face.

"So why will Buford leave some with an empty smile? Maybe it's just the curse of greatness. But for all Buford did at Creighton, he left people always wanting more. He had every offensive skill in the book. But he never did play defense well enough. He could score 40 points. But he could never be consistent enough."

Buford told Shatel that he was proud of his legacy as one of the guys who helped turn around a dead-in-the-water program. One of his regrets, he said, was that the Bluejays had not accomplished what they had set out to do.

That soon would change.

Creighton, which entered the Valley tournament as the No. 3 seed, opened with a 68-63 win over Illinois State, followed by a 78-70 defeat of Southwest Missouri in the semifinals.

Buford led Creighton with 21 points and 13 rebounds in a 70-61 win over Evansville, as the Bluejays locked up their first trip to the NCAA tournament since 1991. Walker added 18 points and 11 rebounds.

"I remember there was still some uncertainty going into that game," Sears said. 'We knew we were good, but we didn't know if we could get over the hump. Ben was big in getting guys fired up, and Rodney really stepped up.

"After that, we had some confidence. We knew what it took and how to get there. Our expectations had been raised."

Buford, a senior, torched Evansville in the Valley title game after a halftime tongue-lashing from sophomore teammate Ben Walker. "He said, 'You're not playing like you should, you're not rebounding, and on the offensive end you've got to take over,'" Buford said. Altman appreciated Walker's help. "Ben should take over the coaching duties," he said.

Fans gave Buford, dubbed "Rodzilla," a happy ride after the Jays won the 1999 Valley tournament and earned a berth in the NCAA tourney, the school's first since 1991. "It was a goal we set at the beginning of the year, to go to the tournament and win it," Buford said. "During the season we had a lot of doubts. But we put it together in the end." The airport crowd that welcomed the team back to Omaha included Mayor Hal Daub, who presented Altman with a key to the city.

Creighton earned a No. 10 seed in the tournament and drew Louisville as its first-round game in Orlando, Fla. The Bluejays trailed 31-23 at halftime and 40-27 early in the second half. The Jays rallied by going on a 22-7 run, taking their first lead on Walker's three-point play with 3:04 to play.

After Louisville tied the game, Buford swung control of the game to the Bluejays when he swished a 3-point attempt with the shot clock winding down. "That was like an ESPN play-of-the-game type of play," Walker said. Creighton then made 10 straight free throws over the final two minutes to finish off a 62-58 win that propelled the Bluejays into a second-round game against fifth-ranked Maryland.

The magic ran out against the Terrapins, who built a 21-point lead but had to fight off a late rally in the second half to record a 75-63 win. Creighton finished 22-9 with a performance that mirrored its season — a good start, a lapse along the way and then a gutsy finish.

"It would have been very easy to throw in the towel," Altman said after the game. "It's about like it was in mid-February when we were 15-8 and it didn't look like we were going anywhere. But then they kind of toughened up and fought a little bit and had themselves a respectable season."

In five seasons, Altman had taken a program that had bottomed out and not only got it back to the NCAA tournament but also managed to win a game there. In doing so, Altman had given Creighton fans a new set of expectations, and nobody knew that better than he did.

Sarver, the longtime athletic department employee, recalled a conversation he had with the coach prior to the Bluejays' first game in Orlando. "I was telling him how great this was, that our fans were unbelievably excited and that if he could find a way to get this done about once every three seasons, they'd build a statue of him," Sarver said. "He looked at me and said, 'If we're only doing this once every three years, then I've failed, and I won't be around here very long.' "

With Walker and Sears back, Altman knew Creighton had a chance to be good as it started preparing for the 1999-2000 season. And while he had to come up with a scoring option to replace Buford, who finished his career as the school's all-time scoring leader with 2,116 points, he thought he had found it in a mop-haired sharpshooter from Pella, Iowa.

Like Buford, Walker and Sears, Kyle Korver didn't have college recruiters banging down his door when he was in high school. Altman recalled how he and assistant coach Greg Grensing drove all over Las Vegas to watch Korver play at a summer AAU tournament.

"He wasn't playing in any of the main gyms," Altman said. "We had to go find him. As we watched him play, Greg and I kept saying, 'Gosh, he really shoots it.' We needed a shooter so bad.

"We were a little concerned about some of the other parts of his game, and we wondered who he would be able to guard. But we kept coming back to that we needed him as a shooter. We also liked how he handled himself. There was an air about him that he knew he could play."

"Kyle Korver" wasn't a widely known name when he came to media day as a freshman.

Korver was the son of a Lutheran minister and a former Iowa high school girls basketball star. His uncle coached basketball at Northwestern College in Orange City, Iowa, and his parents figured that would be where Kyle would wind up.

"All my family played basketball at the Division III level and loved it at a smaller Christian school," Korver said. "I figured I'd play some ball, meet a girl and get married. That was kind of the plan back then."

That all changed when Korver, his father, Kevin, and mother Laine made an unofficial visit to Creighton in the fall of 1998. The Korvers met with Altman in his office at the Vinardi Center, and the Creighton coach offered Kyle a scholarship.

Korver finished his freshman season averaging 8.8 points a game while starting just one game. He was named to the Valley's all-bench, all-newcomer and all-freshman teams.

"I told them we wanted to sign Kyle in November," Altman said. "They smiled and kind of looked at each other."

One of Altman's assistants showed up to take the Korvers on a walking tour of campus, and Kyle and his mother got up to leave. So did Kevin Korver, but he stopped and shut the office door. He looked at Altman and asked the coach if he really thought his son was good enough to play at the Division I level. Altman still smiles when recalling the moment.

"I said, 'Mr. Korver, I'm a nice guy, but not that nice a guy,'" Altman said. "If I didn't think your son could help us, I wouldn't be offering him."

Kyle learned years later what his father had asked Altman that day.

"It took us by surprise, because I don't think any of us had really given much thought to pursuing (basketball) further than Northwestern," Korver said. "But when we were walking around campus, I remember my dad telling me that he thought I could do this, that Creighton would be a good place for me. That was kind of the first time that it sunk in that this might be the right thing for me to do. Creighton was the only Division I school that was on the radar at all for me."

Korver's commitment was another example of unexpected good fortune that Rasmussen said came Creighton's way early in Altman's tenure. Like Sears, Korver probably would have jumped at the chance to play for one of the four Division I schools in his home state of Iowa.

Korver's father had asked Altman during their private meeting why he thought his son could play at the Division I level when Iowa, Iowa State, Northern Iowa and Drake didn't. "Not only did those schools pass on Kyle," Rasmussen said, "but his mom and dad were questioning whether he could play at this level. Sometimes, you just have to get lucky."

Korver made his debut in a Creighton uniform when the Bluejays opened the 1999-2000 season in a game at Itta Bena, Miss., against the Mississippi Valley State Delta Devils. He played 10 minutes and missed all five of his shots from the field. He made two free throws, grabbed two rebounds and had two turnovers. He would make just one start as a freshman, but he played an average of 18 minutes per game and began to demonstrate the shooting ability that had caught the eyes of Altman and Grensing.

As Korver found his legs in Division I, the Jays' veterans found ways to win.

In Creighton's fourth game of the season, the visiting Bluejays trailed Baylor of the Big 12 by 14 points with three minutes to play. Walker's basket at the buzzer capped a furious rally, and Creighton went on to post a 77-76 overtime win, with Walker finishing with 19 points and 15 rebounds.

2000: ANOTHER VALLEY TITLE

Ryan Sears had 15 points, four assists, five rebounds and three steals in a 57-45 victory over Southwest Missouri State in the 2000 Missouri Valley tournament championship game. The win gave Creighton consecutive Valley tourney titles for the first time. "Nothing's unbelievable anymore," Creighton junior Justin Haynes said. Altman celebrated with daughter Audra and wife Reva.

Seniors Donnie Johnson, left, and Matt West watch their careers come to an end in an NCAA loss to Auburn. "Coach Altman is doing a real good job with the program," Johnson said. "I can look back and say I was part of it when he was rebuilding. I appreciate him for making me a part of that."

The Bluejays didn't lose until the season's 10th game, a 20-point loss to host Hawaii at the Nike Classic, but struggled with inconsistency the rest of the season to finish fourth in the Valley. But Creighton defeated Bradley, Indiana State and Southwest Missouri in the conference tournament to earn back-to-back trips to the NCAA tournament for just the second time in program history.

No. 24 Auburn led the Jays 72-63 with 12.8 seconds to play in a first-round game in Minneapolis. The Tigers inserted team manager Jimbo Tolbert, who had joined a roster limited by injuries and a suspension.

A 3-pointer by Sears trimmed the lead to six with 6.5 seconds to play, and Tolbert turned the ball over on the inbounds pass. Freshman Terrell Taylor then countered with a 3-point basket to pull Creighton within three points with 3.8 seconds left. Another turnover gave the ball back to the Bluejays, but 7-foot Auburn center Mamadou N'Diaye blocked Walker's 3-point attempt at the buzzer to preserve the victory.

"If we would have had more time, we would have won the game," Sears said. "I think we showed we were the tougher team and the better team, but we just got ourselves in a hole early in that one."

The 72-69 loss ended Creighton's season at 23-10.

Sears and Walker, both named to the All-Valley second team, had evolved into the Bluejays' new dynamic duo, a pair of hard-nosed competitors who did whatever it took to help their team win.

"We both played hard," Sears said. "That's just who we were."

Korver's 63 3-point baskets set a school record for freshmen, and his 8.8 scoring average ranked third on the team behind Walker's 12.0 and Sears' 11.9 at the end of the year. Korver and Taylor earned spots on the league's all-newcomer team, and both moved into the starting lineup the next year.

Creighton, with Sears and Walker returning as seniors for the 2000-01 season, was the consensus favorite for the Valley championship.

The Bluejays won 10 of their first 12 games, with one of the victories being their first at Nebraska since 1932. They went 5-4 in the first half of the league race but won the last nine games to claim their first Valley regular-season championship in a decade.

Creighton opened the conference tournament with a 63-41 victory over Southwest Missouri, but its bid for a third straight championship in St. Louis ended with an 87-74 loss to Indiana State. With a 24-7 record and an RPI of 23, the Bluejays were awarded an at-large bid to the NCAA tournament, making Sears, Walker, Alan Huss and Justin Haynes the first Creighton players to play in three NCAA tournaments in their careers.

For the third straight year, the Bluejays were given a No. 10 seed for the tournament, drawing Iowa for a first-round game in Uniondale, N.Y. The No. 24 Hawkeyes led by two points at halftime, but Creighton opened the second half with a 12-0 run. The Bluejays then went cold from the field, allowing Iowa to go on a 26-8 run that sent the Hawkeyes to a 69-56 win. Creighton made just one of 15 3-point attempts in the final 20 minutes, with Korver missing seven of his last eight shots from behind the arc.

"That definitely is a game we'd like to have another crack at," said Sears, who scored eight points and had four assists in his final game as a Bluejay.

Walker led the Bluejays with 11 points in spite of playing the final five minutes of the game with a compound fracture of his right ring finger. He first dislocated the finger while grabbing a rebound, then a few moments later slapped at the ball and the disfigured bone broke through the skin.

"I looked down, and it was bleeding like crazy," Walker said. "I looked at it and went, 'Whoa.' I put my hand behind my back so the ref wouldn't take me out. I looked at it again and said, 'This is pretty bad.' "

Creighton senior center Alan Huss is pressured by Hawkeyes Jared Reiner and Rod Thompson. The Jays led by 11 points with 14 minutes left in the NCAA tourney game but missed 17 straight shots at one point in the second half. "We feel like we've accomplished a lot, but we just weren't quite ready for it to end there," Huss said of the departing seniors.

Walker finally came out of the game to have the finger taped and returned to score Creighton's final basket. That left him with 1,238 points for his career. He also had 677 rebounds, 288 assists and 148 steals. Sears finished with 1,309 points and set program records with 570 assists and 283 steals.

Their value to the Bluejays hasn't diminished over time in their coach's mind.

"Sears and Walker really gave us the feeling like we had a chance every game," Altman said a dozen years after their careers ended. "They gave me everything they had. Everyone talks about culture, and I'm not sure what culture is. But if there were any two guys that changed ours or got it to where we wanted it, it was Sears and Walker. They had games where they didn't play well, but they never had games where they didn't compete. People that missed that part of Creighton basketball missed two guys that meant more to bringing this program along than anybody."

Walker and Sears leave the court together for the last time. "Our expectations were very, very high," Walker said of the Iowa game. "We wanted to come in here and do something no other Creighton team has done, like go to the Sweet 16. It's just a bad feeling."

Never a spotlight-seeker, Sears looked back on his career with a big-picture focus.

"We had a bunch of good guys, talented players who had roles," he said. "I loved being on a team that was sold out for a common goal. I appreciate that more and more the further I get away from it. Man, those were some really good times."

Korver had led the Bluejays in scoring that season, averaging 14.6 points and setting a school record by making 100 3-point baskets.

With Walker and Sears gone, juniors Korver and Taylor, a gifted guard from Bridgeport, Conn., seemed destined to become the leaders of the 2001-02 team, which did not have a senior on the roster.

Korver averaged 15.1 points in helping Creighton earn a share of the league championship. He was named the Valley's player of the year and won the most valuable player award at the conference tournament, helping the Bluejays win the title that put them in the NCAA tournament for a fourth straight season.

2001: BATTLE OF THE BIG MEN

Creighton center Brody Deren held his own against 7-foot-1 Chris Marcus in a 94-91 double overtime win over No. 17 Western Kentucky at the Civic Auditorium. Deren finished with 21 points and 11 rebounds in a victory that sent Creighton students spilling onto the court. Bluejays DeAnthony Bowden and Larry House did back flips at half-court as part of the celebration.

Taylor contributed, too, but not to the extent that many had envisioned. A starter in 29 of 32 games as a sophomore, Taylor did not start a game during the 2001-02 season. He averaged 12.6 points, made 67 3-point baskets and was named the Valley's sixth man of the year. During the season, Altman cited a lack of practice intensity as the main reason for Taylor's change in status. After the season, it became clear that other factors figured into the coach's decision to cut back on Taylor's playing time.

Still, it was Taylor who provided Creighton with its shining moment of the season. In its NCAA tournament opener, the 12th-seeded Bluejays faced 15th-ranked Florida in Chicago's United Center, where NBA superstar Michael Jordan had built his legend.

Taylor grew up idolizing Jordan and wore No. 23, just like Jordan. He had a Jordan tattoo on his arm. To prepare for the game, he watched a DVD of, you guessed it, Jordan.

But Taylor had an un-Jordanlike performance in the first 20 minutes, missing all six of his shots as the Bluejays fell behind 38-31. "The rim," Taylor said later, "was the size of a doughnut. I had too much excitement and anticipation for the game."

After halftime, Taylor made 10 of 14 shots, including eight 3-pointers.

Taylor sent the game into overtime when he nailed a 3-point shot with 35 seconds to play in regulation for a 69-69 tie, and each team scored four points in the first extra period. Creighton opened the second overtime with starters Brody Deren and Kyle Korver on the bench with five fouls and with a lineup that included four guards and power forward Mike Grimes.

Florida took an 82-80 lead and had the ball with 30 seconds to play when Creighton forced a five-second violation on the inbounds pass.

The Gators took a timeout, allowing Altman to call a play he had designed a few days before his team won the Valley tournament. There was only one problem: The play was to give the last-second shot to Korver, who had fouled out with 1:10 left in the first overtime.

The ball instead went to Taylor, but not before Florida twice knocked it out of bounds, the second time coming with about four seconds to play. Creighton point guard Tyler McKinney then inbounded the ball to Taylor, who started toward the middle.

"I was going to drive but couldn't," Taylor said. "I got a good look and took what came to me."

Taylor fired a 3-point attempt over the outstretched arms of a Florida defender. The ball swished through the net with two-tenths of a second to play, giving Creighton an 83-82 lead. Florida got the ball inbounds but couldn't get a shot off, leaving the Gators the highest-ranked victim in Altman's eight seasons as head coach.

Scoreless at halftime, Taylor matched his career high with 28 points, and his eight 3-point baskets on 15 attempts both tied school records. "It must have been the shoes," Taylor said after the game, mimicking the TV commercial for Air Jordans. "Sometimes, I even feel like Jordan."

On that one afternoon in March, he even played like Mike and cemented a spot for himself in Creighton basketball history.

"The game basically came down to us not having an answer for Terrell Taylor," Florida Coach Billy Donovan said after the Bluejays' victory.

Two days later, 13th-ranked Illinois used a 12-0 run midway through the second half to take control of the second-round game against the Bluejays. The Illini's 72-60 win ended Creighton's season at 23-9, but the Bluejays left Chicago juiced about their prospects for the next season.

With no seniors, Creighton expected to have all of its players back for the next year. That changed shortly after the team returned to Omaha when, in the normal end-of-the-season meetings Altman held with every player, the coach and Taylor agreed the time had come to part ways.

"He said maybe it was time for him to go somewhere else," Altman said. "And I said, 'I can't argue with you.' He had two years for us where he didn't have any problems. Then, he started having problems. We tried to help him."

A World-Herald check of Douglas County Court and Omaha Police Department records after the 2001-02 season indicated that between January 2001 and April 2002, Taylor had been convicted of 12 misdemeanors, ranging from not carrying his driver's license to reckless driving, and had been briefly jailed four times. Police found him with alcohol before his 21st birthday twice and with marijuana twice.

Rasmussen and Altman said they knew of some, but not all, of Taylor's legal problems. Taylor missed no practices or games, although Altman admitted after the season that Taylor's off–the-court problems did affect his role on the team.

"What happens off the court is very important," Altman said. "I make decisions on playing time on a lot of variables, including how guys handle themselves off the court."

Larry House has his shot blocked by Illinois' Robert Archibald. "It's really tough to lose a game that ends your season," Altman said in the locker room afterward. "We had our opportunities. We just didn't take advantage."

2002: BLOCK PARTY FOR DEREN

Brody Deren blocks Husker Nate Johnson's shot, one of Deren's three blocks in the Bluejays' 81-73 victory in Lincoln. Kyle Korver buried back-to-back 3-pointers to end Nebraska's hopes for a rally in the second half. He finished with six 3s and 25 points, as Creighton claimed its fourth straight win in the series.

Even without Taylor, Creighton appeared loaded as it prepared for the 2002-03 season. The Bluejays returned five starters in Korver, Deren, McKinney, Michael Lindeman and Larry House. DeAnthony Bowden, Joe Dabbert and Grimes were experienced substitutes, and Altman saw big-time potential in incoming freshman Nate Funk.

Creighton was an overwhelming favorite to win the Valley championship in a year that featured a dash of added significance — the Bluejays' last season at the Civic Auditorium.

In 2000, Omaha voters had approved a $216 million bond issue for the construction of a new arena and convention center, and private organizations and individuals raised an additional $75 million for the project. The arena was to seat 15,500 for basketball, 6,000 more than the Civic.

Altman and Rasmussen were adamant that Creighton needed to move to the new arena. Others on campus were just as steadfast in their opposition.

"That was a battle," Altman said. "My position was if we didn't go, you were putting a cap on how successful you thought we could be as a program. My position was that I thought we could do bigger things, and we needed the new arena to help us do that. If we wouldn't have held our ground, that would have set us back a bunch."

Rasmussen believes that if the move to the new arena had been blocked, that would have led to a quick exit by Altman. "And I probably wouldn't have stayed, either," Rasmussen said.

In the end, Creighton officials approved the move to the bigger arena, which was scheduled to open for the 2003-04 season. In order to build some momentum for the transition, Creighton needed to do something special in its final season at the Civic.

Korver and his teammates complied. They opened the season with 10 straight wins, including victories at Nebraska and over Notre Dame in the championship game of the Guardians Classic in Kansas City.

The Bluejays were ranked 15th when they squared off against No. 19 Xavier in a New Year's Eve showdown in Cincinnati.

Creighton's Mike Grimes pressures Notre Dame's Matt Carroll at the Guardians Classic championship game at Municipal Auditorium in Kansas City. "Just because we're the school from the Big East, we don't have the program that they do right now," Irish coach Mike Brey said. "That's a Top 25 team there."

The Musketeers' best player was forward David West, who would be a first-round NBA draft pick in the summer of 2003. He and Korver staged a classic shootout, with the Creighton senior making eight 3-point baskets and scoring a career-high 32 points. West finished with 28 points, the final two coming with 4.1 seconds to play to secure a 75-73 Xavier victory.

Creighton bounced back to run off six straight wins, including an 85-76 victory over Southern Illinois on Jan. 18 that left the Bluejays alone atop the Valley standings. They came back two days later to beat Illinois State just hours after learning that they had climbed to a program-high No. 10 ranking in the Associated Press poll.

At 16-1, Korver and the Bluejays were getting national attention. Locally, Creighton, which had never averaged more than 7,900 fans for a season, was becoming a hot ticket. Seven of the team's first 10 home games drew crowds of 8,000 or more, with the Southern Illinois game attracting a standing-room-only turnout of 10,184.

"We had been gaining momentum through the Walker-Sears years, but things really took off in Kyle's senior year," said DeVries, the former Northern Iowa player who had joined Altman's staff as an assistant. "The timing was perfect."

Joe Dabbert (21) and Tyler McKinney (24) block the path of Wichita State's Randy Burns. Creighton announced the next day that it had sold a record 1,102 all-session tickets for the Missouri Valley Conference tournament. Bradley had set the previous record of 650 in 1996.

The nation's No. 10 team stumbled badly in a Jan. 23 game at Evansville, a team the Bluejays had hammered 93-56 in Omaha eight days earlier. The Purple Aces pulled off a 74-66 upset in the rematch, leaving their fans storming the court and partying to Kool and the Gang's "Celebration."

Creighton rebounded to win nine of its next 10 games to set up a March 1 showdown for the Valley regular-season title at Southern Illinois. The Salukis, who had tied the Bluejays for the championship the previous season, rode a dominant defensive effort to a 70-62 win that clinched at least a share of the title. They would win it outright by defeating Illinois State in their final regular-season game.

The Jays also won their last game, routing Wichita State 86-60 before a crowd of 9,244 in Creighton's final regular-season game at the Civic.

2003:
DEFENSE DOES IT

Fresno State's Renaldo Major knocks down Kyle Korver as he fights for control of the ball with Joe Dabbert during Creighton's 67-66 win in a Bracket Buster game. The Jays shot just 40 percent for the game but turned up their defensive intensity in the second half to hold the Bulldogs to just five field goals in the final 14 minutes. "It was good to see our team find another way to win a game," Altman said. "On a day when we did not play well offensively, we played well defensively and on the boards."

Afterward, school officials had former coach Red McManus "turn off the lights" in a farewell ceremony. It was a fitting honor for the man whose 1961-62 Creighton team was the first to play its entire home schedule at the auditorium. While he had resigned under pressure more than three decades earlier, McManus had never strayed far from the program. Blessed with almost total recall about basketball, he was a walking history book, not only for his era but also the ones that followed.

McManus had become the unofficial patriarch of Creighton basketball.

"Red's a huge part of the tradition," said Kevin McKenna, who first met McManus when he played for Creighton in the late 1970s and early 1980s and became reacquainted as a Bluejay assistant coach on Altman's staff. "It's good to let our guys know about Creighton going to UCLA and playing and going to New York and playing, and some of the guys like Paul Silas that played for him.

2003: MCMANUS MEMORIES

Red McManus' role in Creighton basketball was recalled during the Bluejays' final weeks at the Civic Auditorium. But he also made his mark as a fan after he stopped coaching. Altman remembered McManus making a road trip and taking a seat at the end of the bench alongside buddy Dr. Lee Bevilacqua. As the action heated up, the two men started to get on the officials. Finally, one of the officials had enough and approached Altman, telling him he needed to get the "two old guys on the end of the bench under control or he was going to T them up." Altman walked down to the two men. "We weren't very good at the time," he said. "I told them, 'Fellas, we have enough problems without you guys adding to them. You're going to have to quiet down a bit.' "

"I think it's important for our guys to know they're not the first ones to play in the NCAA tournament and that there is some tradition here."

As he usually did, McManus made the trip to St. Louis to watch the 26-4 Bluejays play in the 2003 Missouri Valley tournament.

Creighton, which already had broken the school record for wins in a season, picked up its 27th victory by surviving a 57-56 nail-biter against Indiana State in the quarterfinals.

The Bluejays also struggled to get past Wichita State in the semifinals before pulling out a 70-69 win.

"We hadn't played well in the first half," Korver said. "Coach came in and broke a marker against the board at halftime. That got us pretty fired up."

Beating the Shockers put Creighton into the championship game against Southern Illinois.

Larry House shoots over Southern Illinois' Brad Korn in the Valley title game. House led the Jays with 20 points and helped hold Kent Williams, the Salukis' leading scorer, to 4-of-12 shooting.

Both teams were headed for the NCAA tournament, regardless of the outcome, but this one was going to be for pride.

Playing in front of a then-record crowd of 14,911, the Bluejays blew out to a 42-16 lead after the first 20 minutes. Creighton limited Southern Illinois to 15.6 percent shooting in the first half. Nothing the Salukis tried slowed the runaway freight train that was Creighton that night.

The Bluejays wound up winning 80-56, with House scoring 20 points.

Korver had 12 points and 10 rebounds to add the tournament's most valuable player award to the player of the year honor he had gained a few days earlier.

"A lot of times, you want that one to be a close game where you win when you hit one at the buzzer," Korver said.

DeAnthony Bowden puts an exclamation point on the win over Southern Illinois with a dunk in the final minutes.

"But I just loved beating the stuff out of those guys," he said, punctuating the statement with a cackle. "That was always my all-time favorite game."

The victory secured a fifth straight trip to the NCAA tournament, and the basketball committee rewarded the Bluejays with a No. 6 seed for their outstanding 29-4 season. Creighton's first-round opponent at Salt Lake City was Central Michigan, the Mid-American champion. Beat the Chippewas, and a high-profile meeting with Duke likely would follow in the second round.

Altman's team missed 22 of its first 29 shots in the 2003 NCAA tournament and never recovered. "We were flat," he said afterward. "Central Michigan was the aggressor. That's not the best basketball we can play."

Central Michigan used a 12-2 spurt at the start of the second half to turn a 38-22 halftime lead into a 50-24 advantage, but the Bluejays went on a 32-13 run to pull within seven points with 9:17 to play. The comeback stalled, but Creighton had one more run left, scoring 10 straight points in 2½ minutes to slice an 11-point deficit to 72-70 with 1:38 to play. But Mike Manciel's jumper and three Creighton turnovers — the Bluejays finished with 18 — in the final 65 seconds finished off the 79-73 loss. It was Central Michigan that got the chance to play Duke, and Creighton's season came to a stunning end.

Asked a decade later whether that would be the one game in his Creighton career that he would like to do over, Altman replied, "Absolutely."

"That was a good enough team that we should have played on," Altman said. "For whatever reason, I didn't have them ready that night. We looked stuck in the mud at the start. I don't know if our expectations were so high or what. We were prepared, but we just didn't have them ready to go. That still bothers me."

In addition to winning a school-record 29 games, Creighton spent 15 weeks in the national rankings and finished No. 15 in the final poll. "So many great things happened to us," backup forward Joe Dabbert said the morning after the loss. "Being in the Top 25 most of the season, winning the conference season, going 29-5. You can't complain."

Said House: "The good times we've had override the bad times, and I wouldn't trade it for the world. Even though we didn't go as far as we wanted, you can't beat what we were able to do."

House and Bowden were part of 52 wins in their two-year Creighton careers. Korver played in 99 wins and four NCAA tournaments in his four years.

An AP second-team All-American as a senior, Korver finished his career with 1,801 points, fifth best in school history. He made five 3-point baskets in his final game to push his career total to 371. In 2003, only five players in NCAA Division I history had made more shots from beyond the arc.

No player, Altman said the day after the game, had meant more to the program in his nine seasons as coach. Korver's value would transcend the time he spent on campus.

Creighton averaged a school-record 8,246 fans for its 17 home games in Korver's senior season. The excitement he and his teammates were able to generate would prove crucial as the program prepared to make a giant step forward the next season.

"Even though Kyle never played in the Qwest Center, his senior year really pushed us over the top in how we were successful early in our move to the new building," said Sarver, the longtime athletic department employee. "And I think it's a big reason why we're still successful."

TYLER MCKINNEY

The 6-1 sophomore point guard scored only 5 points a game, but his assist-to-turnover ratio of 2.6 ranked second in the Missouri Valley. "My role is to get the ball to whoever's open," McKinney said. His leadership and steady play were on display when the Jays won a Valley tournament title. He was fourth all-time in assists when his career ended.

ON THE BIG STAGE

Dana Altman's veteran team started the season by winning the Guardians Classic tournament, beating Notre Dame 80-75 in the championship game in Kansas City. The Jays added wins over Nebraska, BYU and TCU in the nonconference schedule, but the most exciting game was a 75-73 loss at No. 19 Xavier. Creighton won 15 games in the Valley, good enough only for second that year behind Southern Illinois. But the Bluejays put together their best game of the season in dismantling the Salukis in the MVC tourney final and advanced to the NCAA as a No. 6 seed. The season ended in a crushing loss to Central Michigan in the first round. The Bluejays had a school record 29 wins and spent 15 weeks in the ratings, including a Top 10 rating at one point. "This is an outstanding group," Altman said. "I've been fortunate to have a group like that to work with."

BRODY DEREN

Deren, a 6-8, 250-pound center, led the Missouri Valley in blocked shots but didn't make the league's all-defensive team. "That upset me," Deren said after blocking four shots against Wichita State in a conference tournament game. "When he's focused, he's pretty good," Altman said. Deren wasn't alone inside, combining with 6-11 junior Joe Dabbert and 6-7 junior Mike Grimes to give the Jays a rotation that averaged more than 21 points, 11 rebounds and three blocked shots per game.

LARRY HOUSE

The 6-4 senior guard was second on the team in scoring, and his drives to the basket provided an alternative to Korver's long-range shooting. House averaged more than 11 points a game while shooting over 50 percent. Altman called him "our X-factor, especially when he plays on the defensive end." He scored his career high of 28 points in the final regular-season game at the Civic Auditorium and left the court to chants of "Larry, Larry, Larry." Asked later about Bluejay fans, he said, "They showed they love me, and I love them."

DEANTHONY BOWDEN

The 6-1 guard provided a boundless supply of energy to the team. "When Dee is playing efficiently, our energy level goes way up," Altman said. Bowden scored 6.7 points a game off the bench and took on tough defensive assignments. "I want to be remembered as a guy who, every time he took the floor, he went out there and tried to guard somebody and make things happen for his team," Bowden said.

KYLE KORVER

Korver led the Jays in scoring, rebounding and steals his senior season. He was named to the Associated Press All-America second team, was a candidate for the John Wooden national player of the year award and repeated as Missouri Valley Conference player of the year. He led Creighton to a school-record 29 wins and ended his career by becoming the first player in school history to play in four NCAA tournaments. He finished his career with 1,801 points and a school record 371 3-point shots. Altman saluted his work ethic. "He'd take setbacks and come back stronger the next day," he said. There's a persistence there that a lot of players just don't have."

A big, new stage for the Bluejays

When Omaha's Qwest Center opened in the fall of 2003, it was everything the Civic Auditorium was not in terms of fan-friendliness: wide concourses, spacious seats, clean restrooms and well-stocked concession stands.

It also had 7,000 more seats than Creighton had ever averaged for a season. Even with the unprecedented run of success over the previous five seasons, Creighton's season ticket sales had plateaued at about 5,500. Sarver said Creighton couldn't capitalize on the success it was having on the court, because the majority of the Civic's seats were either in the end zones or in the upper tiers.

"There was a perception that there were about 900 good seats in a venue that seated 9,000," Sarver said. "People repeatedly came to us requesting more tickets but were unwilling to buy, because we couldn't get them seats in a premium location."

Tyler McKinney said Altman had asked him to be a leader as practice began in 2003. "I'm ready for that," he said.

In pressing their argument to move to the new arena, Rasmussen and Altman convinced school officials that they could sell out all 9,000 seats in the lower bowl of the Qwest Center. "People told me all the time they wouldn't buy tickets at the Civic, because they couldn't get in the lower bowl," Altman said. "At the Qwest, we had 9,000 tickets in the lower bowl. All we had to hope was that people were sincere in what they were telling us. They were."

Creighton played its first regular-season game at the Qwest Center on Nov. 22, 2003, and a crowd of 12,255 watched the Bluejays hammer San Diego 79-44. Creighton drew just two crowds below 10,000 the rest of the season and four times topped the 14,000 mark. The topper was the 15,561 — a state record for a basketball game — that showed up for a December win over Nebraska.

The San Diego win was the first of 12 straight by Altman's veteran team to start the season. While the Bluejays had lost Korver, Bowden and House, they returned fifth-year seniors in Dabbert, Grimes, Deren and Lindeman. McKinney was back for his third season as the starter at the point, and Funk, who had played sparingly as a freshman, was primed to play a much larger role.

The 2003-04 season began successfully, but a medical issue threatened to derail hopes for another big season. McKinney had used tap water to clean his contacts while the Jays were on a preseason trip to Canada for a series of exhibition games, and his right eye became infected. It was first thought to be a minor irritant, but by the time the Bluejays played their eighth game of the season on Dec. 22 at Wyoming, McKinney could hardly tolerate the bright lights in the arena. On Christmas Day, a camera flash caused him to scream in pain.

Creighton pulled out a 72-66 overtime win over the University of Nebraska at Omaha in the Jays' first competition at the Qwest Center. The 2003 exhibition game drew a crowd of 9,684.

He came back to play in two games after Christmas, but his vision continued to deteriorate. In a Jan. 5 win over Bradley, McKinney stepped three feet out of bounds because he didn't see the baseline, and doctors later recommended a cornea transplant. The infection recurred after the transplant, leaving him in intense pain and dealing with side effects from drugs.

At one point, McKinney told his parents, "I don't care if they have to take my eye out. I don't want to deal with it anymore." His season ended when he was told to undergo a second transplant. As encouragement before the surgery, a doctor mentioned to him that a lot of people lead successful lives with only one eye.

Brody Deren had 11 points and nine rebounds against Northern Iowa in 2004, as the Jays' home winning streak hit 28.

The Bluejays kept plowing along without McKinney. An early February win over Northern Iowa improved Creighton to 17-2, the same record it had compiled after 19 games the previous year.

The season went downhill after that. The Jays lost five of their next seven, including a double-overtime loss at Drake and an embarrassing 70-46 rout at Southwest Missouri State.

Creighton closed out the regular season with a win over Wichita State but headed to the conference tournament knowing it needed to at least reach the title game to have a chance to extend its streak of NCAA tournament appearances. Southwest Missouri put an end to those hopes, pinning an 84-75 loss on Creighton that sent the Bluejays to the NIT.

The NIT, in search of games that might draw big crowds, paired Creighton against in-state rival Nebraska. The Bluejays, who had beaten the Huskers 61-54 in December, led by 9 points with 6:26 left but missed their final seven shots from the field in a 71-70 loss before 13,483 at the Qwest Center. Nate Johnson's basket with 12 seconds left produced the winning points for Nebraska, and Jake Muhleisen preserved the victory by blocking Funk's jumper at the buzzer.

"This is how our season went toward the end," Grimes said afterward. "We gave teams good games, but we couldn't find ways to finish it off. Ending it like this to Nebraska leaves a bad taste in our mouth."

The defeat left Creighton with a 20-9 record, but there was another number to ponder as the Bluejays headed into the offseason. In its first season in its new home, Creighton finished 29th nationally in attendance, averaging 12,016 for its 16 home games.

"We knew we would have a huge increase with the move," Sarver said. "We weren't sure how huge, but we were sure that we would have enough to make the move revenue-neutral. We went way over the top." Altman knew sustaining the surge in attendance would be dependent on continuing to put a winning product on the floor. That would be a challenge in 2004-05, as he would have to replace four players — Deren, Grimes, Lindeman and Dabbert — who had been a part of teams that played in three NCAA tournaments and one NIT.

Coming off a sophomore season in which he led the team in scoring and assists, Funk figured to be the Bluejays' marquee player. Creighton also returned a starter in Johnny Mathies and a top reserve in Kellen Miliner and had high expectations for Anthony Tolliver, a 6-9 forward who had seen limited action as a freshman.

The wild card would be McKinney. His second transplant was successful, and his recovery was so rapid that doctors waived the normal yearlong ban on contact sports that customarily followed such surgery. He received a standing ovation when he was announced as a starter for the season opener against Alcorn State. Nine days later, he made the game-winning shot to beat Ohio State 65-63 in the championship game of the Guardians Classic.

McKinney had another game-winning basket in the next contest as the Jays squeaked past Xavier 73-72, and he assisted on Miliner's game-winning basket to beat Nebraska 50-48 in Lincoln.

"I appreciate little things a lot more," McKinney said after the first month of the season. "Even being able to practice."

Even with the ultra-steady McKinney in control of the offense, Creighton found it difficult to perform with any consistency after seven straight wins to start the season. A 71-67 loss to Southern Illinois in mid-February was the 10th in 18 games, leaving the Bluejays sitting at 15-10. They followed a win at Wichita State with a 100-68 BracketBusters clubbing of Chattanooga in which they made a school-record 20 3-point baskets. It seemed as if every Bluejay played well, with one exception.

Kellen Miliner scored a game-high 20 points against Nebraska in December 2004. "It felt good, but I thought it was going to be short," he said of the game-winner.

Tolliver failed to score, had one rebound and fouled out after playing just nine minutes. "It was the worst game I ever played," Tolliver recalled.

Altman met with him before Creighton's next game and delivered a message: Your team needs you to rebound and play defense. Anything else, the coach said, will be a bonus.

The memories of that meeting — and the legend born of it — bring a smile to Tolliver's face. "Over the years, I've heard so many different things about what supposedly took place," Tolliver said. "He kicked me off the team, he wanted me to transfer, he threatened to bench me. It's amazing how some of that stuff got started.

"The truth is, the only thing Coach talked about that day was how important it was for me to focus on defense and rebounding. I do remember him saying that if I didn't think I wanted to do that and wanted to look somewhere else after the season, he'd do what he could to help me. But he said he really needed me here."

Tolliver went out and grabbed 13 rebounds as Creighton defeated Evansville to extend its winning streak to three. He had a dozen more in the next two games, victories over Indiana State and Illinois State that sent the Bluejays to St. Louis riding a five-game winning streak.

Anthony Tolliver goes up for a slam dunk in an 83-82 win over Northern Iowa in 2005. He finished with just 4 points in the game played two weeks before Altman sat him down for a talk.

Creighton opened the Valley tournament with a 69-52 win over Illinois State. Funk scored 20 points in the win, and the Bluejays got an unexpected boost from Jimmy Motz, a sharpshooting backup forward who didn't miss from the field in a 15-point night that included three 3-point baskets.

Motz stayed hot in the next game, making three of four 3-point shots, as Creighton outlasted Wichita State 70-60 to reach the championship game. Motz then capped a three-day performance that earned him a spot on the all-tournament team by scoring 12 points in the 75-57 win over Southwest Missouri State that put the Bluejays back in the NCAA tournament for the sixth time in seven seasons.

"When we were 15-10, nobody believed it," Tolliver said after the game. "Now, here we are, going to the Big Dance."

Jimmy Motz made 10 of 14 3-point shots in the 2005 Valley tourney. In one game, Motz hit a 3-pointer that prompted an opposing coach to turn to his assistant and exclaim, "We're going to get beat by Jimmy (expletive) Motz."

In the first round of the 2005 NCAA tournament, McKinney goes in for a basket against West Virginia, which advanced to the Elite Eight.

As a No. 10 seed, Creighton was paired against No. 7 West Virginia in a first-round game in Cleveland on St. Patrick's Day. The game was tight throughout, and the Bluejays found themselves with the ball in the final seconds with the score tied 61-61.

Creighton worked to get Funk the shot, and the junior guard thought he had a good one when he let it fly with about seven seconds to play. "I had a good look," Funk said. "It seemed like he came out of nowhere."

"He" was West Virginia's Tyrone Sally, who blocked Funk's shot, retrieved the ball and scored on a breakaway dunk with 2.4 seconds to play. Creighton got one last attempt, but Funk's desperation shot from about 22 feet flew harmlessly over the rim at the buzzer to seal the 63-61 loss.

"That's one I'm going to think about for seven or eight months," Funk said in a tearful Creighton locker room.

The game was the last one for Miliner and McKinney, who finished his career fourth in assists.

With four starters and several key reserves returning, the Bluejays had high hopes heading into what would prove to be a banner 2005-06 season for the Missouri Valley.

The direction of Creighton's season took a dramatic turn four games in when, late in a 15-point loss at DePaul, Funk tore the labrum in his shoulder while diving for a loose ball. He had scored a career-high 38 points in his previous game, leading the Bluejays to a dramatic 91-90 double-overtime victory over Dayton.

Funk missed Creighton's next five games, including the Bluejays' annual meeting with Nebraska. Creighton dressed just nine players for the game at the Qwest Center, as injuries also kept reserves Motz and Pierce Hibma on the sidelines.

"We were coming off a loss against Chattanooga, and Nebraska came in here feeling good," said DeVries, the Creighton assistant coach. "They actually had set up a meal at the arena for after the game. They ended up canceling that meal."

The largest crowd (15,621) to see a basketball game in Nebraska watched the Huskers lose their appetite, as Creighton rolled to a 70-44 win. The Bluejays held the Huskers to 11 first-half points in building a 20-point halftime lead. Mathies scored a career-high 29 points, and forward Dane Watts chipped in nine points and a dozen rebounds.

DeVries, left, and Funk welcome Mathies back to the bench after he finished with 29 points against Nebraska in 2005. "All the odds seemed to be stacked in their favor, but we just played harder and wanted it more," Mathies said.

That game showcased Altman's leadership, DeVries said.

"Every time it seemed like our backs were to the wall — and it happened almost every year — that's when Coach was at his best," DeVries said. "He was so good at rallying guys and almost willing them to win in those type of moments."

Funk returned for a pair of early-January conference games and scored a total of 25 points in the two contests, but he wasn't satisfied with his play and opted for season-ending shoulder surgery. Even with their star sidelined, the Bluejays managed to remain a contender in the Missouri Valley race. Freshman Josh Dotzler showed why Altman had offered him a scholarship as a high school sophomore by taking over at the point and providing solid direction.

Tolliver, who had finished the previous season on a high note following his mid-February meeting with his coach, began to emerge as a go-to player for the Bluejays. After averaging 2.6 points and 3.0 rebounds in his first two seasons in the program, Tolliver was averaging 12.5 points and 6.2 rebounds at midseason.

"I never really worried about scoring after we had our meeting, but I became a much better scorer," Tolliver said. "It's funny how those things work."

Tolliver's biggest basket of the season came in a late-January game against Wichita State. The Shockers hit town on a roll and roared to a 25-6 lead after 10 minutes.

Creighton closed the deficit to seven points at halftime and took its first lead since the early seconds when Tolliver made a layup for a 48-47 advantage with 7:38 to play. The two teams battled back and forth down the stretch, with Wichita State's miss on a 3-point attempt setting the stage for the finish with 23 seconds left and the score tied at 55.

Tolliver (44) set off a celebration at the Qwest Center with his game-winning shot against Wichita State in 2006.

Creighton ran the clock down and got the ball to Tolliver, who drained a jump shot from the right baseline at the buzzer for a 57-55 win.

That started the Bluejays on a four-game winning streak, and they entered a Feb. 11 showdown at home against Southern Illinois with first place at stake. The Salukis' 74-67 win snapped Creighton's 16-game home-court winning streak.

More important, Dotzler suffered a season-ending knee injury when he became tangled with a Southern Illinois player.

A buzzer-beating, 3-point basket by Wichita State's Matt Braeuer sent Creighton to its second straight loss. The Bluejays split their final two league games to finish in a three-way tie for second behind the Shockers.

Creighton, seeded fourth for the Valley tournament, drew red-hot Bradley for its first game in St. Louis. The Bluejays held a seven-point lead early in the second half, but the Braves came back to post a 54-47 win.

While it was a disappointing conference season for Creighton, the league never had it better. Bradley upset Wichita State in the semifinals before losing to Southern Illinois in the final. For the first time in history, the league placed four teams in the NCAA tournament — the Salukis, the Braves, the Shockers and Greg McDermott's Northern Iowa club. Bradley and Wichita State advanced to the Sweet 16. Creighton had to settle for a trip to the NIT along with Missouri State, which the NCAA passed over in spite of 21 wins and an RPI in the low 20s.

The Bluejays won their first NIT game since 1942 by posting a 71-60 home win over Akron in the first round.

Up next was Miami. The Hurricanes' defense dominated as Creighton scored just 19 points in the first half, the fewest it had in 49 games at the Qwest Center, and 52 for the game, the fewest at home since 1996. Still, the game was tied with 2.6 seconds left when Creighton's Watts was called for a blocking foul that drew a loud protest from Altman. Miami's Guillermo Diaz made one of two free throws to give his team a 53-52 lead.

Altman unloads on officials after a foul was called on Dane Watts with 2.6 seconds left against Miami in a second-round NIT game at the Qwest Center in 2006.

On the game's final play, Diaz collided with Mathies as he tried to get off a last-second 3-pointer, but there was no call. The referees ran off the court as fans threw things onto the floor, and Altman ran onto the court to protest. He apologized after the game. "That's just the way the game goes," he said. "I shouldn't have lost my composure."

Creighton had lost four of its last seven games after losing Dotzler but still ended the season with 20 wins for the eighth straight season. The school also finished in the top 20 nationally in attendance for the first time. The Bluejays' average of 13,901 for 17 home games placed them right behind perennial power Connecticut, which was 19th.

Mathies earned a spot on the All-Valley second team, as did Tolliver, who also was selected as the league's most improved player. That remains a point of pride for Tolliver.

"Everyone always talks about what can happen if you work hard," Tolliver said. "I'm an example of that."

His emergence, along with Funk's return, sent expectations for the 2006-07 season skyrocketing, good news considering the Qwest Center was adding 1,518 more seats to raise its capacity to more than 17,500 for basketball.

Altman unsuccessfully tried to rein in talk that this was a team bound for the Sweet 16 — or beyond — but Creighton's first-ever preseason ranking only fueled the fire.

2006: UPSET OF THE MUSKETEERS

Dane Watts fights for one of his 10 rebounds in a 73-67 victory over No. 24 Xavier at the Qwest Center. "They're a very difficult team to play against at home," Musketeer coach Sean Miller said. "When you look at their history, it's a tough place to walk in and win."

The Bluejays started the season ranked 19th in the AP poll and opened with a 78-42 rout of Mississippi Valley State that actually dropped them a spot in the ratings. A 73-61 loss at Nebraska sent Creighton tumbling out of the rankings altogether and set the tone for the first two months of the season.

The Bluejays would play well for a game or two before slipping up. From mid-January on, they began to play like the team they had been expected to be and closed the regular season with a 71-54 drubbing of Wichita State. They headed to St. Louis as the No. 2 seed for the conference tournament.

A 21-point win over Indiana State put Creighton into the semifinals against Missouri State. With Funk, Tolliver and Nick Porter combining to score all but 10 of the team's points, the Bluejays rolled to a 75-58 victory and a spot in the championship game.

Funk delivered a virtuoso performance against the Bears, scoring 33 points — the most by a Bluejay in a Valley tournament game — to go with eight rebounds, three assists and two steals.

"We've had a lot of good performances here, but I'm not sure if we've ever had a better one," Altman said of Funk after the win.

Creighton's championship opponent was old nemesis Southern Illinois. The Salukis brought a 13-game winning streak into the final and had beaten the Bluejays in the last eight meetings dating to the championship game of the 2003 tournament.

Funk had played a minor role as a freshman in the 2003 win. This time around, he was the catalyst for the 67-61 win that locked up his third trip to the NCAA tournament. His 19 points pushed his three-game tournament total to 66 and earned him the most valuable player award.

"I didn't want to go out a loser," Funk said. "It hasn't been a picture-perfect year for me, but to play this well toward the end, put three games together and have a decent tournament, it feels pretty good."

Funk missed out on one more chance to be a Bluejay hero.

Dead-eye Nate Funk shoots over Southern Illinois' Jamal Tatum in the 2007 Valley final.

Nate Funk (10), Anthony Tolliver (44) and Nick Porter (3) played their last games as Bluejays against Nevada in the 2007 NCAA tournament.

Facing Nevada in the first round of the NCAA tournament in New Orleans, Creighton found itself in a 59-59 tie when it forced a turnover with 19.6 seconds to play. Altman didn't call time out. He didn't need to. Everyone at the New Orleans Arena knew the ball was going to Funk. He brought the ball down, dribbled around the perimeter and, as the clock dipped under 10 seconds, made his move.

As he went up to take a fade from about 15 feet — his bread-and-butter shot — he lost control of the ball. He caught it in midair and threw up a shot that fell short. Tolliver grabbed the miss but lost it to Nevada, which missed a backcourt shot at the buzzer.

The game slipped away in overtime, with Nevada pulling out a 77-71 victory to send Creighton home with another first-round loss.

"It's just disappointing," said Funk.

"We had our opportunity," Altman said. "We just came up a little short."

Funk led the Bluejays with 23 points to finish his career with 1,754. He had been named first team All-Valley twice in his career.

"We rode Nate Funk hard those years," Altman said.

Tolliver also was named first-team All-Valley as a senior. He recalled his early struggles when he learned of the honor.

"When I first got here, I don't know if I ever thought I would reach this level," Tolliver said. "If they had a last-team All-Valley, I probably would have made that."

The selection of Tolliver and Funk to the all-conference first team marked the first time that Creighton had two players named All-Valley in the same season since Bob Harstad and Chad Gallagher earned the honor in 1991.

Creighton also continued to make news off the court as it topped the 200,000 mark in attendance for the first time. The Bluejays averaged 15,909 for their 14 home games to finish 13th nationally in per-game attendance.

Upon returning to Omaha, Altman began preparing for a 2007-08 season that had the makings of a rebuilding year.

Funk and Tolliver were gone. So was Porter, a gritty junior-college transfer who blossomed as a senior.

As usual, Altman held his end-of-the-season meetings with the players and set up the spring workout program. It was business as usual in early April when Bluejay fans heard the news they had feared for years.

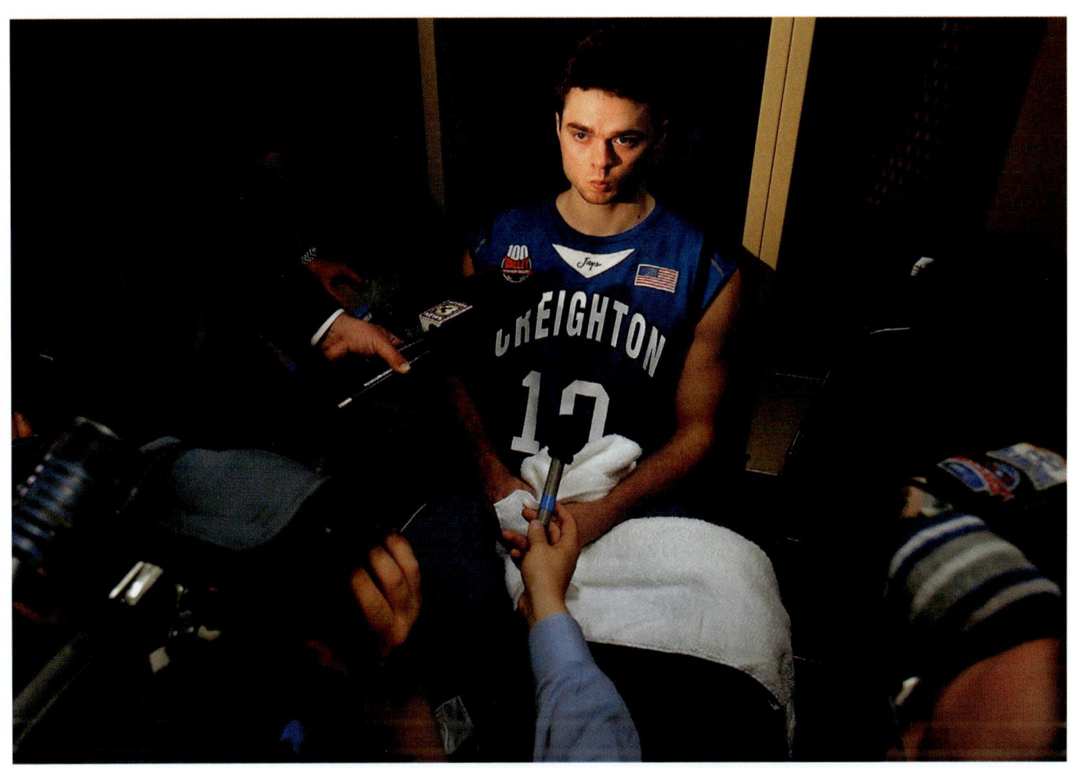

Funk was asked by reporters whether he had been fouled on his shot attempt at the end of regulation against Nevada. Altman downplayed the no-call. "Part of the game," he said. "You have to fight through it. I thought the officials did a good job."

A change of heart, and another change of heart

Altman's success at Creighton had made him a hot commodity on the coaching market over the years. Miami, Illinois, Georgia, Arizona State and Tennessee were among the schools that had made serious attempts to land him as their next coach. Each time, he turned them down.

"My family was really young, and we were building something here," Altman said. "I never really gave those offers much consideration. I'd think about them, and I was never really close to leaving."

But at the 2007 Final Four in Atlanta, Altman received a phone call that caused him to do more than just think. Arkansas Athletic Director Frank Broyles — who 33 years earlier had plucked Eddie Sutton away from Creighton — called Altman to inquire whether he would be interested in coaching the Razorbacks.

Altman walks away from the Vinardi Center in April 2007 after informing his players that he was leaving.

"He got off the phone and said, 'You won't believe who just called,'" Reva Altman said. "When I saw the look on his face, I got excited for him."

The Altmans met with Broyles and his wife for dinner. Broyles called Rasmussen to ask permission to talk to his basketball coach and then offered Altman the job.

On Monday, April 2, Altman accepted.

A whirlwind day began for the Altmans, who flew from Atlanta to Omaha on a private jet provided by Arkansas. Altman met with his players and others associated with the program. From there, the Altmans, accompanied by daughter Audra, headed to Fayetteville.

At 5:14 p.m., Altman, Broyles and Arkansas Chancellor John White walked into Bud Walton Arena as the Arkansas fight song blared on the public address system. Minutes later, Altman was introduced.

"This just felt like the right situation at the right time for myself and my family," Altman said. "I am thankful for the opportunity that Coach Broyles gave me. At 48, I wanted to make one more run at things."

Although no contract terms were disclosed, sources said Arkansas had lured Altman to Fayetteville with an offer of $1.5 million per year for five years.

Altman had turned down big offers before, and it was estimated he was making $1 million at Creighton. The difference this time, he said, was that Arkansas provided him with an opportunity that money couldn't buy.

"Maybe it's the chance to get that one special player that we couldn't get at Creighton," he said. "We've had great players and been so close. Kyle Korver, Nate Funk, Rodney Buford — those guys could play anywhere.

"There's not a lot of difference, but maybe it's that one player, that special guy that you have the opportunity to recruit that puts you over the hump."

Altman prepares to board a plane for Arkansas.

In introducing Altman, Broyles called him the "greatest coach in America." He then led the crowd in welcoming Altman with an Arkansas tradition — the calling of the hogs. Altman participated in chanting "pig sooie" and raising his hands skyward, although he wore a slightly embarrassed look as he went through the ritual.

"That's not really my style," he said later as he met with reporters from The World-Herald and from an Omaha television station who had made the hasty trip to Fayetteville. During the interview, Altman seemed more melancholy than overjoyed about the decision he had just made. He talked about what he had accomplished at Creighton and the good times he had in Omaha. He talked about how difficult it was to be parting ways with his boss and good friend, Bruce Rasmussen, and the players.

"You don't stay at a place for 13 years and in 72 hours change your feelings about a special place and a special group of players that I had," he said.

Back in Omaha, Rasmussen set about the task of picking the program off the canvas after a gut-punch. His first priority was the players, because Altman's meeting with them hadn't gone well. Many were in class when the news first broke, and they were upset that they had learned of his leaving from classmates or the news media.

Rasmussen knew the players would have questions about what the next move would be. "I told them I wasn't going to take calls, I'm going to make calls," Rasmussen said. "I told them I was going to call their moms and dads and answer their questions. I was going to have to start thinking about hiring a coach, but taking care of them first was more important. I told them to trust us for a while."

Rasmussen spent the rest of the day making phone calls. When the battery on his cellphone died, he switched to his office phone. He finally arrived home around 2 a.m. He plugged his cellphone into the charger and told his wife to make sure to get him up if he didn't hear the alarm he had set for 5 a.m.

"Dana said, 'I have to get out of this. I can't do it. It was a mistake.'"

— **Bruce Rasmussen**

Shortly after rising, Rasmussen heard his cellphone. It was Altman, who had been trying to reach him continually since the previous evening.

"Dana said, 'I have to get out of this. I can't do it. It was a mistake,'" Rasmussen said. "He said he hadn't signed anything. I told him, 'Coach, you get this way a lot. You just need to sit on it for a while.' He was adamant that he had to get out of it."

The two men continued to talk until finally Rasmussen told Altman that if he could get out of the Arkansas commitment, he would have a private plane in Fayetteville around midday. That proved to be a bit of a challenge.

Rasmussen first tried booster David Sokol, but his plane was in New York. He next tried another booster, Howard Hawks. "He was in a board meeting, with board members from all over the world," Rasmussen said. "I told his secretary, 'You have to trust me on this, but you have to interrupt that meeting.'" Hawks took the call, and Rasmussen told him he needed his plane. "He says, 'What for?' I told him, and he said we could use it on one condition: He wanted to be on the plane."

Altman spent the day meeting with Arkansas officials to inform them of his intentions. Less than 24 hours after Altman's half-hearted "pig sooie" call, the news of his return to Creighton started to leak out. Back in Omaha later that night, Altman held an emotional meeting with his players at the Qwest Center.

"A lot of people think the players rolled out the red carpet for him when he came back," Funk said. "The reality was it wasn't that easy for everybody. A lot of emotions went through guys over those few days. There were some hard feelings that had to be addressed."

Nick Bahe said some players, upset that they had heard from secondhand sources that Altman was leaving, were ticked off again when they learned of his return the same way. "When you have 15 guys on a team, you're going to have people feeling different ways about what happened," Bahe said. "Some guys didn't hold back, but he said he wanted us to be honest."

Altman addressed the challenge of rebuilding trust with his players and with the Creighton community when he met with reporters at a press conference two days later.

"It's going to take some time to build that relationship back with my players, with the fans and even with the media," Altman said. "I hope we can build that back. I know I have some rebuilding to do with a lot of people, and that process starts today." And he announced that he intended to finish out his career at Creighton. "This is home," he said.

The athletic director and the coach at a press conference upon Altman's return. "My ego and money affected my decision" to take the Arkansas job, Altman said. "But it was something my heart just wouldn't allow me to do."

Altman's first 13 seasons at Creighton had been relatively free of criticism from those outside the program. That was about to change, in part because the rise of social media provided fans with more of a voice in how they thought the program should be run and in part because of a drop in the Bluejays' on-the-court production.

Dane Watts was the Bluejays' lone returning starter heading into the 2007-08 season. Only three other players had played meaningful minutes the previous season. Altman's 14th Creighton team would be his least experienced.

"With only four guys having any real experience," Altman said, "it's important that our newcomers are ready to go."

Those newcomers included a pair of junior-college transfers, Booker Woodfox and Cavel Witter, and three true freshmen — P'Allen Stinnett, Kaleb Korver and Kenton Walker. Of the group, Stinnett was the most highly regarded, a four-star recruit who originally had committed to Iowa State but backed out when the Cyclones had a coaching change.

Stinnett turned in an impressive debut, scoring 23 points, all in the second half, to rally Creighton to a season-opening 74-62 win over DePaul. The Bluejays would win nine of their first 10 games, losing only to No. 21 Xavier.

But Creighton never was able to play consistently once the conference schedule began. The Bluejays lost their first two Valley games, won five in a row and then dropped three straight. Three more wins at home were followed by three losses on the road.

They headed into the regular-season finale needing a win to keep intact a string of 10-win seasons in conference play. They got it by outlasting Bradley in a 111-110 double-overtime shootout in which Witter scored 42 points.

Creighton won a rematch with the Braves six days later in the conference tournament before Drake, enjoying its finest basketball season since its Final Four run in 1969, posted its third win of the season over the Bluejays in the Valley semifinals.

Junior point guard Josh Dotzler, wearing a knee brace after two injury-plagued seasons, had five assists in a 2007 victory over DePaul.

An NIT invitation followed, and Creighton pulled out a 74-73 win over Rhode Island when Witter made a 3-point basket with 3.2 seconds to play. The Bluejays had trailed by 12 points with 3:10 on the clock and by seven with 1:31 remaining before rallying to keep their season alive.

The win earned Creighton a trip to Gainesville, Fla., to face a Florida program that had won national championships in 2006 and 2007. Although these Gators were a couple of notches below the quality of their title-winning clubs, they had little trouble in hammering out an 82-54 win. Nick Calathes recorded the first triple-double by a Creighton opponent by scoring 11 points, grabbing 13 rebounds and handing out 11 assists for Florida.

Stinnett became the first freshman since Buford to lead Creighton in scoring, and his 416 points were five shy of Buford's freshman scoring record. He earned both the Valley's freshman and newcomer of the year awards while receiving honorable mention on the All-Valley team, and Woodfox was named the league's sixth man of the year.

Cavel Witter launches the game-winning 3-point shot against Rhode Island in the 2008 NIT.

Booker Woodfox scored 20 points in Creighton's 74-70 win over Illinois State to gain a tie for the 2009 MVC regular-season title. The Qwest Center crowd serenaded Woodfox with "M-V-P" chants after the game. "I could care less if I had zero points," said Woodfox, whose four free throws in the final 18 seconds helped seal the win. "We haven't won it in seven years, and to get this win and be co-conference champions is amazing."

It would be Woodfox, a 3-point marksman, who would emerge as the leader of Creighton's 2008-09 team. He would lead the team in scoring with a 15.8 average and finish second nationally by making 47.6 percent of his 3-point attempts.

After back-to-back road losses at Arkansas-Little Rock and Nebraska left Creighton 3-2, the Bluejays ran off nine straight wins. They hit the midpoint of the conference season at 5-4, then strung together 10 straight wins — nine in league play — to earn a share of the Valley championship with Northern Iowa.

Seeded second for the conference tournament, Creighton appeared in control of its quarterfinal game against Wichita State, building an 18-point lead with 6:52 to play. The Shockers staged a furious rally, outscoring the Bluejays 25-6 over the next 6:43 and taking a 62-61 lead on Toure' Murry's 3-point basket with nine seconds to play.

Creighton got the ball to Antoine Young, who missed a jumper with about three seconds to play. The rebound went out of bounds, off Wichita State, and after the officials reviewed the videotape, 1.9 seconds were put on the clock.

Creighton inbounded the ball to Woodfox, who took two dribbles before launching the buzzer-beating basket that gave the Bluejays a 63-62 win.

Wichita State coach Gregg Marshall thought the officials put too much time on the clock. Then he argued that the timekeeper was slow to start the clock after Woodfox touched the ball.

"We got beat on a great shot from Booker Woodfox after two dribbles and a ham sandwich," Marshall later said.

The win was Creighton's 26th of the season, the second-most in school history. In spite of that, the Bluejays knew they needed to reach the championship game to ensure themselves a spot in the NCAA tournament because of a so-so RPI.

Instead, Creighton laid an egg in the semi-finals, as Illinois State rolled to a 73-49 victory. Eight days later, the Bluejays learned that their 26-7 record wasn't good enough to earn an at-large bid to the tournament and instead had to settle for a return trip to the NIT.

"That one stung," said DeVries, the Creighton assistant coach. "I think that year showed how hard it is to sustain things at the mid-major level. We went 14-4 in the league, won 26 games and were left out of the tournament.

"We really liked that team."

Creighton's record did earn it one of the four No. 1 seeds for the NIT, and the Bluejays opened their 10th appearance in the event with a hard-fought, 73-71 win over Bowling Green. After trailing by 14 points in the first half, Creighton shot 63.6 percent from the field in the final 20 minutes. Woodfox's 3-point basket with 4:44 to play gave Creighton its first lead of the second half, and the Bluejays took the lead for good when Justin Carter buried a 3-point shot with 1:36 to play.

P'Allen Stinnett had 18 points and a career-high six assists in the 2009 NIT victory over Bowling Green.

The victory advanced Creighton to a second-round home game against one of college basketball's true bluebloods, the University of Kentucky. The Wildcats' visit to the Qwest Center drew a crowd of 16,984 and produced an atmosphere unlike any seen before at the venue. The sheer size of the building lends itself to a somewhat sterile atmosphere no matter how many bodies are packed into the place. But on that night, the fans turned out juiced and jazzed.

Josh Dotzler reaches in to tip away a pass to Kentucky's A.J. Stewart in the 2009 NIT.

They saw a game that came down to the wire. Creighton led for all but 4½ minutes and for all but 36 seconds of the final 14:24. But it was Kentucky that emerged with a 65-63 win when Jodie Meeks did what All-Americans are supposed to do with the game and a season on the line.

His three-point play with 10.6 seconds left decided the game. Meeks took an inbounds pass, slipped his defender and drove hard to the basket. Carter blocked his path, leaving Meeks to ad-lib his final shot that finished off a 16-point night.

"I saw the guy trying to take a charge, so I tried to avoid him any way possible," Meeks said. "I went sideways, heard a whistle and tried to throw it up. It was a lucky shot, but I'm glad it went in." Meeks' basket put the Wildcats up by a point, and he added a free throw to put his team ahead by two. Creighton called timeout with 7.5 seconds left and called a play that put the ball in the hands of Woodfox, its best 3-point shooter.

"When I saw him free up and get open, I thought he was going to hit it," Altman said. "He's done it for us a number of times, and when it left his hand, I thought he hit it."

Woodfox's final attempt of his two-year career was instead inches long. The ball ricocheted off the iron to Meeks, who clutched it as time ran out.

Creighton wouldn't have needed any last-second heroics had it made free throws in the final 3½ minutes. Stinnett missed three attempts and Carter two, with his misfires coming right before Meeks hit his winning shot. Overall, Creighton made 11 of 19 free-throw attempts.

Woodfox led Creighton with 18 points against Kentucky but afterward focused on the shot he missed at the end. "Coach set up a good play," Woodfox said. "I just didn't knock it down."

"We should have won, and it's really hard when you have that opportunity and you don't finish it," Altman said.

The final-game turnout pushed Creighton's total attendance to a Valley record 302,676. The Bluejays' per-game average of 15,930 also set a league record and left them ranked 12th nationally.

The Kentucky game, although disappointing in its finish, was Creighton's last big moment under Altman.

Altman was aware of the potential for a rocky beginning to the 2009-10 season. The Bluejays had to replace starters in Woodfox and Dotzler, a steady and sometimes underappreciated point guard. Creighton also had a key backup, forward Kenton Walker, transfer during the offseason, leaving the Bluejays thin on the front line.

In addition, the Bluejays faced a challenging nonconference schedule with road games at Dayton, George Mason and New Mexico and a tournament in Florida in which they would face Michigan, with the possibility of games against Marquette, Xavier, Alabama, Baylor and Florida State.

With three veterans injured or ill and a fourth — point guard Antoine Young — hobbled by a knee injury, Creighton opened the season with a 90-80 loss at No. 21 Dayton. The Bluejays won a pair of home games before heading to Florida to face No. 15 Michigan in the first of three games in a tournament at the Walt Disney Sports Complex.

Antoine Young, who had battled a sore knee, played 35 minutes with only one turnover in a 2009 victory over Nebraska. "I liked the way Antoine was handling the ball," Altman said.

Creighton let a chance for an upset slip away, squandering a five-point lead in the final four minutes and needing Young's runner at the buzzer to force overtime. The Bluejays couldn't stop Manny Harris in the extra session, as the Michigan star scored half of the Wolverines' 14 points that secured an 83-76 win.

"We had our opportunity, but we had a couple of bad turnovers, and we couldn't get a defensive rebound," Altman said. "Our guys played hard, but we just didn't play very smart."

Creighton then lost 80-67 to Xavier, leaving the Bluejays playing Iona for seventh place in an early Sunday morning game that attracted a crowd of about 200. In a horrid performance, Creighton turned the ball over 21 times and got just 35 field-goal attempts in losing 63-55.

"I thought we'd respond better than we did," Altman said.

Creighton returned home to defeat Nebraska, then fell 75-72 at George Mason in a game that had turned on a technical foul called on Altman.

Stinnett said the coach apologized to the team after the game.

"But it shouldn't have come down to that," said Stinnett. "You don't think about turnovers and missed free throws until a time like this." Creighton committed 16 turnovers — four on its final 12 possessions — and 28 fouls. The Bluejays also missed three free throws in the final three minutes of the game.

A week later, Creighton traveled to Albuquerque to take on New Mexico at "The Pit," the school's legendary home court. For the first 20 minutes against a Lobos team that was 11-0 and ranked 19th, the Bluejays showed what kind of basketball team they could be. For the last 20 minutes, Creighton showed what kind of team it was, allowing New Mexico to rally from a 12-point halftime deficit and post a 66-61 win.

Stinnett tries to plead his case to Altman after receiving a technical foul against Missouri State in 2010.

"Hopefully, our basketball team can learn from this," said Altman, again apologetic. "We're soft. The coach is soft, the players are soft, and we have to get better."

Creighton closed its nonconference schedule with a win over Houston Baptist to improve to 5-6. The Bluejays opened Valley play with losses to Northern Iowa and Indiana State, then came back to win five of their next seven.

The fifth win would prove to be the final game Stinnett would play as a Bluejay.

Altman's brand of disciplined play chafed Stinnett, a free spirit on and off the court. He and Altman had clashed at times in the past, and Stinnett missed a game in 2008 because of "disciplinary action" from a locker-room incident after a loss to Arkansas-Little Rock.

But some of Stinnett's teammates thought the coach tended to cut him too much slack.

In a late-January game against Missouri State, Stinnett was called for the ninth technical foul of his career. Stinnett and referee Curtis Shaw exchanged words near the Missouri State bench midway through the second half. Two reporters seated near the bench heard Missouri State coach Cuonzo Martin tell Shaw that Stinnett had "cussed" at the official. Shaw hesitated briefly, then called the technical foul on Stinnett. The referee and Altman had a brief conversation, and Altman removed Stinnett from the game.

The coach put Stinnett back in for about a three-minute stint late in the contest. He finished with eight points while playing 19 minutes in the 76-72 win. The next day, Altman suspended Stinnett for conduct not acceptable to the team. He declined to comment about what led to the suspension or its length at the time. Nor did he comment about it at any time during the season.

Stinnett issued an apology in a text message to The World-Herald.

"I need to find some way to play hard and channel my emotions in a positive way," he said. "I apologize to Creighton, to my team and my coaching staff in my failure to represent the university with the respect and attitude I should."

Kenny Lawson had 17 points in a 2010 CIT victory over Fairfield at the Civic Auditorium.

Stinnett's absence proved to have no major impact on the Bluejays' play. They continued to win at home and lose on the road. A close win at Southern Illinois against a struggling Salukis team enabled them to finish 10-8 in the Valley, keeping alive the streak of 10 conference wins.

Their stay in St. Louis was short, though, as Bradley turned around an 11-point loss to Creighton in the regular-season finale and hammered out a 19-point win in the conference tournament. At 16-15, Creighton would have found its string of postseason appearances in jeopardy had it not been for a pair of alternative tournaments that had started up.

The CollegeInsider.com Tournament and the College Basketball Invitational offered opportunities to play on for teams not selected by either the NCAA or the NIT. Neither provided the participants with much glamour or publicity, but Creighton chose to play in the CIT.

Because the Qwest Center was unavailable, Creighton had to return to the Civic Auditorium for its opening-round game against South Dakota. The Bluejays won 89-78 in front of 4,348 to earn a second-round game against Fairfield, also at the Civic. Creighton won that, too, posting a 73-55 victory before 3,824.

In spite of being assured by CIT officials that conference opponents would not be paired up until the final, Creighton found itself traveling to Missouri State for its semifinal game. The Bluejays never led but managed to tie the game at 52-52 with 6:18 to play. Missouri State then scored the next 10 points and earned a spot in the CIT title game with a 67-61 victory.

Creighton ended the season 18-16, having played in a second-year tournament that most fans were not excited about, especially since the Jays didn't win it.

The 2009-10 season had turned out to be a hodgepodge of missed opportunities and bungled execution. By the end, the coveted streak of 20-win seasons was gone.

"This wasn't what we had in mind coming into the season," Creighton center Kenny Lawson said. "But we can all learn a lesson from it, not only in future years but in life also."

A month later, Lawson and the Creighton basketball community would be adjusting to life without Dana Altman.

Oregon, which was having difficulty finding a replacement for Ernie Kent, had turned its attention toward Altman, and on April 24, news broke that he was considering an offer from Oregon.

Altman welcomes Casey Harriman back to the bench in his last game in Omaha as Creighton's coach.

Creighton point guard Antoine Young was playing pickup games at Bellevue University when he checked his phone. He had multiple text messages asking for information about Altman leaving for Oregon. "In your head, at that point," Young said, "you're thinking, huh? How can they know before I know? I'm on the team."

Rasmussen called the players together that evening for a meeting at the Vinardi Center. Accompanied by DeVries, he broke the news to the seven players in attendance.

"Everybody was dead quiet," guard Josh Jones said. Altman is upstairs in his office, Rasmussen said, if you want to talk to him. All seven players crowded into the coach's office. Nobody said an ill word, Jones said. They thanked the coach and congratulated him on his opportunity. "He was real emotional," Jones said. "He said he appreciated his time with us."

Josh Jones and Kenny Lawson talked to reporters after learning of Altman's departure to Oregon.

Altman's 16-season stay at Creighton officially ended the next day when he accepted Oregon's offer. He was introduced as the Ducks' new head coach on April 26, 2010. At his introductory press conference in Eugene, he mentioned that he had said he wanted to finish his career at Arkansas when the Razorbacks hired him. He said he also had wanted to finish his career with the Bluejays when he returned to Creighton.

An Oregon official then handed him a "letter of intent." Altman scribbled his name, made his opening statement and invited questions. Reporters wasted no time asking about Arkansas.

"I think that's why they had us sign those papers," said Altman, earning laughs from the audience.

More than a few folks in Omaha found little humor in that exchange. A segment of Bluejay fans was upset by Altman's decision to leave. "I think there is a small percentage of people that are bitter about it to this day and haven't gotten over it," Sarver said.

Another segment of the fan base remains convinced that something changed after Altman returned from Arkansas, that he lost some of the fire in his belly and let things slide. Those closest to the coach say that's almost laughable.

"I've heard that, and I've never agreed with that," DeVries said. "Being around him, I thought he was just as passionate and motivated as he ever was to try to take Creighton to that next level, to take that next step."

But he might not have been as lucky, Rasmussen said. Altman had been able to jump-start his program by landing some under-the-radar recruits such as Kyle Korver, Rodney Buford and Ryan Sears who developed into great players.

Later, Altman was in the running to land a number of high-profile recruits. One was Russell Westbrook, who was ready to sign with Creighton, Rasmussen said, after a visit in the fall of 2005. Westbrook decided at the last minute to wait until the spring and wound up signing with UCLA. He became a first-round NBA draft pick, a three-time All-Star and an Olympic gold medalist.

"We were lucky with Korver and Buford and Sears and unlucky with Westbrook and some other guys that could have made a difference," Rasmussen said. "Even then, we were close. While it seemed like we were a long way away in those last three years under Dana, the reality was we weren't that far away."

> "While it seemed like we were a long way away in those last three years under Dana, the reality was we weren't that far away."
>
> **— Bruce Rasmussen**

Altman left Creighton with a school-record 327 victories, including 182 in league play. His teams won one outright Missouri Valley regular-season championship and shared two others in addition to claiming six conference tournament titles. Each of his last 13 teams participated in postseason play.

"I don't think people, to this day, give him enough credit for how driven he was to get this turned around," Sarver said. "For him to do what he did, with all the circumstances we were facing and as low as we were at the time, is just remarkable."

Altman treasures the 16 seasons he spent at Creighton. His relationship with Rasmussen developed into a deep friendship, and Altman credits the athletic director with much of the success on his coaching watch.

"When you're talking about Creighton basketball, Bruce Rasmussen is as big a figure as anyone," Altman said. "He allowed me to work, and he allowed me to do our job. It was never, 'You better get this done.' It was always, 'Coach, we have to figure out a way to get this done.' "

The bottom line is that they both got it done. Altman took a program that had been kicked to the gutter, pumped some life into it and took it to some unprecedented heights.

CREIGHTON
VALLEY

2010-13

A big-time player

Doug McDermott made his Creighton debut in a 2010 exhibition game against Northern State.
He led the Bluejays with 18 points, making six of nine shots from the field and all six of his free throws.
Teammate Kenny Lawson's assessment after the game would be repeated over and over.
"He's not the most physical player out there, but he's very efficient."

Doug McDermott celebrates a basket against North Texas in 2012.

Another secretive road trip

BRUCE RASMUSSEN KNEW DANA ALTMAN'S OREGON JOB wouldn't be a repeat of 2007, when Altman left for Arkansas and returned one day later. This time, the divorce was going to be final, and Rasmussen was going to have to find himself a new basketball coach.

Because Altman had been sought by other schools throughout his time at Creighton, Rasmussen had always been updating his list of possible candidates. Names were added to the list over the years, others were subtracted. One had always stayed at the top.

Greg McDermott spent four years at Iowa State after earlier coaching at Northern Iowa. He also had head coaching jobs at Wayne State and North Dakota State.

Greg McDermott's success at Northern Iowa — he had guided his alma mater to three straight NCAA tournament appearances — had led to his hiring by Iowa State in 2006. Four seasons of frustration followed for McDermott and Iowa State fans. The Cyclones struggled mightily in the competitive Big 12, going 6-10 in league play in his first season and 4-12 in each of the next three seasons. McDermott's overall record stood at 59-68 after four seasons, with finishes of seventh, 11th, 10th and 11th in conference standings.

The inability to retain talent in Ames compounded the coach's frustration with losing. He had several players transfer, including one, Wesley Johnson, who went on to become the Big East player of the year and a first-team All-American at Syracuse. McDermott also had to ask other players to leave because of violations of team rules.

Still, McDermott thought things were looking up a bit for the Cyclones in late April 2010. The players returning for the next season were attacking the offseason program with renewed commitment, and he and his staff were welcoming three recruits on visits to Ames.

"In retrospect, it was probably one of the better weekends I had had all winter and spring because of those kids we had on campus and because of the guys I had in the program," McDermott said. "I felt like we really had a chance to start moving forward."

McDermott was spending a quiet Saturday night at home — wife Theresa and daughter Sydney were out of town, oldest son Nick was still away at college and younger son Doug was out with friends — when the phone rang.

The caller was Rasmussen, making good on a promise he had made years earlier. Rasmussen had approached McDermott in 2005 after his Northern Iowa team had just lost in the first round of the Missouri Valley Conference tournament. " 'If Dana Altman ever leaves CU,' " McDermott said Rasmussen told him, " 'I don't care where you're coaching, you're going to be my first call.' I just kind of passed it off as Bruce trying to make me feel better."

But five years later, Rasmussen was on the phone explaining to McDermott that Altman was headed for Oregon.

"One of the first things he said was, 'I told you that you'd be my first call,' " McDermott said.

Rasmussen said he had one reservation when he placed the call: "He had a good job."

But McDermott also had a good sense of his situation at Iowa State. Cyclone fans were not yet banging at his door with pitchforks and torches, but another season like the previous four would likely be the end.

"I had five years on my contract, so contractually, I was on solid ground," McDermott said. "From a happiness standpoint, I was not. I've been in this business long enough to understand that we had gone four years without an NCAA tournament appearance and that we failed to really compete in the Big 12. If those things happen for a fifth year, your chances of surviving in this business are slim."

Rasmussen and McDermott agreed to meet the next day at the Marriott Hotel in West Des Moines.

In the morning, Rasmussen told his wife, Jill, that he was leaving on a trip. As she did 16 years earlier, when Rasmussen had headed to Wilber to meet Altman, Jill Rasmussen asked where he was going. Can't tell you, he replied. When will you be back? she asked. Can't say, he replied.

McDermott and Rasmussen talked for about three hours on that Sunday in West Des Moines, the interview made easier because of the relationship the men had built over the years. In addition, McDermott had become more familiar with what Creighton had to offer outside its basketball program because the school had tried to recruit his son Doug the previous summer.

Bruce Rasmussen said the Creighton head-coaching job attracted a lot of interest, but he declined to discuss any of his other contacts.

By the end of the meeting, McDermott said he was pretty sure he would accept Rasmussen's offer to replace Altman but needed a little more time. "I wanted to visit with my family about it," he said.

Part of that discussion involved son Doug, who had committed to Northern Iowa. Greg McDermott knew that if he took the Creighton job, his son would want to play for him.

Doug McDermott had blossomed into a Division I prospect in his junior season at Ames High School. Creighton recruited him, but because the Bluejays' immediate need was to sign a center and not a forward, the CU coaches wanted him to walk on his first season with the promise that he would receive a scholarship for his final four seasons.

"Even though we didn't have that extra scholarship available for him, Doug was a guy I felt very strongly about," said Creighton assistant coach Darian DeVries, who was in charge of McDermott's recruitment. "I told Coach (Altman) that best-case scenario, Doug was a guy who would develop into a really good Missouri Valley player for us. Worst-case scenario, he'd play a ton of minutes for us."

Greg McDermott did not try to recruit his son to Iowa State, in part because of advice he received from other coaches who had sons play for them. If you're going to play your son, McDermott was told, make sure he's either one of your best players or one of your worst. Doug didn't project to be either, so Iowa State was eliminated from his list of schools. Greg McDermott also admitted that he didn't want to expose his son to the culture that had developed within the Iowa State program.

Doug McDermott ultimately picked Northern Iowa — coached by his father's former assistant and close friend, Ben Jacobson — over Central Florida and signed in the fall of 2009.

McDermott walks through Creighton's campus with the Rev. John Schlegel, university president, on the way to the press conference announcing his hiring.

So Jacobson was the next to receive an unexpected call in April 2010.

"When we talked about Doug, he totally understood what is best for our family," Greg McDermott said. Jacobson later released Doug from his scholarship to UNI.

When Rasmussen returned home, he discovered that his veil of secrecy had been lifted. "Our girls tell me you met with Greg McDermott today," his wife said.

As it turned out, an Omaha television cameraman who was finishing an assignment was checking out of the Marriott in West Des Moines about the same time Rasmussen was arriving to meet with McDermott.

The cameraman started checking around, and soon other reporters were onto the story.

Meanwhile, McDermott was planning meetings with his boss, Iowa State Athletic Director Jamie Pollard, and with Cyclone players. "In a situation like this, there are always a lot of things to think about and a lot of things you need to do the right way before it becomes public or there are going to be hurt feelings," he said.

On Monday afternoon, McDermott called Rasmussen and accepted the Creighton job. The next day he was introduced as Creighton's 16th basketball coach.

Sort of. Rasmussen mistakenly referred to Greg as Doug in introducing the coach to the crowd. Given what would transpire over the next three seasons, Rasmussen's slip would become a recurring joke between the two men.

"The way it's turned out," McDermott said, "it's hard to be hard on him about that."

"The Creighton opportunity is something that would have intrigued me at any time," McDermott said. "Does that mean I would have taken it at any time? I can't say that."

Rasmussen has a stock answer whenever Greg McDermott brings up his introduction. "One of the roles of a good athletic director is to see things before they become obvious to others," Rasmussen said. "I just saw the reality before it was obvious to anyone else."

Greg McDermott's work at Iowa State had some Bluejay fans less than overjoyed about Rasmussen's choice to succeed Altman. At the press conference, Rasmussen disputed the notion that he had rushed into a decision.

"Even though it appears that this has been a quick process," Rasmussen said, "in reality, Coach has been interviewing for this job the last 20 years."

In regard to McDermott's record at Iowa State, Rasmussen said, "You look beyond results. I think he did a great job at Iowa State with what he had and was putting together a solid foundation. Sometimes we judge people too much by the final score and don't pay enough attention to the process. Greg consistently has done a great job with what he's had."

McDemott began the assessment of his first Creighton team. The Bluejays returned seniors in center Kenny Lawson Jr., forwards Wayne Runnels and Casey Harriman and guards Darryl Ashford and Kaleb Korver. But he faced a decision on whether the team would include another senior, P'Allen Stinnett, who had been suspended in late January. Stinnett had been working out on his own when the spring conditioning program began, with the idea that he might be able to rejoin the team.

After meeting with Rasmussen and other staff members, McDermott told Stinnett in May that the suspension would not be lifted. Stinnett had scored 1,024 points in less than three seasons, but he had caused his coaches and teammates too many headaches.

Greg McDermott gathers with his new team for the start of practice for the 2010-11 season.

McDermott had a talented group of underclassmen to mix with his five seniors.

Antoine Young was coming off a solid year as a sophomore starter at the point, and Josh Jones and Ethan Wragge had moved into the starting lineup near the end of their freshman seasons. Creighton also had added a Canadian recruit, Jahenns Manigat, who signed days before Altman announced he was leaving. Manigat stuck with his decision.

Adding intrigue was massive center Gregory Echenique, who joined the program the previous January after transferring from Rutgers. The 6-9 native of Venezuela had been heavily recruited by Creighton as a high school player out of New Jersey but had decided to enroll at the Big East school. He started 30 games as a freshman, averaging 8.4 points and 8.4 rebounds against some of the premier big men in the country. After playing seven games as a sophomore, he suffered a detached retina that required season-ending surgery. Echenique decided to transfer and considered a number of schools before enrolling at Creighton at the start of the second semester. Because he was unable to work out after undergoing the eye operation, his weight ballooned from 270 pounds to around 300.

McDermott's initial reaction when he met Echenique?

"I told him someday I hope we can get his weight lower than mine," the coach recalled, suppressing a laugh.

As he continued to get to know his players, McDermott added a transfer from Gonzaga. Grant Gibbs wouldn't be eligible for the 2010-11 season, but the coach believed the 6-5 guard would be a key to future success.

While at Iowa State, McDermott had unsuccessfully tried to recruit Gibbs, who as a junior led Linn-Mar High School to an Iowa Class 4-A state championship. "He was a huge priority," McDermott said. "Probably more than anything what attracted us to him was the intangibles he brings to the table that impact a program in positive ways. At that point in our Iowa State program, we desperately needed a guy like him."

Unfortunately, McDermott found himself fighting an uphill battle. Gibbs grew up a Gonzaga fan and had told his middle-school teachers that he would one day play for the Zags in Spokane, Wash. Before he committed to Gonzaga in November 2007, shortly before the beginning of his senior season at Linn-Mar, he called McDermott.

McDermott remembers the conversation and a subsequent one he had with Gibbs' mother, who was an Iowa State graduate. He admits that he recruited mom almost as hard as son.

"She wanted Grant close to home, but she also knew that he grew up a huge Gonzaga fan," McDermott said. "When Judy and I talked, she was a little distraught. As was I. She was crying. I wasn't, but I was close."

> "I told him someday I hope we can get his weight lower than mine."
>
> **— Greg McDermott, relating an early conversation with Gregory Echenique**

Gibbs wasn't happy with his role at Gonzaga, and injuries limited his court time. A torn labrum in his shoulder that required surgery forced him to redshirt as a freshman. He came back to play in 24 games during the 2009-10 season, averaging nine minutes, 2.2 points and 1.9 rebounds a game. A severe case of tendinitis in his knee hampered his effectiveness when he did get on the court.

Shortly after the season ended, Gibbs knew he wouldn't be returning to Spokane. He was granted his release and narrowed his decision to Creighton or Northern Iowa. He ended up picking Creighton because he wanted to play for McDermott, the coach, and with McDermott, the player.

"I think the relationship that Grant and I had during his recruitment in high school helped," Greg McDermott said. "But I think the relationship Grant developed with Doug really was the difference. I think he felt that Doug was going to be a pretty good player."

Gibbs had made another assessment, Greg McDermott said. "I think Grant saw the pieces here that had the makings of a very good basketball team."

When Doug McDermott first stepped onto Creighton's campus in June 2010, no one was quite sure what to make of the slender, 6-7 Iowan. In high school, he had played on the junior varsity his first two seasons before becoming the sixth man on the varsity as a junior.

While he had blossomed as a player in his final two seasons, he was best known for being a teammate of Harrison Barnes, considered one of the country's top recruits. Barnes had created a stir when he announced in the fall of 2009 that he was headed for North Carolina.

McDermott showed up at Creighton weighing 190 pounds. Many, including his father, believed he was a candidate for a redshirt season in order to gain the strength needed to survive in the more physical style of collegiate play.

He was still on the redshirt bubble when Creighton started preseason practice in the fall. That started to change when Wragge missed practice time with a foot injury. McDermott looked good in a closed scrimmage the Bluejays had with Colorado, then scored 18 points and grabbed seven rebounds in a 79-67 exhibition victory over Northern State.

"Doug's a talented offensive player, and he's a work in progress on the defensive end," Greg McDemott said after the game. "His lack of strength hurts him at times on the glass, and that's why I think he could benefit from a redshirt (season). But the more I've been around this team, we probably need his offensive punch in the lineup."

Some Creighton fans got their first look at incoming freshman Doug McDermott during summer-league games.

Greg McDermott's players were coming together on the court, partly because of what was happening in the locker room.

The Bluejays were convinced that better chemistry could improve their performance from the previous year, when an 18-16 campaign ended an 11-year streak of 20-win seasons. Many of the shortcomings could have been blamed on lack of execution and missed assignments, but lack of cohesion off the court also may have contributed to the breakdowns.

"Something was a little different, but I'm not going to get into all that was wrong," Young said. "I'll just say it's a lot better this year. We all hang out together. We're just a big family right now."

Several insiders said a rivalry between Stinnett and Cavel Witter had created a tense locker room. Players said that when it came to chemistry, the teammates who had arrived were just as important as those who had left. "We brought in some new guys this year, and they all seem to fit in well," Wragge said. "They're here for the team and not for their individual priorities."

Players enjoyed McDermott's upbeat approach, but they also reported grueling practices, especially a "boot camp" that started drills in the fall of 2010. "It was rough," Kaleb Korver said. "Someone puked about three stations in."

The final factor was the new coach. "It feels a lot different," Young said. "He lets us play, and he interacts with us. He understands our generation and has fun with us. That helps on the court."

Creighton opened its 2010-11 season against Alabama State, and the Doug McDermott redshirt questions ended. He started, becoming the first freshman since Ryan Sears in 1997 to start his first game. McDermott scored 16 points and grabbed seven rebounds in 32 minutes, while Young led the Bluejays to a 71-57 win with 21 points in 34 minutes of play.

The game was the first of four the Bluejays played in the Global Sports Hy-Vee Challenge, which had been arranged by Altman's staff. The tournament called for Creighton to play three home games against low Division I opponents with one feature game — a neutral-site meeting in Des Moines against Greg McDermott's old Iowa State team.

While McDermott might have found it uncomfortable to face his old players, fans were treated to an entertaining game from start to finish. Creighton got double-figure scoring from all five of its starters and led by a dozen points early in the second half, but Iowa State rallied to go ahead 88-85. Scott Christopherson had a chance to close out the win at the free-throw line with nine seconds to play, but he missed the first shot of a one-and-one, and Young pushed the ball up the court before getting fouled on a drive to the basket with 3.7 seconds to play. He made the first free throw and intentionally missed the second, ran down the long rebound and was fouled again. Young tied the game with two free throws with 1.6 seconds left.

Antoine Young had 21 points and six assists against Iowa State in 2010. On the facing page, the backboard lighting shows that time had expired before the game-winning shot.

Iowa State forward Jamie Vanderbeken won the game with a 30-foot shot that dropped through the net at the game's end. Whether Vanderbeken's shot beat the buzzer was uncertain. The officials had no courtside monitor to review the play, so the shot counted. Pictures shot by newspaper photographers and video recorded by television cameramen later indicated that Vanderbeken still had the ball in his hands when the red lights in the backboard lit to signal that time had expired.

"It's unfortunate because you hate to have a game decided when you don't know for sure," Greg McDermott said.

Creighton won its next game but lost its next three — at Northwestern, at home to No. 21 Brigham Young and at Nebraska. The Bluejays did succeed in holding high-scoring BYU guard Jimmer Fredette to 13 points, which would prove to be his season low.

VANDERBEKEN
23
DOC

A bounce-back win over St. Joseph's featured a pair of outstanding individual efforts by Lawson and Wragge. Lawson scored a career-high 30 points and set a Qwest Center record with 18 rebounds in the 82-75 win. Wragge, still slowed by the foot problem, made six 3-point baskets, including four in five possessions in one second-half stretch, and scored 22 points.

The win left Creighton 5-4 and was significant in that it would be the last game the Bluejays would play without Echenique. The center became eligible at the end of first-semester classes, and he made his long-awaited debut in a Dec. 18 game against Idaho State.

Echenique scored 12 points, grabbed five rebounds and blocked three shots in the 66-60 win. Two plays in the game illustrated what Echenique could bring to the Bluejays. The first was when Young ran 6-0, 170-pound guard Kenny McGowen into a screen set by Echenique. McGowen might have had a better chance getting through a concrete wall, hitting the floor like a rag doll after running into Echenique. The second play came late in the game when Idaho State's Chase Grabau tried to drive to the basket. Echenique didn't just block the shot. He spiked it volleyball-style, sending the ball out to midcourt.

Greg McDermott praised Kenny Lawson's work ahead of the St. Joseph's game. Lawson was the Missouri Valley Conference preseason player of the year for the 2010-11 season.

"He's a force on defense," Doug McDermott said. "He gets a hold of that one, and he's throwing it into the seats. He's an animal."

Greg McDermott said Echenique was bringing a different dynamic to the Bluejays both offensively and defensively. His size, the coach said, makes him difficult to handle one-on-one.

"I know because I've tried to guard him a couple of times," McDermott said.

He had chosen to avoid running through an Echenique screen, however. "I was born at night," said the coach, a smile coming to his face. "But not last night."

Gregory Echenique had 12 points and five rebounds in his Bluejay debut against Idaho State in 2010. He also had three blocked shots, including one that he spiked like a volleyball out to half court.

Creighton closed out its nonconference schedule with two more wins, leaving the Bluejays 8-4 heading into Missouri Valley play. But they faced their conference schedule without Wragge, whose foot injury — which had been diagnosed as plantar fasciitis — had again flared up and left him unable to play.

The Bluejays opened league play 4-1 but then came a series of tough-luck losses — a 2-pointer at Indiana State when an opponent hit an over-the-shoulder follow-shot at the buzzer, a 1-pointer in front of a packed house at Missouri State when Doug McDermott lost his man on an inbounds play, a 5-pointer at Northern Iowa and a 3-pointer at Drake.

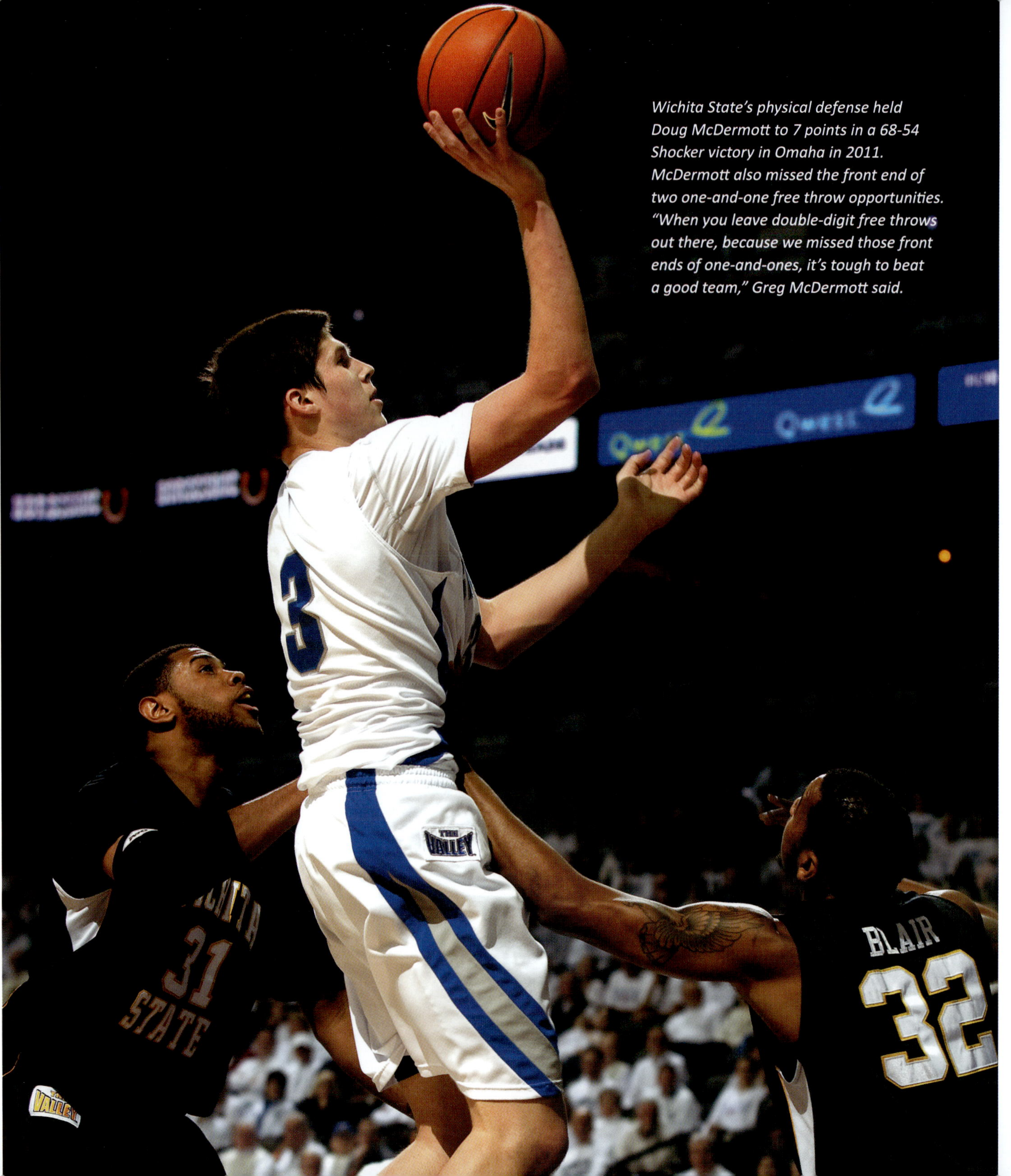

Wichita State's physical defense held Doug McDermott to 7 points in a 68-54 Shocker victory in Omaha in 2011. McDermott also missed the front end of two one-and-one free throw opportunities. "When you leave double-digit free throws out there, because we missed those front ends of one-and-ones, it's tough to beat a good team," Greg McDermott said.

Games were slipping away, and it wasn't just because the Bluejays were getting outmanned on the court. Greg McDermott sensed a lack of leadership and didn't see an immediate remedy. But he suspected that the leader his team needed might be a player who wasn't even practicing at the time. Gibbs was still recovering from an offseason knee operation, so he spent the bulk of practice working with trainers or sitting on the sidelines.

"I did spend a lot of time talking with Coach Mac that year," Gibbs recalled. "He told me the one thing we were lacking was a guy that could lead. He said that more than anything next year, no matter how much I played, that he needed me to be that kind of guy. I started seeing things from a coach's perspective."

At the same time, he was laying the foundation with his teammates to assume such a role.

"When you're not playing, you can't go around getting into everybody's stuff," he said. "I just started trying to build relationships with everyone on the team, so guys could get to the point where they could trust me."

He also texted his coach with ideas on how he could help. "Obviously, I knew I was still going to have to go out and prove myself on the court, but I think what I did during that season really paid off."

A couple of mid-February home wins left Creighton with 17 victories, but the Bluejays played poorly in a BracketBusters game at Akron and let a chance for a big upset at Wichita State slip away. Echenique's basket had tied the game at 65-65 with 1:11 to play, and Creighton had a chance to take the lead, but Doug McDermott missed a one-and-one free-throw opportunity with 33 seconds to play.

"He knows he has a lot of areas in which he can improve, and that's the great news with him," Greg McDermott said of freshman son Doug. "He's far from reaching his ceiling."

The Shockers' Aaron Ellis then made a layup with two seconds left, giving his team a 67-65 victory and handing Creighton its seventh loss of the season by five points or fewer. The Bluejays closed out the regular season by defeating Northern Iowa at home, running its streak of winning at least 10 games in league play to 15 consecutive seasons.

Three days later, Doug McDermott made some Missouri Valley history when he became the first freshman to earn first-team all-conference honors since Wichita State's Cleo Littleton in the 1951-52 season. McDermott also was named the league's freshman and newcomer of the year. Young gained a spot on the All-Valley second team, Echenique was picked to the all-defensive team and joined McDermott on the all-newcomer team, while Manigat and McDermott earned spots on the all-freshman team.

McDermott finished the regular season fourth in scoring in the Valley and second in rebounding. Perhaps the most striking aspect of McDermott's first season was its consistency. He scored 10 points or more in 26 of Creighton's 31 regular-season games, ranking in a tie for second in the nation for most double-figure scoring games by a freshman. He scored 15 points or more and grabbed seven rebounds or more in a Valley-best 11 of 18 conference games. His eight double-doubles led the league.

McDermott and his teammates knew they would have to win the conference tournament to make the NCAA field in 2011, and they opened their bid with a hard-fought 60-57 win over Northern Iowa in the quarterfinals. The victory advanced the Bluejays to the semifinals against Missouri State, which had ridden its veterans to a league championship.

Creighton was sniffing an upset, leading 39-27 early in the second half, when it worked McDermott free for a wide-open 3-point attempt. His shot didn't go down, but Kyle Weems' did on the Bears' next possession, trimming the Bluejays' lead.

"I just couldn't get it to go down, and it kind of turned things down," McDermott said afterward.

Missouri State held Creighton to three baskets in the final 11 minutes and 51 seconds in grinding out a 60-50 win, leaving the Bluejays 19-14 and pondering their postseason alternatives.

The Jays' record ruled out the NCAA and the NIT. Creighton officials indicated that they would be open to playing in either the pay-to-play College Basketball Invitational or the CollegeInsider.com Tournament. The CBI required host schools to meet a minimum financial guarantee of $70,000, the CIT $30,000.

Eventually, the Bluejays picked the CBI. So did Oregon, which had made a late-season charge under first-year coach Dana Altman.

The Ducks had been 8-10 midway through January before going on a 6-2 spurt that included victories over eventual NCAA tournament qualifiers Washington and Southern California. They then lost their last four regular-season games before wins over Arizona State and UCLA, another NCAA team, got them to the Pac-10 tournament semifinals. Washington eliminated Oregon, leaving the Ducks to enter the CBI at 16-17.

Jahenns Manigat tips the ball away from Marcus Jordan of Central Florida.

Because of the Altman connection, Creighton and Oregon arranged with tournament officials that the only way they would play each other would be in the event's unique best-of-three championship series.

Creighton opened its CBI run with an 85-74 win over San Jose State, then scored a season-high 102 points in turning back Davidson by 10 points. Playing a third straight home game, Creighton faced Central Florida for the right to advance to the championship series.

With rumors swirling throughout the Qwest Center that former NBA great Michael Jordan would show up to watch son Marcus play for the Black and Gold Knights, Creighton put on another dominating offensive showing in racing to an 82-64 victory. His Airness failed to make an appearance in Omaha.

Meanwhile, Oregon had won home games against Weber State, Duquesne and Boise State.

Altman was predictably uneasy about having to play the opening game of the championship series in Omaha.

"I don't want to play Creighton," Altman said. "I know the guys, the staff, 'Ras.' You never like playing people that you're that close to."

Altman and his team arrived at the Qwest Center about 75 minutes before the March 29 game. He headed for the visiting locker room — a place he said he had never seen during his time in Omaha — and then did something he almost never does.

Altman's normal pregame routine is to stay in the locker room until just before game time. This time, he sought out his old players as they warmed up on the floor. He shook hands with Harriman and Korver and Young.

Oregon coach Dana Altman sought out his old Bluejay players on the court before the game.

When he threw an arm around Lawson, Altman choked up. "You spend a lot of time with those guys," Altman said later.

Creighton had drawn a total of just more than 14,000 for its first three CBI games. A crowd of 12,381 showed up for Altman's homecoming, and the warm applause he received seemed to surprise him.

Young said the sight of his former coach on the other bench was a little weird.

"He was calling out plays that I knew from last year," Young said. "I knew what they were running, because I ran it here."

Did it help?

"It didn't hurt," Young said.

Doug McDermott scored 21 points for Creighton, while Echenique had 15 points, nine rebounds and four blocked shots. Young and Lawson turned in strong efforts, but the shot of the game might have been the dagger that Jones threw in late in the 84-76 victory.

Creighton was clinging to a 4-point lead late in the game when the Bluejays broke the Ducks' press and found Jones all alone in the corner with about 27 seconds left on the shot clock. The conventional play would have been to pass the ball out and run time off the 35-second clock.

Jones, though, was no conventional player. The sophomore guard let a shot fly that swished through the net to expand Creighton's lead to 7 points with 1:23 left. So, Josh, what were you thinking when you took that shot?

"I wasn't thinking," he said, smiling. "I know that the safe play would have been to pull it out, but I was wide open. There wasn't anyone on my side of the court. Except for the time and the score, it was a great shot."

Darryl Ashford defends against Oregon's Garrett Sim. On the facing page, Altman congratulates Josh Jones after the 2011 game, which drew a CBI record attendance of 12,381.

Jones was right in front of the Creighton bench when he launched the shot and said he heard several teammates yell, "No, no, no!" before he let loose. A collective "Yes!" followed after it dropped through the net.

Greg McDermott admitted he was one of those yelling no.

"He plays without fear," McDermott said.

Altman said after the game that he appreciated the fans' kindness — and perhaps their forgiveness.

"I was here 16 years, and we did what we could," Altman said. "It didn't end the way everybody wanted it to. I know a lot of people are disappointed in me. But for 16 years, people were unbelievable to us here. ... Tonight was no different."

The teams headed to Eugene, Ore., for the final two games of the series. After an off day, Oregon evened the series with a 71-58 win. Doug McDermott spent most of the game in foul trouble and attempted just four shots, finishing with 6 points.

For the first time in program history, Creighton played a basketball game in April when it took the floor at Matthew Knight Arena for the final game of the series. With the score tied at 69, the Jays had a chance to get the game's final shot when Young stepped into backcourt on the new arena's avant-garde court, which featured a fir tree outline and a thin, almost invisible, half-court line.

Greg McDermott said the midcourt line was difficult to see from the coaching box just a few feet away. "This is a beautiful building," he said. "I just wish they had a visible half-court line."

Oregon got the ball on the turnover and put the game in the hands of E.J. Singler, who drove hard to the basket before pulling up to launch the game-winning basket.

The 71-69 victory ended Altman's first season in Eugene with a championship.

Altman admitted that the win left him with mixed feelings. "There are four or five guys over in that other locker room that I got very close to over the years," he said.

No one on the Creighton side felt good about losing the final game, but the CBI experience allowed the Bluejays to finish the season on an up note. Creighton had shown signs of progress throughout Greg McDermott's first season as coach, but winning four games and finishing second in the tournament appeared to alter the mentality heading into the offseason.

"I think our players are in a lot better place mentally, individually and as a group, than they were three weeks ago," Rasmussen said after returning to Omaha. "I think our fans are in a better place and more enthused about next year and future years."

> "I think our fans are in a better place and more enthused about next year and future years."
>
> **— Bruce Rasmussen, after the Bluejays' runner-up finish in the 2011 College Basketball Invitational tournament**

The tournament also allowed the Bluejays to finish with a 23-16 record, a source of pride to the players who had seen the 20-win streak end in the spring of the previous season.

Another positive was that the tournament had provided the Bluejays with a glimpse of what the next season would bring in terms of style of play. McDermott had focused on defense throughout his first season in Omaha, believing a grind-it-out style gave this group the best chance to win.

In the postseason, he opened things up offensively, and the result was that the Bluejays averaged 88 points in their first four CBI games.

"The tournament meant a lot to this team," said Young, who finished the season with 511 points, giving Creighton two 500-point scorers for the first time since Bob Harstad and Chad Gallagher in 1990-91. "We got some experience. We took advantage of it."

Creighton's other 500-point scorer, of course, was Doug McDermott. He finished the season with 581, the most by a freshman in Missouri Valley history. Longtime followers of the program were starting to talk about McDermott as the best freshman in Creighton history.

"It's definitely been a good year for me, but I can't be worried about comparisons with other guys," McDermott said. "What we've done is not acceptable to the expectations we have here at Creighton. I'd rather be known as the guy that took Creighton to four NCAA tournaments rather than the guy that led Creighton in scoring."

Doug McDermott's 581 points during the 2010-11 season ranked ahead of Rodney Buford's 421, Kyle Korver's 291 and Bob Harstad's 289 as freshmen. McDermott also became the first Creighton freshman to score 30 points or more in a game since Buford in 1995.

Adjusting to higher expectations

The anonymity that accompanied Doug McDermott into his freshman season was gone in the fall of 2011, replaced by expectation.

In the previous decade of college basketball, only two other freshmen — Carmelo Anthony and Kevin Durant — had matched McDermott's feat of at least 525 points, 270 rebounds and 40 3-point baskets. Both had become stars in the NBA.

McDermott followed his stellar first season by earning a spot on the United States' under-19 national team, which finished fifth in the world championship tournament. The team was a disappointment, but he wasn't, emerging as one of its most consistent players and finishing second in minutes played.

Creighton freshmen, from left, Austin Chatman, Avery Dingman, Nevin Johnson and Geoff Groselle arrived on campus in 2011.

McDermott seemed unaffected by the attention that suddenly was being directed his way.

"I'm not a guy that reflects on the past," McDermott said. "I'm about coming to work each day and trying to get better. I can't really think about all the recognition because I know, as a team, we have a lot of expectations on us."

The Bluejays started working on meeting those expectations in midsummer when they began practicing for an exhibition trip to the Bahamas in August. Creighton had a core of experience for the 2011-12 season, with four returning starters — McDermott, Young, Echenique and Manigat — along with top reserve Jones.

Plenty of new faces, though, had to be integrated into the rotation. Ethan Wragge hadn't played since Christmas. Gibbs had a year of transfer rust to shake off. Will Artino, a slender but skilled big man, also was coming off a season of inactivity after redshirting, while four scholarship freshmen — Austin Chatman, Avery Dingman, Geoff Groselle and Nevin Johnson — needed to learn the system.

Creighton had 10 days of practice before leaving for the Bahamas. They played four games against so-so competition. While that helped the players' confidence, the team gained something else from the trip.

"I don't think anyone could look at how we played on the trip and say, 'This team is going to win a lot of games,'" Gibbs said. "But as far as the chemistry we established, I think the way guys got along and played together on that trip gave us a glimpse of our potential. We could see that guys were going to buy in."

Gibbs' Gonzaga experience had soured him a bit, and teammates' selfish attitudes had made life miserable at times.

The trip to the Bahamas, Gibbs said, re-energized him.

"All the guys hung out together," he said. "It reminded me of playing in high school. You've grown up with those kids, and you've played with them your whole life. Somehow, we were able to develop that same kind of chemistry."

The expectations continued to grow as Creighton began preseason practice. So did the sense of urgency for Young, the Bluejays' three-year starter at the point. The senior had joined the program two seasons after Creighton had made its last NCAA tournament appearance in 2007.

"I'm tired of sitting at home and watching it," he said.

Antoine Young goes up for a dunk at the 2011 Bluejay Madness event before the season's start.

In Young, McDermott and Echenique, Creighton arguably had three of the best players at their positions in the Missouri Valley. Young had earned second-team All-Valley recognition the previous year while averaging almost 36 minutes per game. He led the league in assist-to-turnover ratio for the second straight season and became the first player since 1993 to lead the Valley in assists while also ranking in the top 10 in scoring.

Greg McDermott figured Young's effectiveness as a senior could increase with the addition of Chatman, a lightning-quick freshman from the Dallas suburb of The Colony. Chatman could provide Young with some much-needed relief at the point, and the coaching staff planned to play them together at spells in the coming season.

"Having both of them will allow us to play faster, and I think that fits Antoine's game," McDermott said. "Antoine will have to adjust to playing faster but not in a hurry. And if he makes sure he's a point guard first and a scorer second, he's going to have a great year, and we're going to have a great year."

The 2011-12 season opener against North Carolina A&T turned into a laugher for Josh Jones and Doug McDermott. The Bluejays won 97-65.

Young had the offense geared up in the opening two games as the Bluejays hung 97 and 95 points on a pair of overmatched opponents at the CenturyLink Center, Omaha's newly renamed arena. Creighton then headed to Birmingham, Ala., for its first road trip. Alabama-Birmingham was coming off an NCAA tournament appearance and had won 38 straight non-conference home games.

Creighton led by 12 points early in the second half, but Alabama-Birmingham rallied to tie the game at 50 with 5:55 to play. Creighton then closed the game with a 20-10 spurt to walk away with a 70-60 win that, in all likelihood, would have been a 15-point loss a year earlier.

"When they made that run at us ... last year, and I'm speaking for myself, I would have hung my head and given in to it," said Doug McDermott, who led the Bluejays with 27 points. "But tonight, in the back of our minds, we knew we were going to win this game."

That victory, Gibbs said two years later, has kept on giving.

"I think a lot of people have forgotten about that game, but I still revert back to that one when I think about the success we've been able to have here," Gibbs said. "That was our first road test, and they had a decent team. We found a way to win that one by grinding our way through it and making some big shots and having everyone contribute. After the game, it was like we realized that we have a shot here to win a lot of games if things go our way."

Gregory Echenique (00) had 15 points, nine rebounds and two blocked shots in the 82-59 rout of Iowa.

IOWA
35
00
16:47
1ST
IOWA
ARENA
Follow us on
IOWA
5
12

McDermott goes inside on Nebraska's Bo Spencer, left, and Toney McCray to score 2 of his 24 points, 17 of which came in the second half.

Creighton followed that performance by embarrassing Iowa 82-59 in Des Moines, before hanging 104 points on Campbell in Omaha.

The Bluejays were a confident group when they headed to San Diego State for a game that would close out November and test their toughness.

They fell behind by 17 points in the first 15 minutes to put some added juice into the sellout crowd of 12,414 at Viejas Arena. Creighton used a 16-4 run to pull within four at the end of the half, then outbattled the Aztecs in the final 20 minutes to pull out an 85-83 win.

"We stopped taking it from them and started throwing punches back," said Wragge, who scored 19 points off the bench. "We quit letting them push us around, and then when we started knocking down a few shots, we built on it." Wragge's putback with 16 seconds to play gave Creighton an 84-81 lead. Known for his marksmanship from beyond the arc, Wragge actually had three 2-point baskets to go along with his four 3-pointers. He also turned in a couple of key defensive plays in the second half.

"He isn't known for his defense, but he came up big on that end tonight," said Doug McDermott, who scored 25 points and had 12 rebounds in becoming the first Bluejay to string together five straight games of 20 points or more since Rodney Buford in 1996.

McDermott made it six in a row — and also became the first Creighton player to post three straight double-doubles since Nate King in 1994 — when he scored 24 points and had 12 rebounds as the Bluejays improved to 7-0 with a 76-66 win over Nebraska.

St. Joseph's handed Creighton its first loss, using its perimeter athleticism to post an 80-71 victory in Philadelphia. The Bluejays bounced back to close out their pre-Valley schedule with wins over Houston Baptist, Tulsa and Northwestern, with McDermott scoring 87 points in the three games.

He had 35 in the 83-64 rout of Tulsa, leaving Golden Hurricane coach Doug Wojcik proclaiming after the game: "I thought that guy single-handedly broke the spirit of my team. He's a really, really, really good player."

How good was McDermott against Tulsa?

"Doug was ridiculous," Gibbs said. "I say a lot of times that Doug gets a quiet 25 (points). There wasn't anything quiet about him tonight. He was spectacular."

Creighton's quick start and McDermott's play pumped life back into a fan base eager to end a five-year NCAA tournament drought. Season-ticket sales and attendance had slipped slightly the previous two seasons, along with the Bluejays' level of success. But with McDermott second in the nation in scoring and the team ranked in the top 25 in both national polls, a Creighton basketball ticket once again became a hot commodity.

Austin Chatman tries to get past Missouri State's Anthony Downing, who scored 26 against the Jays. "They came into our house, punched us in the mouth, and we really didn't do anything about it," Greg McDermott said.

A crowd of 17,665 — third-largest in program history — turned out for the Bluejays' Missouri Valley opener against a young Missouri State team. They left disappointed after witnessing career scoring nights by the Bears' Kyle Weems (31 points) and Anthony Downing (26), as Missouri State pulled off a 77-65 upset.

The loss was doubly troubling because Creighton was scheduled to play next at Wichita State, the team expected to challenge the Bluejays for the conference championship. The players knew an 0-2 start would leave them working against history: No Missouri Valley team that had lost its first two conference games had won the championship since the 1992-93 season, when Illinois State did it.

"We definitely put ourselves in a tougher position performing like we did against Missouri State," Gibbs said. "But there's no panic with our guys."

Fans' fingers might have been inching closer to the panic button when the Shockers' hot 15-minute stretch turned a 17-9 deficit into a 46-39 lead, leaving the sellout crowd of 10,506 in a frenzy. But the defense that had deserted Creighton against Missouri State reappeared. The Bluejays held Wichita State to 29 percent shooting in the final 20 minutes and turned the game with a 21-5 spurt that featured 8 points by Jones and 7 by Gibbs.

The Shockers held McDermott to a season-low 12 points, more than 12 under his average.

CREIGHTON
00
PROSSER
44
SHAYOK
23
3

Jahenns Manigat celebrates a 3-point shot over Illinois State's Tyler Brown in a victory at the CenturyLink Center. The Bluejays coupled a 10-of-11 shooting start from the field with defensive tenacity to break out to an 18-point lead eight minutes into the game. Manigat finished with 11 points, one of six Jays in double figures.

"We had talked before the game that it was important for guys to step up," said McDermott, who took just nine shots and made four. "We got some other guys going tonight, and I just tried to impact that game in different ways."

The win started the Bluejays on an 11-game winning streak. McDermott scored 44 points in a win at Bradley. Young burned Northern Iowa for 21 when the Panthers paid too much attention to McDermott. Gibbs had 12 points, 10 assists and seven rebounds in a victory over Illinois State. The Bluejays survived a furious rally at Missouri State to pull out a one-point win. McDermott had 30 points in a win at Drake, overcoming a Bulldog student section that chanted, "You're adopted (clap, clap, clap-clap-clap)," as he prepared to shoot free throws.

Creighton came close to matching its season-high scoring total when it had six players score in double figures in a 102-74 clubbing of Illinois State on the first day of February, and the Bluejays appeared to be reaching a historic level of play for the program. The win boosted Creighton to 12th and 13th in the national polls with a 21-2 record.

Gregory Echenique found pink shoes to his liking, contributing 14 points and 10 rebounds in a win over Bradley. The 2012 "pinkout" game, an effort to raise cancer awareness, drew 18,436. The cause was special to Greg McDermott, whose wife, Theresa, had been diagnosed with breast cancer six years earlier.

The streak came to an end on a cold, gray day in Cedar Falls, when Northern Iowa's Anthony James' step-back 24-footer beat the buzzer to give the Panthers a 65-62 win, touching off the biggest celebration in the six-year history of the McLeod Center. The victory was especially sweet to the Northern Iowa fans, still stinging over the loss of one-time recruit Doug McDermott to Creighton.

The loss to the Panthers might have seemed at the time like just a speed bump for Creighton's championship hopes. But the wheels were coming off the Bluejay Express.

Playing three days later at Evansville, Creighton scored just one point in the final five minutes and 25 seconds and lost 65-57 to the 13-13 Purple Aces. The Bluejays had gone from being alone atop the Missouri Valley standings to trailing Wichita State by a game heading into their meeting at the CenturyLink Center.

The deficit grew to two games by the time the Shockers were finished with an 89-68 dismantling that left the record crowd of 18,735 silent.

Things unraveled on the Bluejays to the point where father and son almost butted heads as Greg McDermott delivered a stern lecture to his son. "He had the right to," Doug said afterward. "I wasn't playing well."

Worse than playing poorly, the coach didn't think Doug was playing hard. "He's one of our best players, and there's a lot that goes with that," Greg said. "That's being able to compete your tail off on the defensive end when shots aren't falling."

The Bluejays were in shock after being routed at home by Wichita State.

The win left Wichita State with a two-game lead with three to play. It was Creighton's worst home loss since Nebraska also won by 21 points in December 1995 and the Bluejays' worst loss at home to the Shockers since a 22-point setback in 1953.

Creighton's February fizzle left the Bluejays in a delicate spot with two weeks left in the regular season. Barring a Wichita State collapse down the stretch, Creighton had lost its chance to win a championship. Its once sunny NCAA tournament hopes were starting to fade.

But while voices outside the program were calling for changes, Greg McDermott did what his coaching instincts told him the situation required: Stay the course. The calendar told McDermott that this was not the time for radical changes on offense or defense.

"If this were the first week in December or we were six or seven games into our season, and we had lost some games we were supposed to win, then maybe you might be able to risk trying to juggle some things," he said. "But when you're in the middle of February, and you've been successful for the first 23 games, it really makes no sense to try to reinvent the wheel."

That steady approach produced wins in the final four regular-season games, although three of them tested the cardiac worthiness of the followers of the program.

After an easy win over Southern Illinois, Creighton escaped its BracketBusters meeting with Long Beach State when Young's basket with one second to play produced an 81-79 win.

Young got to celebrate Senior Night three days later when Jones, his longtime buddy, buried a jumper with 22.8 seconds to play in overtime in a 93-92 shootout with Evansville. The Jays had to overcome an arena record 43 points by the Purple Aces' Colt Ryan, who made 17 of 24 shots. He missed his last one, with Jones guarding him.

Young releases the winning shot against Long Beach State in 2012. "I've kind of dreamed about making big shots in front of the home crowd in my hometown," the Bellevue West graduate said. "It's crazy that it actually came true."

"I've known Antoine since the fifth grade," Jones said. "I needed him to go away with this (win). You don't want the last memory for someone you care about so much to be something so sad."

Creighton closed out the regular season with a 61-60 victory at Indiana State. The Sycamores had a shot at the win, but Dwayne Lathan missed a jumper at the buzzer to leave Creighton 25-5 and heading to the Missouri Valley tournament as the No. 2 seed.

Jones and Young celebrate after the Bluejays' overtime victory over Evansville. Jones' game-winning basket came three days after Young's against Long Beach. Against the Aces, Young's shot late in regulation had rimmed out, but Gregory Echenique tipped it back in to force overtime. "I don't remember much after Antoine took the shot," Echenique said of his tip-in.

A methodical quarterfinal victory over Drake set up a third meeting in less than a month with Evansville. After winning at home and playing Creighton to a one-point decision in Omaha, the Purple Aces had no answers for the suddenly reinvigorated Bluejays, who roared into the championship game with a 99-71 rout.

The Bluejays got a giant boost inside from Echenique, who scored a season-high 20 points, blocked three shots and had nine rebounds. "That's the best game — offensively, defensively and rebounding — that Gregory has played this year," Jones said.

The win put Creighton in the tournament championship game for a 12th time, but the Bluejays' opponent wasn't the top-seeded Shockers, who were upset by Illinois State in the semifinals.

The athletic Redbirds, trying desperately to play their way into the NCAA tournament, gave Creighton everything it could handle. After nine ties and 14 lead changes, the No. 25 Bluejays pulled out an 83-79 overtime victory. McDermott scored 33 points and Gibbs added a season-high 20 as Creighton assured itself of a return to the NCAA field for the first time since 2007.

"It's good to have Creighton basketball back where it needs to be," said Young, who at the start of the season had complained that he had grown tired of watching March Madness on television. "To get it done this last year is just tremendous," the senior said.

Wragge tries to screen two Redbirds as Gibbs prepares to launch a 3-point shot. Gibbs' 20 points topped his previous season high of 12. "When I go back and watch it this week, I think I'll appreciate what a great game it was and how well our guys executed on both ends of the court," Greg McDermott said after the Valley title game. "But when you're in the middle of it, you're just trying to grind it out."

Creighton spent the week between its tournament championship victory and Selection Sunday contemplating where it might be seeded and what team it might play in its opening NCAA tournament game. Some of the excitement and anticipation were doused when the pairings and seedings were finally announced.

The NCAA basketball committee paired the 28-5 Bluejays against Alabama of the Southeastern Conference in Greensboro, N.C. The winner of that game most likely would face No. 1 seed North Carolina in a game that would be played 50 miles from the Tar Heels' campus.

"I'm not thrilled with our seed," Greg McDermott told the crowd of 1,700 that had assembled to watch the selection show at D.J. Sokol Arena.

While most bracketologists had Creighton slotted as a No. 5, 6 or 7 seed leading up to the official announcement, the basketball committee decided that the Bluejays warranted only a No. 8 seed. That touched off speculation that the committee was trying to possibly set up a made-for-TV matchup of former high school teammates Doug McDermott and Harrison Barnes.

The Jays lined up for a photo after practice in Greensboro, N.C. Young, on the facing page, had ended the workout with a dunk.

"There is a part of me that knows the NCAA tournament is a great event but that they also look for a story once in a while," Greg McDermott said. "Obviously, Harrison and Doug in the same regional is quite a national story. I'm thrilled to be back in the NCAA tournament, but I really think these guys earned more than an eighth seed."

Of course, a Barnes-McDermott matchup would be moot if the Bluejays stumbled against Alabama, which finished fifth in the SEC and sported a 21-11 record. The Crimson Tide ranked among the country's top defensive teams, while Creighton had spent the entire season in the top 10 offensively.

It didn't take Creighton long after arriving in Greensboro to realize that it would be playing on anything but a neutral court. The chanting started as the Bluejays were nearing the end of their open practice at Greensboro Coliseum.

"TAR ... HEELS!" "TAR ... HEELS!" "TAR ... HEELS!"

"That was pretty awesome," Young said, referring to the crowd of about 500. "They had a pretty good fan base show up just for a shoot-around." North Carolina took the court after Creighton finished its 40-minute workout. By then, the crowd had swelled to a couple of thousand. That's when they let another team in blue have it:

"DUKE ... SUCKS!" "DUKE ... SUCKS!" "DUKE ... SUCKS!"

CAA® SECOND AND THIRD ROUNDS
24

McDermott and Echenique double-team Alabama's JaMychal Green, who had 12 points. Despite a 7-point halftime deficit, Gibbs was confident. "I just thought if we could get our pace going and knock down a couple of shots, we could change the momentum of the game," he said. "We wrote on the board at halftime: 'Stick with the plan.' We just stuck with it, and we were able to turn the game around."

It made for an entertaining sideshow, but the Bluejays' focus was on Alabama, which in 32 games had held its opponents to a season-low scoring total 11 times.

Only 13 opponents had managed to score 60 or more points against the Crimson Tide, while five had failed to score 50.

"Our identity is defense," Alabama forward JaMychal Green said. "That's our game, and we're going to stick to it."

The Crimson Tide's plan worked in the first half against the Bluejays. Alabama's grinding offensive style put it up by 7 points at halftime, and the Crimson Tide led by 11 points after scoring on its first four possessions of the second half.

Normally, Greg McDermott would rather give blood with a rusty needle than stray from using a man-to-man defense, but at this point the Creighton coach ordered his team into a zone. The switch to a 2-3 zone worked, as the Bluejays held Alabama to 13 points over the next 14 minutes and 17 seconds.

Still, the Crimson Tide led 50-43 with 8:44 left before Jones and Wragge knocked down 3-point shots. Doug McDermott, who led Creighton with 16 points, gave Creighton the lead with a layup. A Jones free throw, another McDermott layup and Jones' 3-pointer from the wing pushed the run to 14-0 and left Creighton with a 57-50 lead with 2:44 to play. But 'Bama wasn't finished and pulled to within a point with 19 seconds left.

Jones then missed two free throws with 8.4 seconds remaining but made up for it with his defensive work against Trevor Releford on the game's final play. Jones said he got a piece of Releford's final shot, although Crimson Tide fans later argued that Jones got a piece of Releford. Regardless, the attempt fell short of the rim, and Creighton had a 58-57 win that moved it on to the next round.

"If they think I fouled, the refs didn't blow the whistle," Jones said. "It was a clean play. Just good defense."

Gibbs gets a hug from Avery Dingman after Alabama's final shot fell short. The Crimson Tide had gotten the ball to Trevor Releford (12), its sophomore point guard. He dribbled to his right, and Jones closed in on defense. "Josh did a really good job," Greg McDermott said. "He got into Releford's right hand and made him take a really tough shot."

Echenique dunks over North Carolina's John Henson, who was drafted in the first round by the NBA's Milwaukee Bucks. Echenique scored 12 points and was the only Bluejay to make more than half of his shots in the game. "Our shots that normally go in just wouldn't go in," Doug McDermott said.

As expected, North Carolina also advanced, posting a 77-58 win over Vermont. The next day, reporters grilled Doug McDermott and his dad, Barnes and North Carolina coach Roy Williams in an attempt to get all the juicy details about the meeting of the two former teammates from Ames High School.

Meanwhile, Jones was repeating to anyone who would listen a message he first delivered after Friday's win.

"There are a lot of people that doubt us, even President Obama," Jones said. The president had picked North Carolina to win the national championship, but Jones said the Bluejays were out to wreck his bracket.

Greg McDermott just shook his head when told that Jones had called out the president. Young laughed.

"I'm not surprised," Young said. "And if the president reads any of this, disregard anything (Jones) says."

The Bluejays knew they would have to make shots to have any chance of knocking off the Tar Heels, and shooting 41.2 percent — almost 10 percentage points below their season's average — didn't cut it.

Creighton led twice early in the game, but North Carolina took control with some dazzling first-half shooting. The Tar Heels made 14 of their first 19 shots from the field, led by 8 at halftime and then quickly pushed their advantage to 13 points early in the second half.

As it turned out, President Obama's bracket was safe. The combination of too many elite athletes in North Carolina blue and too many missed shots by the Bluejays produced an 87-73 loss that ended Creighton's season at 29-6.

A group of players who had struggled much of the previous season to stay above .500 had taken a giant step forward.

Creighton had changed its style of play under Greg McDermott, ditching the deliberate, set-based system he employed in his first year for a wide-open attack in his second. The result was that the Bluejays developed into one of the highest-scoring teams in the nation. Creighton ranked second nationally in points per possession and also finished in the top 10 in scoring, field-goal shooting, 3-point shooting and assists.

Doug McDermott led Creighton with 20 hard-earned points. He made eight of 19 shots, below his season average of 60 percent, and had difficulty getting good looks inside against the 6-foot-11 Henson, left, and former high school teammate Harrison Barnes. "I'm really happy with the way we fought, though," McDermott said. "We didn't give up. We didn't hang our heads when the shots weren't falling."

There had been concern coming into the season of whether Creighton could handle the quicker pace, but the Bluejays had soon put any worries to rest. Nonconference opponents, with limited time to prepare for Creighton, especially had trouble slowing the Bluejays in transition. McDermott figured Creighton's deep roster was suited to wear down foes, and he was right.

But perhaps the biggest improvement during the year came from the player who least needed to improve.

The Bluejays were a dejected group after the North Carolina loss. "It's a nice way to end, getting a chance to play a team like Carolina for your last game," Young said after his Creighton career ended. "I just wish we could have hit some shots."

Before he headed into the offseason, Doug McDermott nearly needed an accountant to keep track of the avalanche of postseason awards that came his way. He first had been picked as the Missouri Valley player of the year as well as a first-team All-Valley selection for the second straight year. After the season ended, he learned that he had won the Lute Olson national player of the year award and was a finalist for the John Wooden national player of the year award. He earned first-team All-America recognition from the Associated Press, the United States Basketball Writers Association and the National Association of Basketball Coaches.

He had become Creighton's first consensus first-team All-American.

"I'm in some great company, and it's crazy when I look back on it," said McDermott, who finished third nationally in scoring with a 22.9 average.

McDermott also became the second player coached by his own father to earn AP first-team honors. Pete Maravich was a three-time AP All-American while playing for his father, Press, at Louisiana State from 1967 to 1970.

Greg McDermott acknowledged that coaching a son who is the star of the team — a bona-fide superstar at that — created different problems. "It could be a situation where if your son was a borderline player that your fans get upset if you put him in the game," the coach said. "Our fans get upset if I take him out."

Some players would have difficulty handling that rocket-sled ride to stardom, but not McDermott, who four years earlier had been playing on his high school's junior varsity team.

Gibbs, who came to Creighton partly to have a chance to play with McDermott, sees something slightly different in the All-American's approach.

"It's not like he's weird, but he is to the beat of his own drum," Gibbs said. "There are certain things that make him tick. It's like the way he plays basketball — it's like he's off just a step, and that throws other people off because they can't catch his rhythm."

But while he might be offbeat, Gibbs said, there's also order in what he does. Theresa McDermott once told him that when Doug was young, he would walk behind his father while he was mowing the lawn to make sure Greg was cutting in straight lines.

Doug McDermott celebrated the news that he had become Creighton's first consensus All-America basketball player with a 45-minute talk with his father about what he needed to do to improve for his junior season. Then he headed to the weight room.

"I never imagined I would be in this position," he said. "Now I know where I can get, and I know what I have to do and how much harder I have to work to get there again."

Although proud of his team's effort, Greg McDermott said the North Carolina game illustrated the difference between where his program was and where it aspired to be. The Bluejays had closed the gap in the 2011-12 season, but there were still steps to take in pursuit of college basketball's elite programs.

"We have to make some changes if we want to be able to compete at this level. We have to improve defensively," McDermott said. "We've had a very good offensive year, but there are still strides we can make in that area. I think what happened opened the eyes of some guys in regard to how hard we have to work in the offseason."

"I think what happened opened the eyes of some guys in regard to how hard we have to work in the offseason."

— Greg McDermott

More peaks in the Valley

Doug McDermott wanted to take Creighton in the 2012-13 season to a place the Bluejays had never gone before. He worked with a private coach in Indiana and participated in camps run by NBA superstars LeBron James and Amar'e Stoudemire.

His teammates also rededicated themselves to their offseason conditioning. Creighton's only loss from the previous season's team was Antoine Young, the three-season starter at the point. But big things were expected out of sophomore Austin Chatman, who had backed up Young and was set to take over as a starter.

"It's difficult to replace Antoine," Greg McDermott said. "Part of that is that you only learn it by being out there under the lights and doing it when the pressure is on. Austin got a taste of that last year, and that's helped him. But it's definitely an area of concern."

Will Artino receives congratulations for winning the slam dunk contest at the Bluejay Madness event to kick off the 2012-13 season.

But the coach made it clear even before the season's first practice that he would not shy away from expectations. This was a team that was capable of playing in the Sweet 16. Or beyond.

His players embraced the bold talk.

"Coach Mac understands how good this can be, and he's not going to let things slide," junior guard Jahenns Manigat said. "He's going to challenge us, and saying something like that really just helps us think about how good we can be."

The national pollsters backed Greg McDermott's expectations, placing Creighton 15th and 16th in the preseason rankings.
Doug McDermott became the first player from Creighton and the Missouri Valley to land a spot on the AP's preseason All-America team.

An expected difficult opening test with North Texas, and hyped professional prospect Tony Mitchell, never materialized as Creighton cruised to a 71-51 victory. The Bluejays followed with easy wins over Alabama-Birmingham, Presbyterian and Longwood to take a 4-0 record into a pair of much-anticipated games at the Las Vegas Invitational.

First, Creighton showcased its toughness in winning a November game against Wisconsin that had a March feel to it. Though the Bluejays were the ranked team coming in, they needed to prove they were capable of going toe-to-toe with one of the Big Ten's bruisers. Creighton 84, Wisconsin 74.

"I think people were thinking we were overrated, that we hadn't been tested by anybody," Ethan Wragge said. "We wanted to come in here and show what we're all about and what kind of basketball we like to play."

The 14th-ranked Bluejays got 30 points from McDermott, 17 from Wragge and 14 from Chatman as they put up 84 on a team that gives up points grudgingly. "I thought we matched the toughness of a team built on toughness," Greg McDermott said. "That's what their program stands for, and we knew that we'd at least have to be even with them. I thought we were."

The 30-point game was Doug McDermott's seventh of his career. "He made our guys look like they haven't played before," Wisconsin coach Bo Ryan said. "He's like those old-time players you used to see in the Y's and the Boys Clubs. He works, he's smart, he's tough — but I think we knew that before the game. We had his shooting percentage down in the first half, but then he just went to work."

The win advanced Creighton into the tournament's championship game against Arizona State, which had won its semifinal game against Arkansas. What started as a Bluejay blowout turned into a tight game, with the Sun Devils closing an 18-point deficit to 6 with 2:51 to play.

Josh Jones scored all 18 of his points against Alabama-Birmingham in the second half. "That was just part of being a senior," Jones said after the game.

A closing charge finished off Arizona State and secured an 87-73 win. McDermott tacked on 29 points to the 30 he scored the previous night in earning the tournament's most valuable player award, while Wragge, who had 13 against the Sun Devils, also earned a spot on the all-tournament team.

"This is huge for our confidence, especially coming here and getting two wins over big-time teams," Greg McDermott said. "But we know we have a big week coming up. Boise State has only lost once."

Manigat tries to get through a pick by Boise State's Kenny Buckner and keep up with Igor Hadziomerovic.

When the Broncos left Omaha five days later, they still had lost only once. Boise State had let a win at No. 13 Michigan State slip away earlier in the season, but the Broncos didn't let the No. 11 Bluejays escape their grasp, snapping Creighton's season-opening winning streak at six with an 83-70 win.

Derrick Marks led the upset, scoring a career-high 35 points, including 18 straight at one point in the second half. Creighton, which trailed by 13 points with 4:21 to play, trimmed its deficit to 5 with 2:29 remaining before the Broncos pulled away.

"It was obvious who the better team was," Greg McDermott said. "And it wasn't us."

As poorly as they had played against Boise, the Bluejays were just as good when they took the floor against a St. Joseph's squad that returned everyone from a team that had handed Creighton its first loss the previous season.

The Bluejays led by 30 points by the time the game was 16½ minutes old. When it was finished, a dozen Creighton players had scored in the 80-51 romp before a sellout crowd of 17,390 at the CenturyLink Center.

"I think we sent the nation a statement by what we did," Doug McDermott said.

He also was looking forward to the No. 16 Bluejays' next game, against in-state rival Nebraska in Lincoln. "It's going to be a packed house," he said. "It should be a great atmosphere, just like any other Creighton-Nebraska game."

Chatman was proving that he was up to the challenge of replacing Young as starting point guard. He had six assists and just one turnover against St. Joseph.

It was going to be a big game for Josh Jones, the Bluejays' senior from Omaha Central. It would be his last visit to the Devaney Sports Center, where he had led the Eagles to three state championships in high school. His last title had been special. As a high school senior, he had open-heart surgery to repair a damaged valve, and there had been concern whether he would play basketball again. But he returned to finish his career at Central with a championship and had become a valuable Bluejay reserve who had captivated fans with his swashbuckling style of play.

On the bus ride to Lincoln, Jones noticed that he was starting to lose vision in his left eye. He chalked it up to the new contacts he was wearing. Then came a dizzy spell.

"Everything that happened to me," Jones recalled later, "I thought it was off adrenaline."

Avery Dingman assumed Jones' role of first guard off the bench against Nebraska in 2012. "Everyone on the team loves Josh, and it fired us up," he said.

Jones took the court nearly two hours before game time, putting up some shots and playfully sparring with the Husker student section. Suddenly, he felt weird as he tried to do an easy layup.

"My heart was like a snare drumroll," Jones said.

He fell down, then got back up.

Jones approached teammates Grant Gibbs and Alex Olsen and asked how to get to the locker room.

"We said, 'Same way we came in,' " Gibbs said. "I thought that was a little weird but didn't think too much about it. Then, as we started warm-ups, he didn't come back out, and I put it together that it could have been a heart thing."

When the Jays returned to the locker room following their opening round of warm-ups, they found Jones hooked up to a variety of monitors and machines.

"His face didn't look good," Gibbs said. "We asked him if he was all right, and he said, 'Nah, this isn't good.' "

The players moved to a different locker room, where Greg McDermott gave them pregame instructions. As the team headed to the court, the coach grabbed Gibbs and asked, "Are we ready to go?"

Gibbs said he wasn't sure, and McDermott told him the game's start could be delayed if the players needed more time to prepare.

The team captain gathered his teammates. "I asked them, 'We OK?' " Gibbs recalled. "Everybody said, 'Let's play. Josh is going to be fine.' "

Jones was taken to a Lincoln hospital, where he was admitted for tests.

"Once the game began, you get involved in it," Gibbs said. "But there were times I remembered thinking if he was going to be OK. There was a moment there, especially with his previous heart thing, that you just didn't know. It was really scary."

Creighton cruised to a 64-42 win over the Huskers. Afterward, the players talked by phone to Jones, who was hospitalized overnight and released the next day for additional tests in Omaha.

Two days later, with Jones watching from the bench, Creighton pounded Akron to improve to 9-1. On Dec. 12, Jones held a press conference to announce that his basketball career was being put on hold because of an atrial flutter, a type of abnormal, fast beating in the upper chambers of the heart.

The best-case scenario, Jones was told, was returning to the court in a month or so. Worst case? "He's done playing," Greg McDermott said.

Later that day, the Jays boarded a plane to head to the West Coast for a game against California. On the East Coast, news was developing that would drastically alter the basketball landscape.

For weeks, it had been rumored that the seven Catholic universities that were a part of the Big East were considering breaking away from the conference and possibly forming their own league. The seven — Marquette, Georgetown, St. John's, Villanova, Seton Hall, Providence and DePaul — had become frustrated that the conference had become consumed by football.

News of the break became public the morning of Dec. 13, with a formal announcement coming two days later.

Details were sketchy, and questions arose quickly in Omaha. The seven schools would have to add members, but what schools would they ask to join? Would Creighton be one of those schools? When would the league begin play?

McDermott works inside against Nebraska's Brandon Ubel. McDermott's 27 points pushed him into 10th place on Creighton's career scoring chart, moving past Benoit Benjamin. The Jays' 22-point margin of victory was their largest ever in Lincoln.

Athletic Director Bruce Rasmussen and the Rev. Timothy Lannon, Creighton's president, declined to comment, because at that point, there really wasn't anything to say. Bluejay fans began to chat up a storm online, in other social media forums and in the stands during games.

In addition to a schedule with basketball-first schools, the new league also was set to sign a national television contract with Fox, which was set to launch a 24-hour sports channel in nine months.

Out of nowhere, Creighton might get its shot at the big time.

Meanwhile, Greg McDermott and his team were getting ready to play a game against a tough California team, part of a rugged nonconference schedule the Bluejays needed to help their résumé for the NCAA tournament in the spring. The last thing McDermott needed was a distraction. Anyway, he had always figured that Creighton had little chance of being a player in the realignment that had been reshaping the landscape of college athletics in the past decade.

Echenique made seven of nine shots against Tulsa.

"The realignment world was all based on football," McDermott said. "We didn't bring anything to the table, because we didn't have football."

Taking care of what it could control, Creighton handed the Golden Bears a 74-64 loss. Doug McDermott, who had scored 30 points in the win over Akron, led Creighton with 34 in becoming the first Bluejay since Bob Harstad in 1990 to record back-to-back 30-point games.

"Cal is no pushover, and they'll be playing in March in the NCAA tournament," said Manigat, who turned in a strong defensive effort against Cal star Allen Crabbe. Manigat's prediction was correct. Cal made the tournament and beat UNLV before losing to Syracuse.

McDermott couldn't make it three straight 30-point games, scoring 16 in Creighton's 71-54 win over Tulsa, which served as the final tuneup for Missouri Valley play. The win left the Bluejays 11-1, marking the first time in program history that the Bluejays had won 11 games before Christmas. Creighton got a strong game from Echenique, who had 15 points and eight rebounds, while Avery Dingman scored a career-high 21 points in making eight of nine shots from the field.

After a Christmas break, Creighton returned to the practice floor to begin preparing for the start of Missouri Valley play. Jones did not return, however, nor would he ever. Two days after Christmas, he told The World-Herald he was giving up basketball. The procedure he had just undergone had required nine hours to perform and had indicated that the problem might be more serious than an atrial flutter.

Jones' doctors were uncertain what the next course of action would be — he could have another procedure, he might have to undergo another open-heart surgery or he might need to have a defibrillator implanted in his chest. Even with the best-case scenario, he probably wouldn't be cleared until mid-February. By the time he would get back in basketball shape, the season could be over. Of course, a greater problem raced through his mind.

"My life is on the line," he said.

Jones broke the news to his coach before Christmas that he wouldn't return.

As he contemplated life without basketball, he remembered when McDermott gathered the team around him in the fall and talked about legacy.

How do you want to be remembered? McDermott asked.

At the time, Jones was focused on the basketball part of the question. Did he want to be remembered as the guy from Omaha Central who scored a lot of points or played great defense? Or did he want people to cherish the spirit and enthusiasm he brought to the team?

That night in Lincoln changed all that.

"When I look back on it, I know what I want my legacy to be," Jones said. "It's about how a young kid from north Omaha who grew up with nothing but a dream and faced every adversity possible, stayed focused and became successful. If I can do that, it would mean more to me than any basket I ever scored."

"I'm holding back tears," Jones said during a press conference about his heart condition. "I just want everyone to know I'm strong, and basketball has been a blessing to let you guys see the person that I am."

The Bluejays opened conference play with six straight wins, four by margins of 10 points or more. A 3-point loss at Wichita State left the teams tied in the standings, but Creighton dropped a game off the pace with a befuddling 74-69 loss to a Drake team it had beaten by 30 points in Omaha two weeks prior.

After running off wins over Southern Illinois, Missouri State and Bradley, the Jays hit a February funk, as they had the year before. They looked horrid in a 19-point loss at Indiana State, dropped a close game at home to Illinois State and blew a 5-point lead in the final 5½ minutes in a 61-54 setback at Northern Iowa.

In the three losses, Creighton shot 40.7 percent from the field and 28.1 percent from beyond the arc.

"We know that we're capable of doing what we were doing at the beginning of the year," Doug McDermott said. "We've put ourselves in situations these last two games, and we just didn't come through."

McDermott came through in the next game after Evansville had built a 16-point lead in the first half. He scored all of his 21 points after that, rallying Creighton to a 71-68 victory over the Purple Aces. In the process, he became the 15th player — and first junior — in Missouri Valley history to score 2,000 points.

Will Artino had 7 points in six minutes of play in a 75-58 win over Bradley in 2013.

"I credit my teammates and coaches for putting me in position every single night to get points," he said. "It doesn't really mean much to me right now because we're in the midst of the season, fighting for a conference title."

A win over Southern Illinois kept the Bluejays a game off Wichita State's pace, but Greg McDermott delivered a message to his team after the game: Toughen up. "If they have a fault, their fault is that they're too good of guys," he explained later. "I want so much for them to achieve all their goals. But they're going to have to step out of their comfort zone a little bit if we're going to get there."

Doug McDermott received a commemorative ball in a ceremony before the Southern Illinois game for reaching 2,000 career points three days earlier at Evansville. McDermott became just the third Valley player to hit that milestone in three seasons. The others were Oscar Robertson and Larry Bird, neither of whom played as freshmen.

The Bluejays slipped up in a BracketBusters trip to St. Mary's, dropping a 74-66 decision in a game in which they trailed by 17 points in the second half. But Creighton recovered nicely in Peoria, riding a 19-2 spurt to an 80-62 win over Bradley. Coupled with a Shocker home loss to Evansville, the Bluejays had regained a tie for the league lead heading into the final regular-season game.

Creighton and Wichita State carted 12-5 conference records into the CenturyLink Center for the March 2 winner-take-all showdown.

"You can go a whole career as a coach and as a player and not have an opportunity like this," Greg McDermott said.

As if the stakes weren't high enough, it also was the final home appearance for the team's seniors, and perhaps for one junior: Doug McDermott, who was projected as a first-round NBA draft pick.

McDermott's big game against Wichita State overshadowed the performance of Chatman, who had 12 points and six assists and showed toughness driving inside.

Doug McDermott saved his finest hour as a Bluejay for a time his team needed him the most. He scored 12 points in the first 8½ minutes, igniting a CenturyLink crowd of 18,613. He didn't miss a shot in the first 21 minutes.

When Wichita State made a last push, trimming a 15-point deficit to 6, McDermott made back-to-back 3-point shots to widen the lead. His 3-point play with 2:19 sealed the win, punctuated with a layup for Creighton's final points.

Playing perhaps for the final time at home, McDermott scored 41 points as Creighton won its first outright Valley title since 2001 with a 91-79 victory. In the final seconds, the crowd serenaded him with chants of "one more year" in recognition of the decision they knew he would have to make at the end of the season. He would hear the chant over and over in the coming weeks.

McDermott made 15 of 18 shots. Overall, the Bluejays shot 70.2 percent against the Valley's best defensive team.

Greg McDermott couldn't have been prouder of his team.

"We went through some tough times in February, some times that a lot of teams may not have gotten through," he said. "To these guys' credit, they didn't allow all the things going on on the outside to affect the locker room. They never pointed fingers, and because of that, they provided themselves an opportunity to play for a championship."

With the MVC regular-season title in hand, Creighton headed to St. Louis, accompanied by a record following of 6,000 fans.

Talk of Creighton joining the new Big East had grown louder and louder, and many traveled from Omaha knowing full well that it could be the school's final appearance at the tournament.

Butler and Xavier had emerged as locks for two of the three schools that the Catholic 7 would invite for the league's first season of operation.

Bruce Rasmussen still considered Creighton to be a long shot to receive an invitation, mostly because it was the geographic outlier among the schools most mentioned as possible candidates. He had repeatedly shared with Valley commissioner Doug Elgin his belief that Creighton's chances of leaving were essentially nil. Still, Rasmussen and other school officials had been studying the feasibility of Creighton joining the league should it receive an invitation.

CREIGHTON
3
CREIGHTON
00
COTTON
32

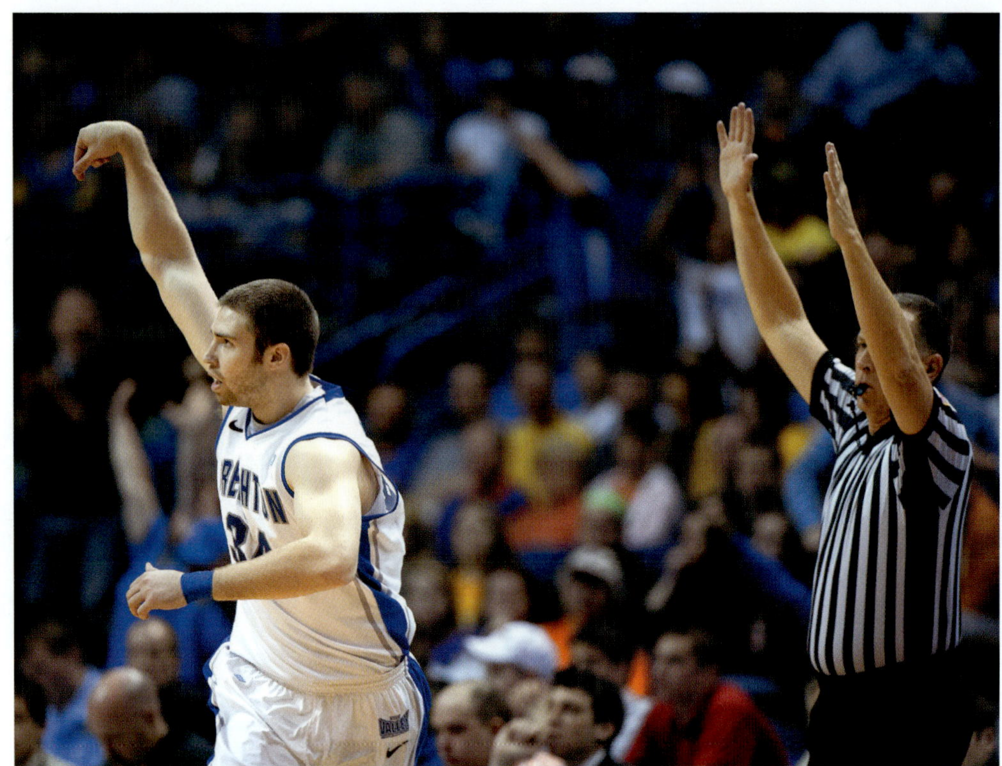

Wragge hit five 3-pointers, including four in the first half, against Wichita State in St. Louis. On the facing page, Manigat scores the last basket against the Shockers, who would advance to the NCAA's Final Four.

The Bluejays worked their way through the bracket in St. Louis by defeating Drake in the quarterfinals and Evansville in the semifinals. Wichita State also won its first two games, setting up a third meeting between the two teams, eight days after their classic showdown to close the regular season.

Creighton won this one, too, pulling out a 68-65 victory to win the tournament for the 12th and final time. The Bluejays led by 12 points with 4:21 to play. But the Shockers rallied, pulling within a point at 66-65, when Malcolm Armstead, a former Oregon Duck who had transferred to Wichita State, buried a 3-point shot with 43 seconds to play.

Creighton called time out after advancing the ball past half-court to set up its possession.

The Bluejays wanted to get the ball to Gibbs, but Wichita State denied that option.

Instead, Manigat found himself with the basketball in front of the Bluejay bench with the shot clock winding down.

"I just wanted to get the ball to Grant and get out of the way," Manigat said. "Everything else got shut down, and I knew I just had to make a play. I decided to put my head down and head to the basket. Fortunately, I got a miraculous shot to go down."

He might have considered it miraculous given his problems making layups throughout his career, but the ball simply kissed off the backboard and dropped through.

Creighton survived Wichita State's last gasp to extend the game when Armstead's 3-pointer — contested by Doug McDermott — hit the side of the rim and bounced away at the buzzer.

12
2
STATE
22
WICHITA
5
STATE
McDERMOTT

Afterward, a World-Herald reporter cornered Lannon to ask him whether this indeed was Creighton's swan song in St. Louis. He would reply that no formal invitation had been extended to the Bluejays. Does he expect one, Lannon was asked?

"Only God knows," Lannon said with a smile.

That invitation came three days later. Lannon was in a campus meeting when he received a call from Dennis Holtschneider, the president of DePaul.

"Tim, I'm thrilled to tell you, I'm calling officially on behalf of the conference," Holtschneider said. "We'd like to offer Creighton membership."

Lannon was ecstatic, repeatedly thanking his old friend. He then called Rasmussen, and for the first time the athletic director allowed himself to believe this was going to happen.

But first, there was unfinished business regarding this season.

With a 27-7 record, Creighton was awarded a No. 7 seed, paired against Cincinnati of the Big East and sent to Philadelphia with a chance to face Atlantic Coast Conference powerhouse Duke later.

"This is a good draw for us," Doug McDermott said. "We're not scared of anyone."

Creighton's opening assignment came against a Cincinnati team that had won its first 12 games but limped into the tournament having lost seven of its last 11. Overall, the Bearcats were 22-11, having played a schedule rated 21st nationally — thanks to the tough lineup of Big East opponents.

"They're a tough team, a physical team," Gibbs said.

The Rev. Timothy Lannon, Creighton's president, was a happy face among the Bluejay fans before the Cincinnati game in Philadelphia.

Creighton found out just how tough the Bearcats were, but Cincinnati likewise learned a thing or two about the Bluejays' mettle.

The same Creighton team that Greg McDermott had called out a month earlier for maybe being too nice traded body blows for 40 minutes with a Cincinnati team that was supposedly bigger, stronger and tougher. In the end, it was the Bluejays who walked, or limped, away with a 67-63 win.

Creighton advanced by outrebounding the Bearcats and holding them to 42 percent shooting from the field. The Bluejays held their own against a bully bunch from the Big East.

"People always question our toughness," Echenique said. "We take it personal."

After the game, Echenique received three stitches for a cut above his eye and five more in his head. Gibbs talked to reporters wearing shorts spotted with blood.

"That was one of our most physical games of the year," Gibbs said. "There were not a lot of easy shots to be had. Buckets definitely were at a premium."

Echenique got Creighton's last basket with 3:04 to play, breaking a 54-54 tie, and the Bluejays closed out the game by scoring their final 11 points at the free-throw line. The win put the Jays into the next round against Duke, their path to the Sweet 16 blocked by another legendary program.

Echenique upends Cincinnati's Justin Jackson on the way to the basket.

McDermott runs into a barrier in Duke center Mason Plumlee.

"We've been working for this moment since we lost to North Carolina last year," Doug McDermott said. "It's every kid's dream to get a chance to play against Duke in the NCAA tournament."

Creighton held Duke to 38.8 percent shooting, hung with the Blue Devils on the boards and took decent care of the basketball — the Bluejays committed 10 turnovers. But Duke never allowed Creighton to get into any type of offensive rhythm. In addition, the officials whistled 46 fouls, leaving both teams spinning their wheels to get anything going offensively. Each team lost a pair of players to fouls.

"It was just so difficult to score," Duke coach Mike Krzyzewski said. "That's the best defense we've played all year. Our guys were really tough. It was just tough to get buckets."

Creighton led 17-15, 19-18 and 21-20 before a 9-2 Duke run, punctuated by a banked 3-pointer at the halftime buzzer, put the Blue Devils ahead 29-23.

"We talk about how sometimes it's as simple as the bounce of the ball," Greg McDermott said. "We missed a wide-open 3 just before the half, and then they throw in a bank shot to go up by 6."

Creighton coaches and players watch the final seconds count down against Duke. Manigat turned away from the court at the end.

Duke held the Bluejays to 30.2 percent field-goal shooting — they missed 17 of 19 3-pointers — and their lowest point total in more than two years. The 66-50 defeat closed out the Bluejays' season at 28-8.

The loss ended the greatest two-year run in school history. The Bluejays won 57 games, including victories in the NCAA tournament in back-to-back seasons for the first time in program history.

The formula for the success? The obvious place to start was Doug McDermott, who added to his personal honors by becoming Creighton's first two-time consensus first-team All-American after the 2012-13 season. His personality was almost as important as his skills. The team's biggest star was one of the guys — and did everything he could to make sure it stayed that way — and that had a big impact on the rest of the players.

"If he were like a lot of guys today that are all about self-promotion, taking pictures of themselves and all that stuff, would this have been possible?" Gibbs said.

"It might have been a lot more difficult. It brings out other people's worst attributes when your star has an agenda. Yet, you're never going to meet a guy more humble than he is."

Greg McDermott counts his blessings, and not just for the opportunity to coach his son. He had known in 2010 that he was one bad season away from a pink slip at Iowa State.

"To have our time in the Valley end the way it did, to play our biggest rival in front of 18,000-plus, it just doesn't get any better than that," he reflected after the season.

"To do it on our home floor was really special, and then to play Wichita again in the Valley tournament and to win that, that was a great way to end a wonderful arrangement with the Missouri Valley."

"It's hard to imagine that things could have gone any better here, outside of a little deeper run in the NCAA tournament," he said.

He also realized that he led a special group of young men.

"We've done it with kids that have been just wonderful to coach," he said.

"It's a group of guys that care about each other and care about the program and what we've built the last three years," Gibbs said. "Part of it is that Omaha and Creighton are such great places to be when you're in college. Everybody is so supportive and wants to see you do well."

That support sometimes leaves Gibbs amazed.

"I'm not flashy or super-talented," he said. "If I were a fan, I would not be my favorite player. I'd be like, 'That dude doesn't do jack.' If I played at wherever, nobody would care about me."

But not in Omaha. "People are always telling me, 'Gosh, you're great.' But I'm just doing my job. That just always befuddles me."

Bluejay basketball history has produced its shining stars in players such as McDermott and Korver and Buford and Silas and Portman. But Creighton also has succeeded with more than its share of under-the-radar guys like Gibbs — intent on parlaying whatever talents they possessed into their shot at the big time.

With the Bluejays poised for a brave new step forward, the question is whether that will still be the formula.

Greg McDermott embraced Gibbs at season's end. "It's going to be a whole new set of challenges next year," Gibbs said after the final game.

Getting ready for the next big step

ALTHOUGH HE HAS BEEN AN ATHLETIC ADMINISTRATOR for two decades, Bruce Rasmussen remains a basketball coach at heart. He understands the fragility of the game better than most, of how an injury can wreck a season, of how a misstep on the recruiting trail can undermine not one, but many seasons. He values timing, both on and off the court.

Rasmussen chuckles as he considers the fortunate timing in a series of events that has transformed Creighton basketball over the past 20 years. If Rasmussen would have had his way, the school would have fired Rick Johnson after a second dreadful season in 1993. If that had happened, Dana Altman probably wouldn't have left Kansas State to end Creighton's boom-and-bust cycles and build a perennial winner.

> "Some people might call what happened good timing. Some might call it luck."
>
> — **Bruce Rasmussen**

If Altman had stayed at Arkansas in 2007, Creighton probably would have hired a coach other than Greg McDermott to replace him. Chances are, Doug McDermott would never have worn Creighton blue. Same for Grant Gibbs.

And if the Rev. Timothy Lannon, Creighton's president, hadn't had close ties to some of the officials putting together a new athletic conference ...

"Some people might call what happened good timing," Rasmussen said. "Some might call it luck." The same could be said of the events that boosted Creighton fortunes as it prepared to make the jump to the new Big East.

Most college basketball observers believed that the Bluejays needed to step up their game for battles against the likes of Georgetown and Marquette. Coach Greg McDermott knew he would face the challenge of the 2013-14 season without Gregory Echenique, the muscular big man who finished his career in the NCAA tournament against Duke. But Gibbs' career most likely also was over. Between Creighton and Gonzaga, he had wrapped up his five years of eligibility. The chances of the NCAA granting a waiver for a sixth year because of injuries appeared doubtful.

The bigger question was Doug McDermott. The Bluejay star could return to Creighton for his senior season or declare for the NBA draft. He had been projected as a first-round pick and would have been in line for a first-year contract worth more than $1 million. McDermott had little more to prove as a collegian. He already had twice earned first-team consensus All-America honors and twice had been the Missouri Valley player of the year. He broke Rodney Buford's school scoring record as a junior.

How difficult was it for McDermott to decide?

Gibbs tells a story about his teammate. "He's not good at ordering food," Gibbs said, laughing. "He'll order a sandwich, and the waitress will ask him what kind of sauce he wants with that. He'll be like, 'Whatever.' He gets frazzled in situations like that."

McDermott agonized for a month over whether to leave Creighton. Finally, on April 24, he told his father what he was going to do. That night he talked only to a reporter from The World-Herald and another from a national publication ("You guys are the only ones I trust," he said) to allow them to prepare stories for the next day.

On April 25, McDermott sent out a message on Twitter that Creighton fans had been longing to hear: "I will be returning to Creighton for my senior year and can't wait to put on that uniform for one more season." He said he believed that he would play in the NBA but that he was willing to wait. "My heart has been telling me all along to stay, but my mind tried to take over a couple of times," he said.

McDermott said Bluejay fans figured prominently in his thought process.

"I care so much about Creighton," he said. "There are a lot of people around here that believed in me. I felt like I owed them one more year."

About two months later, McDermott was in an airport in Istanbul, Turkey, on his way to participate in the World University Games in Russia. He received a text message from his father saying that the NCAA had granted Gibbs a sixth season of eligibility.

"It's been a good summer," Greg McDermott said later. "There was a time in April that I didn't know if Doug was coming back, and I hadn't thought about the possibility of Grant coming back. To have them back on the team is exciting."

Doug McDermott made a lot of Omahans happy with his announcement that he would return for his senior season. "There are a lot of areas that I can get better at, and I just felt I'd be more comfortable doing it here in Omaha," he said.

The return of Gibbs and McDermott gave Creighton key pieces as the Bluejays began their first race for the new Big East championship.

Off the court, Creighton also was preparing to compete at a higher level in the years ahead. Most apparent in that effort was the school's new basketball practice and student-athlete support building, which was begun before Creighton was courted by the new conference. The facility was set to open in 2014.

The fans were re-energized by the previous two seasons. The school finished sixth nationally in attendance in each of those seasons, with the Bluejays drawing a school-record average of 17,155 in 2012-13. That was the highest average attendance of any of the new Big East schools.

"What sets us apart from a lot of schools is 17,000 fans in the stands almost every night," Creighton assistant coach Darian DeVries said. "It's huge in recruiting. A lot of BCS schools are getting five or seven thousand a game and sell out a couple of times a year. We're doing that every single night. Our game last year against Wichita State probably broke every fire code invented. Kids see what we're doing, and they are excited about it."

The timing couldn't have been better for Creighton as it made its move to the new conference. Rasmussen knew from the start that his school couldn't pass up the opportunity if it arrived. But one of the athletic director's favorite sayings is, "With opportunity comes exposure."

> "What sets us apart from a lot of schools is 17,000 fans in the stands almost every night."
>
> **— Darian DeVries**

Creighton had plenty in this venture, starting with what would happen if the Bluejays weren't as competitive in the new league as their fans hoped they would be. Rasmussen and his longtime lieutenant, Kevin Sarver, can still remember the days when empty seats outnumbered paying customers at Creighton games. Would those days return if the Bluejays were to find themselves unable to keep up with the competition?

"I'm sure there are fans out there who think we're still going to be able to go to Madison Square Garden and win seven out of 12 tournaments like we just have," Sarver said, referring to the Missouri Valley tournament in St. Louis. "That's a tall order."

Rasmussen also saw uncertainty when he surveyed the ever-changing landscape of Division I athletics and wondered what Creighton's place would be in a decade or two. But he and his staff didn't have time to worry.

"All I can tell you is that we're going to work our tails off to do what we think we need to do to be successful," he said. "I think a mistake a lot of people make is when they have success, they take a breath. We have to be willing to work hard, to be uncomfortable, do things the right way and be a little lucky. I hope we can look back 10 years from now and say that these last few years were not the highlight, that things have continued to get better."

A cozy spot in the Missouri Valley was traded for a league filled with unknowns. The new Big East was a step up and a chance for Creighton to finally claim the spot in the big time it had coveted since basketballs first started bouncing on the Hilltop.

Confidence begins with the head basketball coach.

"I've said it often the last couple of years that Creighton is a well-kept secret and we're a Sweet 16 away from everyone knowing what we really have here," McDermott said. "Now that we move to a national conference, it's not going to be a secret anymore."

Former Creighton coach John "Red" McManus, who always believed the Bluejays belonged on the biggest stage, died July 23, 2013, at age 88. Pallbearers included Paul Silas, Tom Apke and Bob Portman, all of whom played for McManus during his stretch as the Bluejays' coach from 1959 through 1969. The Rev. Timothy Lannon, Creighton's president, praised McManus for instilling a boldness in Creighton and its basketball program that continues to this day. Motioning toward McManus' casket, Lannon said, "In many ways, we are where we are today because of our friend, Red McManus."

Acknowledgments

I WANTED TO BE PAUL SILAS. The Creighton rebounding machine of the early 1960s was the perfect sports hero for a 10-year-old growing up in Nebraska with an aversion to anything red. Silas was one tough hombre on the basketball court, and it really didn't matter at the time that the only thing we had in common was our Chuck Taylor shoes.

Silas' basketball talent took him to the NBA. Mine took me to the UNO intramural league. It was about that time I decided that my future would be served best by writing about baskets and rebounds rather than trying to make or grab them.

I was fortunate to land a full-time job at The World-Herald while still in college. In the years since, I've tackled a variety of assignments but few have been as enjoyable as spending 16 of the past 21 years as the beat writer for Silas' old school. The assignment has allowed me to chronicle some of Creighton's biggest moments on the basketball court, as well as some of the program's darkest days. I've joked over the years that I don't know if I'll ever get to heaven, but I've already spent five years in purgatory covering Rick Johnson's three years coaching the Bluejays as well as Dana Altman's first two.

Since returning to the beat in 2002, I've covered all but eight of the Bluejays' 372 games. I've had the good fortune of being able to write about two of the program's brightest stars, Kyle Korver and Doug McDermott. All-Americans on the court, Korver and McDermott also are two of the classiest people off it whom any reporter could hope to cover.

But they are just part of Creighton's story. The Bluejays owe their success as much to overachievers as All-Americans. For every Korver and McDermott, there is a Dustin Sitzmann or Taylor Stormberg, hard-working reserves who strengthen the program's backbone with their willingness to sacrifice while asking little in return.

I'm looking forward to tagging along as Creighton prepares to write the next chapter with its move to the new Big East. These are thrilling times for the Bluejays and their fans, as they finally get a taste of the big time they've been pursuing on the Hilltop for a century.

At the same time, I hope the move doesn't cause Creighton to lose its identity. The Bluejays have long prided themselves on being able to do a lot with a little.

"We've always been that small Jesuit school from Omaha," said Bob Harstad, another one of Creighton's all-time great players. "We've had a lot of things working against us, but we've always wanted to show that we're just as good as those bigger schools. And many times, we have."

The timing of the move to the new Big East was the impetus for this book. With so many people excited about Creighton's future, The World-Herald decided to take a detailed look at how the Bluejays propelled themselves to this point.

I appreciate the memories that former players Silas, Korver, Harstad, Fritz Pointer, Tom Garvey, Gene Harmon, Randy Eccker, Kevin McKenna, Ryan Sears and Anthony Tolliver shared with me. Grant Gibbs, who will finish out his career in the new conference, provided great insight, and wit, when discussing the last three seasons.

Tom Apke, who played, coached and served as athletic director at Creighton, was generous with his time, as were former coaches Tony Barone and Altman. Current coach Greg McDermott and assistants Darian DeVries and Steve Merfeld helped add perspective to the Bluejays' recent success. Administrators Bruce Rasmussen and Kevin Sarver, who between them have spent 61 years at Creighton, were invaluable in their sharing of many behind-the-scenes details of the program.

I'm also thankful for the thorough reporting of previous beat writers such as Howard "Howdy" Wolff, Ralph Stewart, Bill Last, Don Lee, Steve Sinclair and Rich Kaipust. Their work set the historical foundation for a project that was the brainchild of World-Herald book editor Dan Sullivan. A Creighton grad, Sullivan's guidance and direction helped define the narrative. His skillful editing sharpened its focus, and the work of his team — designer Christine Zueck-Watkins, editors Rich Mills and Pam Thomas and photo imager Jolene McHugh — transformed it into the finished product you hold in your hands. And thanks to Executive Editor Mike Reilly for giving me the chance to work on this rewarding project.

Finally, the support from the home front — wife Susan chipped in to read proofs — provided much-needed energy and encouragement during the long hours of research and writing. For that, I will be forever grateful.

ABOUT THE AUTHOR

Steven Pivovar has covered sports for The World-Herald for 41 years, including 16 seasons of Creighton basketball.

A proud south Omaha boy, Pivovar is a graduate of Omaha Bryan High School and the University of Nebraska at Omaha. He has covered a variety of sports for The World-Herald, including college and professional football, professional baseball and high school sports.

He has been a member of The World-Herald's College World Series coverage team since 1981 and is the author of "Rosenblatt Stadium: Omaha's Diamond on the Hill," published by The World-Herald in 2010.

His family includes Susan, his wife of 40 years; daughter and son-in-law Stephanie and Steve Grams; daughter Shannon; son Bret; granddaughter Aurelia Grams and grandson Truman Grams.

Credits & Photographers Index

BY STEVEN PIVOVAR

EDITOR
Dan Sullivan

DESIGNER
Christine Zueck-Watkins

PHOTO IMAGING
Jolene McHugh

CONTRIBUTING EDITORS
Jim Anderson
Marjie Ducey
Shelley Larsen
Bob McDonald
Rich Mills
Pam Thomas

RESEARCHERS
Jeanne Hauser
Joe Janowski
Sheritha Jones

INTELLECTUAL PROPERTY MANAGER
Michelle Gullett

PRINT AND PRODUCTION COORDINATORS
Pat "Murphy" Benoit
Wayne Harty

DIRECTOR OF MARKETING
Rich Warren

DIRECTOR OF PHOTOGRAPHY
Jeff Bundy

REPRINT INFORMATION
Omaha World-Herald photos are available from the OWHstore. Call 402-444-1014 to place an order or go to OWHstore.com.

PHOTOS

A Bluejay fast break against Gonzaga in 1963: Chuck Officer, front left, passes between defenders to Harry Forehand (25). Paul Silas (35), Fritz Pointer (33) and Tom Apke trail the play.

Index

CHAMPIONS
THE VALLEY
MISSOURI VALLEY CONFERENCE
CHAMPIONS
VALLEY
CHAMPION
CREIGHTON
1